Theatre of the Oppressed and its Times

Political theatre, like any kind of political action, can only be judged in relation to the political moment in which it tries to intervene. Theatre of the Oppressed (TO) was created to fight against dictatorship and an extremely centralized conception of politics. How does it function now, in a time of social media and so-called participatory democracies?

Providing an in-depth account of the political and cultural context in which TO emerged, this book asks: How do contemporary understandings of concepts like oppression, representation, participation, and emancipation shape TO today? Highlighting the pitfalls of reducing oppression to one-to-one relationships, the book proposes a version of Forum Theatre dramaturgy that portrays oppression as a defining structure of societies. The author also shares specific examples of movements and other organizations that use Theatre of the Oppressed to construct themselves.

Theatre of the Oppressed and its Times is an essential text for practitioners and scholars of TO, applied theatre practitioners, students, and anyone interested in how theatre can concretely assist in the transformation of the world.

Julian Boal is a teacher, researcher, and practitioner of Theatre of the Oppressed. He has facilitated workshops in more than 25 countries and is pedagogical coordinator of Escola de Teatro Popular.

Theatre of the Oppressed and its Times

Julian Boal

Translated by Fabiana Comparato
with Kelly Howe

LONDON AND NEW YORK

First published 2023
by Routledge
4 Park Square, Milton Park, Abingdon, Oxon OX14 4RN

and by Routledge
605 Third Avenue, New York, NY 10158

Routledge is an imprint of the Taylor & Francis Group, an informa business

© 2023 Julian Boal by arrangement with Literarische Agentur Mertin Inh. Nicole Witt e. K., Frankfurt am Main, Germany.

The right of Julian Boal to be identified as author of this work has been asserted in accordance with sections 77 and 78 of the Copyright, Designs and Patents Act 1988.

All rights reserved. No part of this book may be reprinted or reproduced or utilised in any form or by any electronic, mechanical, or other means, now known or hereafter invented, including photocopying and recording, or in any information storage or retrieval system, without permission in writing from the publishers.

Trademark notice: Product or corporate names may be trademarks or registered trademarks, and are used only for identification and explanation without intent to infringe.

British Library Cataloguing-in-Publication Data
A catalogue record for this book is available from the British Library

Library of Congress Cataloging-in-Publication Data
Names: Boal, Julián, 1975- author.
Title: Theatre of the oppressed and its times / Julian Boal ; translated by Fabiana Comparato with Kelly Howe.
Other titles: Teatro dos oprimidos e do seu tempo. English
Description: Abingdon, Oxon ; New York, NY : Routledge, 2023. | Includes index.
Identifiers: LCCN 2022061645 (print) | LCCN 2022061646 (ebook) | ISBN 9781032350493 (Hardback) | ISBN 9781032350509 (Paperback) | ISBN 9781003325048 (eBook)
Subjects: LCSH: Theater and society. | Theater--Political aspects. | Theater--Philosophy. | Boal, Augusto--Criticism and interpretation.
Classification: LCC PN2049 .B56 2023 (print) | LCC PN2049 (ebook) | DDC 792.01/3--dc23/eng/20230307
LC record available at https://lccn.loc.gov/2022061645
LC ebook record available at https://lccn.loc.gov/2022061646

ISBN: 9781032350493 (hbk)
ISBN: 9781032350509 (pbk)
ISBN: 9781003325048 (ebk)

DOI: 10.4324/9781003325048

Typeset in Times New Roman
by KnowledgeWorks Global Ltd.

To my father,

For your ever-changing intransigence

with the order of things,

For being an exceptional agitator,

For having started so many processes,

For being the best-dreamed father.

To Muriel Naessens,

For your smile,

For your struggles,

for your generosity,

For having taught me that fidelity

is to reinvent.

To the comrades of ETP,

Past, present, and yet to come,

For teaching me so much

For our common will

To perform onstage

The equality

We want to see one day

Ruling

The world

Contents

Acknowledgments	*ix*
Introduction	1
On the structure of this text 3	

PART I
Criticizing a Critical Theatre 9

1 For a Political History of Theatre of the Oppressed 11

"Give the oppressed the means of theatrical production" 12
"In a Forum Theatre scene, the center of gravity is in the audience, not on the
  stage" 12
"Forum Theatre is a rehearsal for revolution" 13
Participation 14
Representation 17
Oppression 21
Conclusion 24

2 Theatre of the Oppressed as a Formal Critique of the Brazilian
  Communist Party 27

Elements for a panorama of the Brazilian Communist Party 27
Critique of historical determinism 29
Critique of the historical subject 31
Critique of a hierarchy legitimized by knowledge 32

3 Theatre of the Oppressed and Epic Theatre: Notes on Two Attempts to
  Overcome the Bourgeois Drama 36

A common enemy: Aristotelian theatre 36
Beyond discourses: how production dominates the producer 37
New forms of making theatre: didactic plays and Forum Theatre 38
Narrative interruption as a resource against the bourgeois drama 39
The hero and its interpretations: The general and the particular 40

viii *Contents*

4 Critiques of Theatre of the Oppressed 43

Critiques of oppression 43
Criticism of a moralism manifested in dramatic form 45
Forum Theatre dramaturgy 48

5 Theatre of the Oppressed in Neoliberal Times: From Che Guevara to the Uber Driver 51

Regarding the impermanence of politics 51
Regarding the "bad uses" of Theatre of the Oppressed 53
On guerrillas and micro-entrepreneurs 55

6 Notes on Oppression 64

7 Facilitation/Mechanization 68

PART II
Small Screws, Big Twists 73

8 What Can Art Do in the Anti-Capitalist Struggle? 75

Notes on the capitalist state AND its necessary overcoming 78
Strategy 81
What is to be done (with art)? 86

PART III
Are There No Alternatives? 95

9 Examples but Not Models: Against Well-Made TO and for Well-Adapted TO 97

"It is when the theatre ends that our work begins": The example of Jana Sanskriti in India 97
Óprima! Criticism as a Concrete Practice, or: "We don't give a shit!" 103
A brief history of the Popular Theatre School (La Escola de Teatro Popular—ETP), or: political-theatrical learning in times of collapse 111

10 The Search for a Subjunctive Theatre 119

The limitations of the bourgeois dramatic form 119
Can dialectics break bricks (and help Forum Theatre)? 125

11 Exercises Toward a More Dialectical Practice of Forum Theatre 130

Games and exercises 131
Models for Theatre of the Oppressed 137
Model exercises 137
Models to enrich Forum Theatre by contextualizing the scenes that invite spect-actor intervention 139
Models for forum scenes that involve spect-actor intervention 145

Conclusion 149

Index *150*

Acknowledgments

I thank the people I consider comrades. They are not all found in a single party or in the same movement (sometimes, like me, they do not belong to any), or even all in the same country. We recognize each other in our common political guidelines and in shared jokes. Ironic utopians who can't strategize without joking, "open-eyed romantics" who can neither be satisfied with this small world nor take ourselves completely seriously when our intransigence makes plans. In the midst of sadness, misery, sectarianism, you are a breath. In one way or another, you were fundamental for this book; for my life, you are essential. I just hope I'm on par with the problems we've raised together.

To Kelly Howe, without whom this text would simply not exist, all my warmest thanks. I truly wonder how, beyond your own furious practice, you find all the time, all the care you put into any of the work we do together. This miracle will never cease to humble me. How will I ever be able to repay your companionship?

To Fabiana Comparato, thank you for all your beautiful work across the translation process. May our companionship continue to the point that one day we will even meet each other in person!

To my little comrade José Soeiro, how can I thank the one who read me so much and so well? It's a disgrace that we don't live in the same country; otherwise, everything is "delicia."

Beautiful pals from Óprima!, we are together and have been for a long time! How to forget this vital disorganization? This desire to do things that overcomes everything and, especially, the organizers?

Sabrina, Cora, and Quelo, we know that God was wise not to put us in the same corner. The world would not be prepared for this.

Sanjoy, Seema, and my Indian family, you know that one of the origins of this journey—in which this book is a step—happened in Badu, in a garden full of mangos. I still remember the nights I couldn't sleep because I was so taken by the force of what I saw in Jana Sanskriti's daily life. You have built the place where parallel lines meet, where politics, art, and constructing a distinct life interrelate in a way that has never been seen. The question can never be whether one day it will be possible to forget but how to live up to what has been witnessed.

To Montse and Jordi, I still think that if I'm really, really good in this life, maybe I'll be able to reincarnate as another Forcadas sibling. Of the gifts that Theatre of the Oppressed has given me, meeting you is one of the most precious. Calle Luna, n°6, is a place on the sidelines from which you can plot against the center. Full commitment and thoroughness as ways of life. La M… les saluda!

To Uncle Geeeo, for the conversations in which I forced the argument just to see the eyes widen a little more, for the past partnerships, for those to be built. Ball forward!

To the National Collective of Culture of the Movimento Sem Terra, I will never be able to thank you enough for the trust you had in me. The meeting at Escola Nacional Florestan Fernandes that we organized was one of the highlights of my life in Theatre of the Oppressed, and

x *Acknowledgments*

you were the ones who made it possible. For whatever way I can help, in whatever we can build together, call me! Douglas and Rafael, there will always be conversations to catch up on and processes to construct! To all the people who participated with open hearts in those days, I want to see you again as soon as possible!

To dear Kum Alek, another one to trust me, a rare item. With its limits, which we could only come to know after practice, what we came up with was beautiful. May there always be Safari Bar in our lives!

Claire and Bill, how many beautiful stories heard by your side. The discovery of the glories and miseries of the Left on another continent!

To the friends from PTO, our different worlds and our mutual misunderstandings sometimes only become reasons for greater affection.

To Melissa Kievman and Wendy vanden Heuvel, for making the world less narrow through their solidarity even with people they don't yet know.

To the Companhia do Latão, Sérgio and Helena, what I learned from you can only compare to how much we cried together! For many cries and many more moments of learning, onward!

To Ammar, Marina, Gwen, and Léo, my thesis—which became a large part of this book— would not have existed without our time together. What we saw, what we did, and our unchosen paths are the raw material of these pages. Perhaps too invisible to the unsuspecting eye, Ambaata, GTO-Paris, and Féminisme-Enjeux are the basis of this work.

To Olivier Neveux, whose somewhat alcohol-soaked friendship I miss tremendously, thanks for the texts and conversations, and I send a hug that I hope is big enough to bridge the distance that now separates us.

To Iná Camargo Costa, for the conversations in the form of a flying kick, the discovery of other knowledge as complete as theatre, tangos, and boleros ... I thank you for your patience with the beginner Brazilian that I was and am.

To Nestor, I thank you for your help maintaining both distance and proximity with "that author."

To Priscila Matsunaga, a huge thank you for making me the reader of so many texts that I don't understand. This book would be different were it not for our meeting. Our friendship makes me genuinely happy.

To Marildo Menegat, my PhD director, I am grateful for the always productive disorientation. I will remember for a long time the afternoons after class, in silence, trying to process the vertigo felt as a result of the knowledge in the room. I am happy that with me he discovered a new pleasure in thesis advising: "Seeing the anguished look of the mentee in front of his object."

To Fabian, the orange tones you were able to bring to the afternoons were essential to another productivity.

To Virginia, another sibling, I appreciate wisdom in the form of a joke, and vice versa.

To my mother, endless thanks for helping me in so many ways. It's hard to say in which way you've helped me the most. Perhaps by having opened my eyes to what most practitioners of Theatre of the Oppressed do not see: the importance of Arena Theatre. For your so-often solitary combat, my respect. For so many achievements, my admiration. For your love, mine.

Thanks to Gabriel for everything! In the field of the thesis, I am forever not grateful for the amount of work not done and I am grateful that you were the emergency exit that took me out of this academic alienation to focus on your concrete needs of having a father, your father, me, by your side.

To Joana, the deepest gratitude that can only be found, literally, beyond words. How to thank you for the smiles, the affection, the shared life? May the thirst never be quenched! I want at least another 20 years by your side. Renewable.

Introduction

Political theatre, like any kind of political[1] action, can only be judged in relation to the political conjuncture in which it was born and in which it tries to intervene.[2] Theatre of the Oppressed (TO) was created in order to fight against dictatorship and an extremely centralized conception of politics, so how does it function in a time of social media and so-called participatory democracies? This book tries to add to current understandings of how TO was created and how it can operate today.

TO encompasses both a set of political theatre techniques and a particular way of thinking about the relationship between politics and theatre.[3] Augusto Boal proposed that the oppressed should transgress the boundaries of the roles that have been projected onto them, not only taking possession of theatre but also changing its main functions by totally reconfiguring the division between the audience and the stage. These revolutionary ideas have now been diffused across many parts of the world. TO is practiced in more than 80 countries, and the core texts of A. Boal (as I will often refer to him in these pages) have been widely translated.[4]

A. Boal sometimes tends to account for the discovery of TO as a logical consequence in the evolution of a universal history of theatre. Within that history, TO and other Latin American theatre techniques invented around the same time would be part of a trajectory of theatre turning in on itself, meaning that the separation between actors and spectators framed as constituting theatre in the first place—a separation considered an oppressive contradiction—would be subsumed as theatre moves to a higher plane. And on that plane, the union of the community (spectators and actors as a collective) would be reestablished without losing the instance of theatrical representation. The parallel with a teleology that circulates in a certain Marxism is easy to trace here in the substitution of theatre for the means of production. This teleology sets up a situation in which many of those practitioners do not feel the need to ask today about the validity of techniques created now much more than 40 years ago. To portray the long emergence of TO, which was far from the epiphany sometimes described, to locate it in relation to its historical conjuncture, reveals that it articulated a critique of the Brazilian Communist Party, the Latin American Left in general, and their collapse when faced with the rise of dictatorships.

This book aims to re-historicize TO precisely to help create the conditions for its criticism now. Showing the creation of TO not as an epiphany—but as a process rooted within the cultural and political history of Brazil—can help the reader better understand TO as a response to a specific time and therefore open the question of how it relates to the present moment.

The success of TO is a living paradox. On the one hand, it is certainly rare for the use of a theatre technique to have expanded so far and so relatively rapidly, to the point that most countries in the world have TO groups (or groups influenced by TO). The proliferation of themes explored by such groups is seemingly endless. From domestic violence to the struggle against evictions

DOI: 10.4324/9781003325048-1

2 Introduction

to HIV prevention, hundreds of subjects have been engaged through TO. On the other hand, this proliferation has occurred in a period marked by a reversal of the revolutionary tide on which TO emerged. If Forum Theatre was intended to be, in A. Boal's own terms, a "rehearsal for the revolution," what does it become when the prospect of radical repossession of society seems to be no longer on the horizon?[5] The goal of attempting to explain this paradox is to answer the question: What of TO in neoliberal times?

Neoliberalism's date of birth is often identified as September 11, 1973, with the coup d'état in Chile. This historiographical choice is obviously questionable because political processes do not have dates of birth that are as specific as those of human beings. I, however, was born in 1975—after the death of Salvador Allende, months before the beginning of the bloody dictatorship in Argentina and the end of Portugal's revolution (the last European revolution). The revolutionary processes in which my father had placed his hopes were arriving at a dead end. I do not belong to the same times as my father. Nevertheless, my hopes—certainly different from his—were not smaller in scope. In 1995, the revolutionary winds that were blowing in Chiapas with the 1994 Zapatista revolt arrived in France (where I was living at the time), with one of the major popular uprisings to occur in that country. Those protests arose against the right-wing government, who wanted to pass severe reforms that would reduce aspects of French public services. The 1980s and their massive disenchantment with politics were definitely over. On a more personal level, I also had an epiphany of sorts. After a trip to India, where I witnessed the power and beauty of the people's movement known as Jana Sanskriti, I decided to work with TO. If it was possible to be a part of something similar to what I saw there, then I wanted in!

Unfortunately, to create such an enormous and beautiful mass movement was not as easy as the 20-something version of myself had initially thought it would be. Still, my naivete led me to engage fully in beautiful processes, always using TO: the creation of several collectives, the construction of networks of undocumented workers, of labor organizers, and alongside feminist groups …. In those days, I also had the opportunity to travel a lot with my father as his assistant. I encountered many countries through the very peculiar lens of TO. Many times, I found myself in awe of what I was seeing, but many times doubts started rising, too. Was I really witnessing the finally found form for the emancipated theatre? The question was tormenting me so much that it became one of the reasons why I moved back to Brazil. I came from France to Brazil with the intention of writing a thesis on the use of TO by the MST (Movimento Sem Terra, or the Brazilian Landless Movement). The idea was simple: to encounter finally in that social movement the "true" use of TO—to approach the burning center of the struggle to find within it theatrical weapons forged in a fire so scorching that I could use them to battle other groups who use TO for something that seems more like Interactive Victim Training, where TO is engaged not as a way to create knowledge to change the world but to inculcate—through theatrical games—pre-established notions designed by the powers that be. With those kinds of uses of the techniques—which do not encompass all TO, of course!—TO seems to be one of the fields of work in which what is being created is a curiously interactive form of what Paulo Freire critiqued as a "banking system" in education.

My plan was a simple one, but impossible to realize. The MST did not do TO or any other form of cultural action so often anymore. That inactivity was a reflection and a symptom of a crisis in the movement, which seemed to hesitate on how to continue advancing in this new and so serious situation that is ours. But, worse than that (speaking strictly from my individual perspective), I could no longer see in A. Boal's writings a flawless shield merely awaiting the historical subject capable of wielding it in battle. What if all those reactionary uses of TO were not just a consequence of bad readings of the books?[6] (If this were the case, we should ask if there have been other books in history that have been read so badly ….) What if these practices revealed potentialities that have always been present in those texts? And what if those potentialities now reveal themselves with such frequency due to a change so significant in our political conjuncture that nothing has been left untouched, from economy to nature and even our subjectivities? To what extent do those uses of TO reveal aspects of the felt experience of the new conjuncture in which we now evolve? The texts that follow can be read as a kind of diary of a journey across the seas of politics and theatre. No north pole will be reached, but here you will find notes composed on an always-moving landscape, with the hopes that, thanks to these reflections, others will find their own paths.

On the structure of this text

Though there are core questions and arguments that stretch across this book, the writings included in it represent many different moments of thinking. The range of essays and articles initially arose for various purposes, some as stand-alone essays, some as talks or speeches, some as chapters in my doctoral thesis. Some sections were written as recently as this year. Others I wrote well more than a decade ago and revised them for inclusion here. The style of writing inevitably varies because the original audiences varied. While sometimes I refer in later chapters to information or ideas contained in earlier chapters, readers need not necessarily encounter everything in order.

Part I: Criticizing a Critical Theatre

This book is divided into three sections. The first section, "Criticizing a Critical Theatre," focuses on historicization and re-historicization of TO, critiques of TO (others' and my own), and exploration of core TO terms like mechanization, oppression, etc. For example, the chapter "For a Political History of Theatre of the Oppressed" offers a definition of TO and tries to examine how some of the meanings of its key concepts (oppression, participation, representation, etc.) have changed between the 1970s and today. How do the meanings of those concepts now shape our understanding of how TO operates in the present?

Part of understanding TO today lies in comprehending its evolution over time. As a result, I also hope to expand upon some arguably lesser known aspects of the genealogies of praxis that led to TO. For example, in "Theatre of the Oppressed as a Formal Critique of the Brazilian Communist Party," I consider how a foundational element of TO was in fact the complete failure of the Brazilian Communist Party (the PCB)—the strongest Brazilian political organization of the 1960s—to predict and help prevent the coup d'état. In a way, A. Boal transformed his critique of the PCB into theatrical techniques. The party's intensely centralized and hierarchical organization was opposed by the horizontal organization of TO. The frame of the "people" (conceived by the PCB as an immense and absolutely heterogeneous alliance) as the main subject of the revolution was counterposed against TO's more fluid figure of the oppressed as the agent of change. A history divided into closed categories—where revolutionary change was always delayed—was replaced by the moment of the present as the opener of all possibilities that can be imagined by people no longer considered passive observers of progress.

But TO of course cannot be reduced to a mere critique of a Brazilian political organization. In its very essence, TO is theatre, and it is in the theatre field that we should seek out (and learn more about) forms and methods with similar aims or approaches, so that we can better understand TO's specificities. One of those more widely known influences on TO was Epic Theatre. In "TO and Epic Theatre," I compare two major attempts to overcome the bourgeois theatre, focusing mainly on Forum Theatre and on Bertolt Brecht's learning plays (*Lehrstücke*). Here I

4   Introduction

consider the extent to which Brecht's and A. Boal's respective critiques of Aristotelian theatre are similar and different. I examine their shared critiques of theatre as an institution—a means of production that owns its producers rather than being owned by them—and analyze their common attempts to create new theatrical forms and new means of production. In both forms, interruption plays a major role, but not in identical ways. In this chapter, I also contemplate the role of the "hero" and its remarkable differences in these two theatrical processes.

As many people know, aspects of Epic Theatre were severely criticized by A. Boal in the process of articulating TO. But TO—this peculiar manner of doing theatre that expanded so quickly to all corners of the globe—wasn't beyond the reach of criticism, either. The chapter of this book called "Critiques of Theatre of the Oppressed" attempts to address the two most prominent critiques of TO, one diametrically opposed to the other. The first—which is shared by a majority of critics—is one that praises the interactive and ludic aspects of TO on the way to criticizing it for its political core: its attachment to the concept of oppression, supposedly too Manichean or "over-simplistic" for understanding the current world. From the perspective of this critique, oppression would be merely the result of bad choices made through the powerful free wills of people who would just need some enlightenment to correct their actions. In contrast, the second category of critique—a more radical one—that I explore in this chapter finds fault with the interactivity of Forum Theatre, regarding it as a resource that gives a disproportionate amount of agency to its characters, an agency that would inevitably lead to a depoliticization of any issues presented. According to this latter critique, politics would then be evacuated and replaced by moralism. Such a critique leads then to two other questions upon which I elaborate: Would there be any other dramaturgy that could avoid the pitfalls of moralism? And, if such a critique is right, how do we explain the global success of TO?

It is to try to answer this question that I wrote the chapter "Theatre of the Oppressed in Neoliberal Times: From Che Guevara to the Uber Driver." There I consider TO as a political intervention, and therefore one that is only as good as its fight against the specific articulation of oppression that somehow commanded its creation. The contemporary problems of TO cannot be solved simply by calling them mistakes, treason, or bad use. Using the same method in different times can only lead to different outcomes. In this part of the book, I suggest that Forum Theatre was the theatrical transposition of guerilla principles, particularly the notion that an individual can make a difference by enacting a spectacular gesture of refusal of an oppressive situation, a gesture that would then strengthen the audience/people in their will to fight. Nowadays, when one could argue that no revolutionary perspective is on the horizon, the pathos of the hero would then be absorbed by neoliberal subjectivity, where heroism is the capacity to always fight for your own survival in an environment considered both hostile and uncontrollable.

In the chapter that follows, "Notes on Oppression," I try to elaborate on the concept of oppression to give a working definition of it. Though many people often avoid defining oppression precisely, to do so is nevertheless central to TO. The definition explored in this chapter attempts to avoid all the stereotypical dualistic definitions of oppressed and oppressors by putting forward the primacy of a third term, oppression itself. Oppression is frequently confused with a self-definition (I am oppressed if I say that I am) or a series of acts (I am an oppressor if I do so and so, e.g., enacting violence). The definition that I propose in this text considers oppression as a structural relation within our societies, a relation in which certain social groups take advantage of others. In this chapter, far away from any essentialization, oppression appears as a dynamic process always reconfiguring itself and, therefore, demanding constant adaptation in order to fight it.

In "Facilitation/Mechanization," I consider how—from time to time—certain uses of TO transform a type of theatre that was once critical into something redundant. I return specifically

Introduction 5

to the notion of mechanization, truly foundational in A. Boal's writings and practices. In doing so, I also revisit the theory of the social division of labor. Most importantly, this chapter tries to shed light on an issue not often discussed: the specialization/mechanization of the very practitioners of TO. How is this process affecting us? What happens when TO itself becomes a form of mechanization?

Part II: Small Screws, Big Twists: What Can Art Do in the Anti-Capitalist Struggle?

This text—a longer piece of writing that in and of itself forms the middle section of the book—springs from discomfort that I felt in relation to the 2020 elections for mayors and council members in Brazil. During that time, the Left's only propositions for artists concerned resources, as if all the problems of art could be solved by money alone. This feature of politics seems a profoundly utilitarian deal in which politicians offer resources in exchange for the prestige of artists supporting their campaigns. Upon analysis, this dynamic takes such a form that even the most radical politicians pose in front of artists as merely the managers of the state.

Departing from that observation, this section analyzes aspects of the modern state and why certain changes are impossible within it. I also engage aspects of the meaning of strategy—the collective construction, by the oppressed and of the oppressed, of a transformation project that is radical and total and that enables the mobilization of the masses to conquer state power. This strategy wants to invent ways to go beyond the conquest of the state to foster popular participation, without which the insurrection can, yes, become a moment of redeeming beauty, but one doomed merely to establish a new sequence of exploration. Lastly, this essay argues that art and, in particular, theatre have important roles to play within strategy, aggregating people and allowing the development of human and critical capacities that are not submitted to the dictates of capital.

Part III: Are There No Alternatives?

The final section of the book begins with an exploration of examples of absolutely vital present-day TO work in various countries. The examples I engage, however, are not intended as models. Instead, the idea of this section is to try to foster an understanding that TO can only be as good as it is well adapted to the specific circumstances in which it is used. This section also focuses on a new dramaturgy for Forum Theatre, one more capable of dealing with the contradictions that are the very fabric of life in bourgeois society.

The examples of TO groups that I chose to explore in this third section are not ones that I have selected with the idea of naming them "the best in the world." There are far too many TO collectives and organizations out there for someone to be able to award such a prize. Rather, the groups featured in this section are some of the ones with which I am the most familiar—and that I dearly appreciate, for reasons I try to explain in the text.

The first of these examples could not be any other than Jana Sanskriti—not only because of the personal influence that this group had on me, but also because of the group's importance in and of itself, both in the world of TO and in the sphere of Indian politics. Surely one of the most famous TO groups in the world, Jana Sanskriti consists of more than 30,000 peasants and operates in West Bengal using TO as a core methodology. From the perspective of a long-term collaborator with Jana Sanskriti, this chapter will summarize aspects of Jana Sanskriti's history in the process of trying to analyze its particular aesthetics and politics. Above all, I aim here to describe the expansion tactics of Jana Sanskriti, its very atypical way of implementing itself in new territories, and how TO fits within those tactics. My personal experience with

6 *Introduction*

Jana Sanskriti—informed by traveling to the constituencies that compose their political base six times and organizing several of their tours as well as workshops by Sanjoy Ganguly—has provided me with a particular perspective on the organizational aspects of their work that I believe should be emphasized—and in ways that relate to the broader ideas of this book.

The second part of this chapter is not about a group but about a meeting of a network of groups in Portugal. Óprima! is a yearly meeting that started among many TO collectives from within Portugal, groups that shared more than a technique; they also shared a similar anger and an urge to struggle against a crisis with many layers—social, political, and economic. Óprima! was born in 2012, a period marked by mass movements and strikes in Portugal. This period also necessitated the search for a new repertoire of collective action and forms of organization tending to be increasingly horizontal and fluid, capable of including those who were not part of existing organizations, whether parties, unions, or associations. TO looked like a form that resonated with the spirit of the demonstrations, given that it starts from a critique of the specialization of theatre and politics and that its fundamental device is based on a logic of participation that breaks the separation between actor and spectator, proposing that each person speak and represent their own reality. This chapter attempts to show how Óprima! connected with this period in Portugal, and, most importantly, how the meeting tries to survive its times without any fetishization, neither of TO nor of the meeting in itself.

The last example I explore in-depth is the closest to my heart: a group that I helped create and to which I belong. I describe the development of Escola de Teatro Popular (ETP, the Popular Theatre School). ETP was originally created by activists from various social movements of Rio de Janeiro, mainly housing and youth movements. The primary objective of this school was to teach political theatre, principally TO and Epic Theatre, to activists who would then return to their political movement bases to apply the knowledge acquired. The assassination of Rio de Janeiro City Councilperson (Vereadora) Marielle Franco on March 14, 2018, catalyzed a first twist on the school's initial goals. We no longer wanted to be merely a school *for* activists; we became an *activist school*. From that day onward, there were virtually no marches in which we were not present, doing theatre amid those marching. We performed in occupied buildings, gave workshops for social movements, and created an antifascist cultural front. And despite what thousands of Brazilians did to prevent Jair Bolsonaro's victory, he won the presidential election. Therefore, we launched a new step for the school: no longer just *for* activists and no longer just *an activist school*, now it would be the *school as a network* of ongoing workshops in working-class neighborhoods and *favelas* (the English translation often invoked, "slums," is not a precise one), each one of them related to social movements.

All the exercises, games, and theatrical processes in which Escola de Teatro Popular engages would fall under the banner of TO. Our specific work in that area, however, is informed by critiques of how the dramaturgy of Forum Theatre did not surpass or overcome the ideologies of the bourgeois drama. Such critiques are the very focus of the first section of the chapter "The Search for a Subjunctive Theatre": "On the Limitations of Bourgeois Drama." The kinship between bourgeois drama and Forum Theatre (at least as it tends to be practiced) occurs in the construction of plays that (1) have intersubjective relationships as an insurmountable horizon for the themes presented and (2) deploy dialogue as their most powerful instrument. Though today several groups try to make Forum Theatre without dialogue, the characters in the scenes are still often staged as fully conscious and free subjects. In such scenes, characters who are absolutely transparent to themselves—unaffected by unconscious internal divides or social constraints—face each other, approaching pure drama, which seems to give the human a privileged position, one of almost absolute autonomy and where the only subject relations occur without

Introduction   7

mediation, between individuals. How this kinship with the bourgeois drama limits the scope of Forum Theatre is ultimately the subject of the initial portion of the chapter.

The traditional model of Forum Theatre works in many, many situations; in some others, however, it appears problematic. The creation of a new model therefore seemed like a necessity. The latter section of the chapter "The Search for a Subjunctive Theatre"—"Can Dialectics Break Bricks (and help Forum Theatre)?"—is about my attempt to forge another model. The new dramaturgical structure or schema that I explain here is not a universal solution but one specific to a desire to create a more dialectical dramaturgical approach. The particular focus on developing a dialectical scheme (the oxymoron of this expression is not lost on me) came about for two main reasons. The first is that I believe that, when faced with another dramaturgical possibility for the construction of Forum Theatre, practitioners can think of these schemes as propositions, and it is up to them to know which structure is the most suited to the material they wish to treat—or to invent other schemes so that those dramaturgical structures can correspond in the most finely honed ways to the problems that they want to address. The invention of a new schema is a step, I believe, for such structures to be revealed as tools and not dogma. The second reason for proposing this more dialectical scheme is that I believe that it is possible to find a dramaturgical structure that is—while maintaining interventions by the audience—more capable of dealing with the mediations through which oppression manifests without falling into the opposite of Guevarist voluntarism: a kind of fetishism of an absolute obsolescence of human activity.

This more dialectical approach to Forum Theatre can obviously benefit from being combined with the hundreds of games and exercises that already exist in the arsenal of TO, but it can also use other exercises that have the element of contradiction as a core frame. In the last chapter of the book, "Exercises for a More Dialectical Practice of Forum Theatre," I offer some practical exercises and scenarios designed to highlight contradictions, in case the reader might want to use any of those exercises in their own work. I also illustrate or elaborate on aspects of those exercises by offering examples of some of the dramaturgical/structural principles at their core. As I pose those examples, I often refer to existing works of theatre that have—in their structure or intention—a political content. The exercises are aimed at reimagining scene structures to challenge dominant ideologies directly. This chapter will give examples of these scenic models and how to apply them.

On the one hand, this book explores TO as a phenomenon whose proliferation might arise precisely from its capacity to acquiesce to aspects of neoliberalism (individualism, market frameworks, tests, performance evaluation, competition with others and oneself, etc.). On the other hand, I want to avoid a despairing assumption that such acquiescence is inevitable. I try to steer away from that despair precisely by describing examples of groups whose TO practices give me hope, groups who insist on surrendering only the absolute bare minimum to the logics of our present subjugation. TO might die one day. Hopefully that will be the day when there will be no oppression—if that day ever comes! Until then, we—all of us theatre makers who want to witness the freedom glimpsed on our stages expand in scope until it becomes the law of this world—will need to stay observant about how oppression continues to evolve. We will need to be realistic about how staging oppression effectively is never an easy task. The continual re-elaboration of this world urges us to constantly review the tools we use to imagine what emancipation would look, sound, and feel like. This book is a call to not ever rely completely on the achievements of those who preceded us; however wonderful those achievements or those people themselves may have been. And wonderful they were. We will pay homage to them precisely by staying mindful about how we use and refine our tools in our own times, not by celebrating unquestioningly those who came before us. Instead, we will honor the people from whom we have learned by trying to continue their struggles in an always-shifting landscape.

8 *Introduction*

Notes

1 Politics might be the term that I use most frequently in this book; nevertheless, it is not a term that is easy to define. In the pages that follow, I use the term in two different senses, depending on the specific instance in question. First, especially when referring to political theatre, the use of the word politics in this book tends to imply a representation in which sociability appears to be a construct that depends on larger structures present in society. On a broader level, politics also refers to all the actions that try to construct power relationships in order to manifest the principle according to which everyone is equal to anyone. In other words, the term politics contains a contradiction that makes it capable of designating both attempts to conserve society as it is *and* attempts to transform society radically.

2 I refer to conjuncture in the sense of a collection of factors that—in the particular ways they come together—determine aspects of a situation (like, for example, the political situation of a specific country).

3 To learn more about TO as it was initially elaborated by Augusto Boal, its founder and creator, I recommend that readers also consult his own texts on the subject: *Theatre of the Oppressed*, *Games for Actors and Non-Actors*, *Rainbow of Desire: The Boal Method of Theatre and Therapy*, *Legislative Theatre: Using Performance to Make Politics*, *Hamlet and the Baker's Son: My Life in Theatre and Politics*, *Aesthetics of the Oppressed*, etc.

4 I know that in many contexts it is unusual to repeatedly refer to an author by using both the first initial and the last name. At the same time, my relationship to this particular author—my father, Augusto Boal, whom I so deeply love and respect—is far from the usual relationship between a researcher and a source, so I hope my readers will understand this idiosyncrasy.

5 Forum Theatre is the most well-known TO technique. In ideal conditions, Forum Theatre works as follows: A play is created by a certain group of people who have the experience of a specific oppression as a common denominator. That particular oppression, then, is precisely the subject of the play, in which the protagonist tries to defeat the oppression and fails. Immediately after this performance, the actors reenact the play, this time giving the opportunity for members of the audience to replace the protagonist and try to find alternative ways to struggle against oppression. The most important aspect here is the opportunity to discuss the oppression collectively and witness that it is changeable; the focus is not on finding "the" perfect solution to work against it.

6 The reader might be surprised—or at least I certainly hope they might be!—by the existence of such reactionary uses of TO, which I mention here and will describe more fully later. To give a very general—and therefore abstract—preview here of what those uses are, I could say that what most of them have in common is the complete absence of a more systemic view of oppression and, as a consequence, a complete absence of the prospect of overcoming it.

Part I
Criticizing a Critical Theatre

1 For a Political History of Theatre of the Oppressed

Political theatre is a theatre that has embraced the cause of emancipation. In its attempt to escape idealism and dogmatism, what remains is a theatre at once determined by the sociopolitical conjuncture while also desiring to influence it. It is therefore natural for political theatre to have suffered, to a certain extent, the consequences of the century that saw its development. It is also natural for its possibilities to be restored by a resurgence of a socially and theoretically combative spirit.

Theatre of the Oppressed (TO) did not escape the contradictions of the previous century, nor did it survive them unscathed. While the book *Theatre of the Oppressed* itself was first published in Argentina in 1975, the method of the same name was rooted in Augusto Boal's earlier research and experiences.

A. Boal was a member of *Teatro de Arena* (Arena Theatre). The theatre, founded by José Renato, had the core objectives of staging low-budget productions and carrying out dramaturgical research and experimentation; these were intended as clear alternatives to the high bourgeois theatre of São Paulo, known as *Teatro Brasileiro de Comédia* (Brazilian Comedy Theatre). The significant and unexpected success of the play *They Don't Wear Black Tie* saved the group from ruin and led them to discover a much wider audience interested in themes related to Brazilian politics. *Teatro de Arena* became the great theatrical referent for young people from universities just starting to gain political consciousness. Politicization took on diverse forms, though the dominant discourse of the Left was that of the Brazilian Communist Party or the PCB (Partido Comunista Brasileiro). At the time, the party called for the formation of a great alliance that would bring together all the classes, even parts of the capitalist class, parts that were suffering—according to the party—as a result of the competition from North American imperialists. Only the large-scale landowners and industrialists who were pro-imperialism were left out of this alliance. In this conception, ideology was far more important than class, and intellectuals and artists had no reason to question their distance from "the People." That distance was experienced only as one that separated ignorance from knowledge—knowledge that intellectuals, artists, and others had the duty to spread to the masses.

The following anecdote is well known, at least among practitioners of TO. In a village in the hinterlands of Pernambuco, Brazil, after the presentation of a play about agrarian reform that ended by calling for armed struggle, a peasant came to talk to the theatre group. He thanked them for the play and praised the cast. Then he asked the troupe—who had just sung "we must shed our blood to free our land!"—to grab the gleaming weapons shown onstage and join the peasants in a fight against a colonel and his henchmen the next day. The troupe was evidently unnerved by such a proposal and declined the invitation. The weapons were props; the actors didn't know how to shoot! According to A. Boal, the peasant replied, "So in that song you are singing about our peasant blood, not your blood, the blood of artists?!"[1]

DOI: 10.4324/9781003325048-3

12   *Criticizing a Critical Theatre*

A. Boal always said that this was the moment when he decided to begin a new form of research, one in which theatre would no longer dictate to audiences their identities, their problems and suffering, or the solutions to their issues. The Brazilian dictatorship, the defeat of the Left in much of Latin America, A. Boal's exile in various countries, his experience with the literacy program in Peru and Ecuador, where he learned about Pedagogy of the Oppressed—all of these factors played a part in the creation and maturation of TO.[2] This theatre, this "work method, philosophy of life, technique system," is based on the three fundamental principles that follow.[3]

"Give the oppressed the means of theatrical production"

Actors, specialists in the art of expression, can no longer think of themselves as invisible vectors capable of re-transcribing the story of anyone and everyone. The monopoly that actors hold on the stage must be transgressed. The oppressed must take the stage. By making theatre, oppressed people may recover the intellectual and physical possibility denied to them by the ways that they have been represented. They are able to escape, at least in part, the identity imposed on them by others, by the oppressors. This move to the stage is a kind of reclamation, but also, necessarily, an act of research, an investigation. Constructing one's own representation triggers a crisis in the dominant forms of representation. It is inevitable to fight against "the invasion of the brains," as described by A. Boal in his final book, *The Aesthetics of the Oppressed*. The concern with no longer delegating anything to experts, with bringing marginalized knowledge to the fore, is the same as Michel Foucault's concern with the "active intolerance" studies he promoted within the Prisons Information Group, of which he was one of the founders: "Those investigations are not made from outside, by a group of technicians: the investigators, here, are the very investigated. It's up to them to take the speech, tear down the walls, formulate what is intolerable, and no longer tolerate it. It's up to them to be in charge of the struggle that will prevent oppression from being exercised."[4]

"In a Forum Theatre scene, the center of gravity is in the audience, not on the stage"

The first oppression that TO proposes to fight is precisely the oppression generated by theatre itself. The name TO suggests that there is a theatre that does not belong to the oppressed, a theatre that belongs to the oppressor. TO is, to a certain extent, a fight against theatre. Though A. Boal takes up Brecht's criticism of the "digestive," "hypnotic" theatre that serves as a "compensation office for unlived adventures," the former's criticism is more radical. A. Boal's primary critique of the theatre targets the divide between actors and audience, the immutable division of tasks between those who are authorized to speak, to act, and those who are confined to silence, to darkness: "Aristotle's Poetics is the Poetics of Oppression: The world is known, perfect or perfectible; its values are imposed on spectators. They passively delegate their power to the characters so that they can act and think in their place."[5]

It is no longer enough to stage plays of critical, progressive, or revolutionary content. The relationship between stage and the auditorium must be reviewed in and of itself. Otherwise, all hopes of transforming theatre into a possible instrument of emancipation will fail, particularly given that even Brechtian theatre could spark catharsis.[6] This critique of theatre offered by A. Boal is, of course, inspired by Paulo Freire's critique of education.[7]

Freire, too, is a poignant critic of his reality, that of a "banking" concept of education, in which "the teacher presents himself to his students as their necessary opposite; by considering their ignorance absolute, he justifies his own existence."[8] The pedagogy put forward by Paulo

For a Political History of Theatre of the Oppressed 13

Freire is based on a hypothesis of trust: it is impossible to be absolutely ignorant; the work is to constantly expand knowledge, starting with one's own knowledge. It is also impossible to teach when one considers their student inferior. To consider certain people absolutely ignorant reproduces oppressive ideology. Such a form of belief divides the world into two groups: (1) those who know and were born to be knowledgeable and (2) those who have the truth imposed on them.

"Forum Theatre is a rehearsal for revolution"

It is true that A. Boal's theatre is, in a way, also a theatre that postpones insurrection, but this "delay" can only be understood in light of how it enacts a sharing of adversities, a tactical construction of a plurality of forms of emancipation to be put into play. According to him, "Theatre is not superior to action. It is a preliminary phase. I can't substitute it. A strike teaches more."[9]

A. Boal talks of a "rehearsal for revolution."[10] It is sad to be reminded that a rehearsal in itself is not enough, that rehearsal remains in a way inert until the moment arrives when it can become reality. TO is a moment in a long march toward emancipation. It is not satisfied by its sole existence—were that the case, it would lose itself in its own criticism: momentary contentment, pure aesthetic satisfaction. TO is, by definition, insufficient. But that is certainly part of what makes it interesting: it is not satisfied by scenic closure, by a purely theatrical doing, but instead strives with all its power precisely to overcome the theatre. In this sense, TO is inspired by the Leninist concept of culture: it is a small screw that is part of a great mechanism of revolution.

In the face of today's artistic narcissisms, with many people presenting themselves as heroes when they run little political risk, TO has known its boundaries from the beginning, always identifying its own limitations and acknowledging that it is not a replacement for political struggle. In fact, it has done so also as a way of outlining its own space and power, which would allow it to act politically upon reality. It is partially an instrument of here-and-now liberation, but also of creation and the collectivization of hopes, of images of a world yet to be constructed. This theatre does not replace the strike or the fight. In the best of cases, however, theatre can lead to either one of those, and—who knows?—perhaps it can lend them more reflective and prospective contours.

The three principles cited here led A. Boal to the construction of a coherent system of diverse theatrical forms: Image Theatre, Newspaper Theatre, Invisible Theatre, Rainbow of Desire, and others. Of all these forms, without a doubt, the most practiced and well-known is Forum Theatre. In Forum, a group of people who—ideally—share a specific form of oppression come together and create a performance in which the protagonist tries to fight against a certain manifestation of that oppression and ends up defeated. The presentation happens in two phases. The first time around, the play runs as a play usually would, but in front of an audience with a connection to the specific oppression performed. The second time through, a facilitator (called the Joker) asks members of the audience to replace the protagonist and try out alternative ways to fight against the oppressive structures depicted. There is not a precise number of expected interventions, and the search is not so much for a solution. Rather, Forum aims to study a situation from different perspectives and to turn spectators into what A. Boal termed "spect-actors," active investigators and legitimate voices in a discourse that refutes the fatality of oppression.

TO had a curious destiny. Distinct from Brechtian theatre, which suffered a certain eclipse in the 1980s, TO apparently did not itself suffer from the reversal of the revolutionary political momentum that accompanied its birth. On the contrary, the expansion of TO was dizzying. That phenomenon can be noticed in various ways. A. Boal's books were translated into more than 25 languages. A website registered TO groups in over 60 countries (and I know of many countries where TO is practiced that don't even have groups listed there, so the number of countries is

14 *Criticizing a Critical Theatre*

much larger: more than 80, at least).[11] Many countries have more than one group. On most continents, every year there are encounters and festivals where practitioners from various countries have the opportunity to meet and create a sort of international community of TO.

The expansion of TO is not only geographical but thematic as well. With topics spanning the living conditions of prisoners to the need for agrarian reform to the fight against the privatization of higher education, it seems plausible that there is no relevant issue that has not been used by someone to create a TO scene.

This apparent success is partly due to the co-optation of TO by the capitalist system, which has often defanged it. Regarding the use of TO, A. Boal had already pointed out the need to distinguish between "creative heresies" and "unforgivable betrayals."[12] He objected, for example, to the use of the method as a human resources technique for selecting employees or improving the relationship between workers and managers in a company. But were these the only betrayals of TO?

There are absolutely extraordinary experiences that have originated from TO. Take, for example, the Jana Sanskriti movement in India. With its creation rooted in TO, today Jana Sanskriti includes more than 25,000 peasants fighting for things like land reform and gender equality. It has also founded an Indian Federation of TO, which now has more than 400,000 members, all of them militants in social movements.[13]

At the same time, the existence of these experiences cannot cover up the fact that, for the most part, what is done with TO—I believe—more closely resembles a kind of Interactive Victim Training. By that I mean that, play after play, it seems as though one of the core aims of the actors onstage is to make their audience accept—in one way or another—the reality in which they live, merely asking them to change minor aspects of it but never the whole frame. What made that sort of usage possible? Such broad deployment of the techniques resulted in a TO festival in Austria in 2009—only months after A. Boal's death—where hundreds of practitioners gathered to debate whether TO could or could not be used as a tool to mediate the communication between capitalists and workers. The answer to the question of how TO came to be used in such ways can be found in large part by analyzing the evolution of its historical contexts and by examining the contradictions and ambiguities of A. Boal's own texts, where he articulates in a highly original manner themes like participation, representation, and oppression.

Participation

In terms of participation by non-actors on stage, it is the question of the spectator that generates controversy. Those who contest this cornerstone of theatrical practice—the notion of the spectator—have always been in the minority. The current hegemonic political context only doubles down on that reality: rare are the voices who vigorously affirm that the truth can only be apprehended from the point of view of actors and not by those who examine the scene from a distance. The emancipation of the oppressed can result only from the work of the oppressed themselves. In this respect, valuing the perspective of the actor at the expense of the spectator defies certain trends of our time.

TO's diminishment of the primacy of a purely spectatorial perspective establishes *praxis* as a distinctive and selective element of its criteria. However, the task of defining true emancipatory participation seems more complicated by the day. Just as Roberto Schwarz notes that Brechtian alienation techniques like distanciation and exposing artistic labor have lost much of their critical potential and are now part of the arsenals of advertising and television news, the act of participation itself has also been trivialized and sweetened.[14]

Television shows counting on the active participation of the public are innumerable. In fact, one of the resources of reality shows is precisely the promotion of audience members to the

For a Political History of Theatre of the Oppressed 15

status of main characters who will win or lose depending on the viewers' choices. Talent shows seem to have found the formula for inexhaustible success, news reports seek the opinions of passersby, and A. Boal himself had to fight the confusion that was created between Invisible Theatre and pranks.[15]

What's more, participatory democracy, which aroused international enthusiasm by proposing original formulas for the democratization of power, seems to have become a motto devoid of content. Today, non-governmental organizations (NGOs) are dressed up in the garb of conduct beyond reproach, offering the populations with whom they work the possibility of choosing between ready-made and unquestionable options. The palm branch of ideological falsehood probably belongs to Ségolène Royal, a French Socialist Party candidate in the 2007 presidential election, who promoted meetings under the name of participatory democracy in which citizens were invited to *freely* express themselves on any topic. These assemblies, deprived of any decision-making power, only served to manage thousands of contradictory individual positions that could not be synthesized, as they lacked the common denominator of the debate of any proposals.

Without a doubt, participation is in vogue. Company employees are increasingly asked to surrender themselves completely to their work under the models of the quality control circle or the network enterprise (*empresas em rede* or company networks). According to sociologists Luc Boltanski and Eve Chiapello, this kind of workplace exploration is intensifying, with certain fundamental human capacities—imagination, emotional involvement, flexibility, among others—now also put to work. Before, Taylorism—precisely because it treated men like machines—could not reach or deploy those capacities.[16]

In the world of art, interactive installations have become banal. Countless are the performances that resort to audience participation in one form or another, to the point of making us question whether the emancipatory potential of participation is as ample as A. Boal imagined. Do spectators really take a step toward their own emancipation when they take on the role of actor?

Jacques Rancière invites us to criticize this presupposition and many others in his 2008 book *The Emancipated Spectator*. His main objective is to "reconstruct the network of presuppositions that place the question of the spectator at the heart of the discussion of the relations between art and politics," in order to verify how much these assumptions represent a radical deviation in relation to what he calls intellectual emancipation.[17] The main principle is what most people would imagine. Or, as philosopher Peter Hallward says, "Contrary to all philosophers, sociologists and technocrats convinced that only those with time and authorized to think, think, Rancière argues that the ability to escape oneself and one's space belongs to all."[18]

And this precise principle was denied by political theatre as a form when the genre demanded its audience go from a state of passivity to action. But what passivity are we talking about when we talk about spectators? We only can automatically associate gaze with passivity if we presuppose that someone who enjoys images admires their appearances only and ignores the reality under them, as well as the reality outside the theatre. For Rancière, "[b]eing a spectator is not some passive condition that we should transform into activity."[19] The spectator is not devoid of power; on the contrary, a spectator has a specific power: "It is the power each of them has to translate what she perceives in her own way, to link it to the unique intellectual adventure that makes her similar to all the rest in as much as this adventure is not like any other."[20]

The participation of the audience onstage is therefore disqualified by Rancière as just the new in the guise of the old, where "art was defined by the active imposition of a form on passive material; this effect linked it to a social hierarchy in which men of active intelligence dominated men of material passivity."[21] In fact, many times TO practitioners seem to fall victim to a naive arrogance that leads them to believe that they hold the secret to the liberation of their audience. The audience is usually conceived as an amorphous mass of spectators helplessly

16 *Criticizing a Critical Theatre*

swept up in the incessant currents of image-as-commodity, and liberation is usually imagined to be as simple as active participation onstage. That is why there are increasingly more Forum Theatre performances in which spectators are forbidden from speaking from the audience and sometimes even onstage during their interventions, relegating them solely to pantomime, as if emancipation were only possible onstage or when the spectator gives up speech.

As I see it, Rancière rightly destroys the myth of the all-mighty performance that influences the audience. This destruction is, without a doubt, necessary as a kind of negative lens, as a way to question radically the assumptions on which many forms of political theatre are based. But my first hypothesis is that such destruction comes at the expense of creating another myth, that of the similarly all-mighty spectator ever-capable of maintaining a distance and retranslating what is presented to them. The real challenge, in my view, would be to create a dialectical model that is the transposition to performance studies of Marx's famous line in *The Eighteenth Brumaire of Louis Napoleon:* "Men make their own history, but they do not make it as they please; they do not make it under self-selected circumstances." That model would entail, in other words, thinking of the performance as a stance that retains some level of effectiveness in generating the imagination of a spectator who, on the other hand, is not reduced solely to the role of a passive consumer.

However, another possible reading of the relationship between the audience and the stage, one that "saves" TO, is within the scope of Jacques Rancière's philosophy. This relationship would no longer be one that separates "the living from the dead," but one that opens up space for the possible transgression of a prohibition that constitutes our societies—the prohibition of those who have nothing or are considered nothing from being able to express themselves as those who hold the legitimacy of discourse.[22]

A. Boal's critique of conventional theatre enacts a radical refusal of a hierarchy that defines who is able to go onstage and who would not be considered able to do so. Such hierarchy is not limited to the realm of theatre. It is, on the contrary, one of the foundations of our societies. It pulses throughout life in general, "encouraging a population to become mere spectators of 'exceptional beings' and not discovering the exceptional in each one."[23] And this hierarchy exists above all in parliamentary democracies in which the voter, a spectator of another kind, exercises their power—that of voting—only to see it disappear across the elected-actor's time in office. That is why we "do not accept the voter as a simple spectator of parliamentary actions, even when [those actions] are correct."[24]

In summary, we could say that TO follows Lenin's proposal in *The State and Revolution*: seizing state power is certainly an important objective, but only if it is immediately articulated with its own radical transformation, one where power does not exist as an entity separate from the people. There is no use making theatre itself; it is necessary to transform it so that theatre is not just another space of transmission from those who supposedly possess knowledge to those who supposedly do not.

This other way of reading directly relates to what Rancière proposes as politics, which he defines as something that only occurs in the rare moments in which those who cannot and should not be counted intervene in order to actualize the paradigm in which anyone is absolutely equal with anyone else.

TO would then be a figure of the theatre denounced by Plato. Plato was—according to Rancière—a vehement critic of the tragedy not because the stories would be immoral, but because Plato perceived a direct link between the theatrical fiction and democratic politics. The fact that someone could be something else other than what he was designed for—that a worker could talk as an aristocrat—would introduce the germ of democracy in the polis, functioning as a demonstration, in practice, that all individuals could do more and be more than what the organization of the city allowed them to do and be.

This obstruction and confusion are also at the heart of A. Boal's project, one in which "[e]veryone can do theatre: even actors."[25] From this perspective, we can perhaps overcome the unproductive divide between passive and active to find in participation itself the possibility of an act of critique of the social division of labor, which, according to Marx, "only really becomes a division from the moment that a division between material and intellectual labours is installed."[26] The possibilities of participation and interruption offered by Forum Theatre would therefore be a here-and-now critique, in which, from now on—and not in a communist society to come—it would be possible, albeit fictionally, "to be critical at night" after working during the day.

TO would be a mechanism that works against the hierarchy of the capitalist system, "[i]n other words a hierarchy that no longer is, like in pre-capitalist societies, legitimised by social statutes, but by techno-scientific competencies necessary for the organization of a process of production that has become collective."[27]

Representation

Historically speaking, time and again political crises tend to overlap with economic crises, and cultural crises tend to overlap with political crises. In 1917, the October Revolution brought with it a vast agitprop movement that would attract prominent names like Vladimir Mayakovsky and Sergei Tretyakov. This movement's influence reached revolutionary Germany, where, according to Philippe Ivernel, agitprop's cultural and political strategy was to seek a transformation of content—but also its forms and functions—in order to denounce the illusion that art was a separate activity (an illusion that was functional to maintain bourgeois hegemony). This denunciation was paired with the denunciation of the patented representatives of the working class. The self-directed/autonomous revolutionary German theatre questions who speaks and their legitimacy to speak in the name of others, both on stage and in politics.

In Brazil, according to Roberto Schwarz, the 1964 coup d'état—which limited the vast democratic movement to which a new form of theatre sought to respond—at first allowed the arts to operate with relative freedom. This abbreviated freedom meant that, in a way, the arts became a replacement for the political struggles that could no longer happen on traditional stages. "As it could not be otherwise, the trump card of the same Left, which, on the street, had been beaten down almost without a fight, was to bring to the stage the marks of what had happened, leading to unforeseen directions, like Brechtian experimentations, among many others."[28]

One of these unforeseen directions, borrowing from Schwarz, was A. Boal's use of Brechtian narrative procedures, seeking to provide a critical distance "from vehicles of national, 'epic', emotion, to counterbalance political defeat."[29]

Exile and the successive defeats of the Latin American Left in the face of the coups d'état made A. Boal take Brechtian theatre—and theatre as a whole—in other unforeseen directions, too.

A plausible hypothesis is that—after witnessing how the illusions of the Left were confronted by the violence of repressive state apparatuses and their relative indifference toward the majority of the population, country after country—many exiled intellectuals critically reflected on their errors of interpretation or strategy.

A. Boal's analysis is, in part, that revolutionary organizations and theatre groups of the Left were fated to defeat, since they were not part of the people they addressed: "The people who make theatre belong in general, directly or indirectly, to the dominant classes: their closed visions will then be those of the dominant classes. The spectator of popular theatre, the people, can no longer continue to be a passive victim of these images."[30]

18   *Criticizing a Critical Theatre*

A. Boal's critique of theatre is similar in certain points to that of the state by Marx. In Antoine Artous' reading of this critique, when the state announces modern citizenship, it does so by abstracting citizens from their social differences—in other words, abstracting individuals from their concrete conditions of existence.[31] In doing so, the modern state constructs the notion that individuals are not inserted in antagonistic social groups. The idea of sovereign people, of national common interests, is a reformulation of the classes' contradictions.[32]

In a similar way, theatre invites the audience to identify itself with an imaginary community, where *hamartia* (defined by A. Boal as "the only trait that is not in harmony with what society regards as desirable"[33]) will be purged.

Thus, TO can be seen as an attempt to rupture with the ideological function of theatre by adapting it to a popular invention against parliamentary democracy, an invention then adopted and promoted later by various sectors of the international extreme Left: the Soviets.

With the Soviets, there was no longer a separation between abstract citizens and concrete individuals. The separations of workers from their means of production and of the state from civil society were again questioned. The right to vote, to represent as well as to be represented, was directly determined according to a social statute. Roughly speaking, only a worker from a given factory had the right to vote in that factory, having acquired this right by being a worker.[34] Likewise, in TO, the right to develop a representation, to act and intervene in it, is directly related to a certain condition of oppression. Following this logic, only unemployed people could act in a play about unemployment, only LGBTQIA+ people could act in a play about homophobia or heteronormativity, etc.

This way of conceiving representation is not without its problems. Daniel Bensaïd tells us that the critique generally addressed toward the soviet type of democracy relates to its corporative logic. Effectively, the question of how to create a general will from a sum of particular interests remains open. The corporativist logic is only capable of adding, without ever being able to create a synthesis that goes beyond the interest of a locality or of a factory.

Another question arises: If workers appropriating their means of production (whether theatrical or not) in revolutionary times runs the risk of leading the oppressed toward a corporate vision of their interests, what happens, then, when this appropriation takes place in non-revolutionary times?

The 1917 heritage seems far away. If a specter is haunting Europe today, more than that of communism, it is the frightening specter of Stalinism—not as an intrinsic possibility, but as a negative model of the so-called new social movements. A fair criticism of Stalinist parties often leads to a radical denunciation of the principle of representation itself.

This renunciation of any type of representation also has other roots, one of which is the disruption of the world of labor. According to Boltanski and Chiapello, the deterioration of the labor market made the representation of unions more delicate.[35] The very precarity of labor—beyond the unemployment caused by relocations, the increase in productivity by technology, and the bankruptcy of sectors that were true union bastions—made French unionism face a totally new situation:[36] the restructuring of labor created situations where, within the same factory, workers work for different companies and, therefore, are subject to different statutes. How, then, to create an effectively organized representation of these collectives? This fragmentation of the statutes is a factor that contributed to the disintegration of the labor community by disorienting and disarming the collective struggle.

Increasingly less representative of workers, French unions are progressively seen as a new sort of "nomenclature" or legal classification concerned only with maintaining the illusion of social dialogue in a way that allows them to benefit from privileges granted by the state. This accusation unfortunately cannot be regarded as completely slanderous.

For a Political History of Theatre of the Oppressed 19

Another root of the disdain toward representations that will be investigated here is French philosophy, mainly that which was developed in the late 1960s and early 1970s. Isabelle Garo—in a book on the relationship between Marx, Foucault, Deleuze, and Althusser—categorizes the latter three as postmodernism. For her, "[the] merit of the notion of postmodernity is to focus on the relationship between ideas and reality, defined as mimetic and no longer representative."[37]

In fact, a text presented as a conversation between Foucault and Deleuze addresses the question of representation as one of its main themes. Deleuze states that representation is the turning point between reformism and revolution: according to Deleuze, the very fact of having delegates representing others makes it impossible for the organization to demand something else, something other than a reorganization of power.

> Or the reform is carried out by people who claim to be representative and whose occupation is to speak for others, on behalf of others, and it is a reorganization of power, a distribution of power that is accompanied by increasing repression. Or it is a reform demanded, demanded by those whom it concerns, and then it ceases to be a reform, it is a revolutionary action that, due to its partial nature, is determined to call into question the totality of power and its hierarchy.[38]

For Foucault and Deleuze, there is no possibility whatsoever for there to be an organization in which representatives are legitimate delegates who are actually under the control of the people they represent. In the same text, they add: "We mean that representation was ridiculed, it was said that it was over, but no consequences were drawn from this 'theoretical' conversion, that is to say, the theory demanded that the people whom it concerned speak for themselves."[39] In other words, on the one hand, ideas become reality itself, and, on the other, all representative organizations are condemned as unavoidably reactionary, inevitably reproducing power.

Such discourse is quite widespread today. Two of the authors most read by the alter-globalist movement, Toni Negri and John Holloway, are clearly in favor of a political figure who would dispense with thinking about representation. For Negri, "'the democracy of the multitude' affirms the radical impossibility of representation, since in globalization 'the multitude without a sovereign' is directly opposed, 'without mediation,' by Capital and the Empire."[40]

Recent social movements still in development have invaded the world's squares, often with the common theme of a distrust of forms of representation. In Spain, one of the most followed slogans of the 15M movement was and still is: "Nobody represents us, we represent nobody." If the first part of the sentence is easily understandable within the Spanish political system—in which the alternation of power between the Spanish Socialist Workers' Party and the Popular Party has no significant effect on the neoliberal management of the state—the second part of the sentence (we represent nobody) is more sensitive. What would become of a movement that completely sets aside the intention of representing people outside of it? Wouldn't the intention of a demonstration be precisely to create visibility for a critical claim toward the state, so that people who are not (yet) demonstrating can join the cause? When—in the Plural Manifesto written in the Puerta del Sol—the protesters define themselves as "students, teachers, librarians, the unemployed, workers, etc.," are they not implicitly assuming that the problems that they are naming apply to all these categories and even others, and that, in a way, they, the protesters, are *representing* others, the absentees?[41]

Without a doubt, institutions representative of the bourgeoisie are extremely criticizable, even nefarious. Their tendency toward bureaucratization—toward the separation between those who manage and those who are managed—has spread across the labor movement and across all organizations that hold emancipatory aims.

20 *Criticizing a Critical Theatre*

The radical critique of this division of labor is perhaps one of the most remarkable and positive aspects of the Indignados movement in Spain or the Occupy Wall Street movement. The problem, in my view, is that these movements seem to believe that any type of representation ends up necessarily reproducing this division of labor. General assemblies that do not designate any sort of delegate or representative may work well for a certain time or for certain clusters, but—to cite two examples—how can the working class or women, as collectives, be able to express their voices without thinking about forms of representation? Legitimate criticism of political representation within bourgeois society, at least as I see it, will have to unfold further into a reflection on a practice of other possible forms of representation.

While the thesis that negates the value of representation may answer a real question of how not to deprive the oppressed of their own word, it leaves several other questions open. Some may seem trivial, but the issue of controlling spokespeople so that they are not co-opted by the media, for example, seems to me of great relevance. Informal delegations often turn out to be the worst.

How to avoid falling into what Bensaïd calls the "illusion of the social," the notion of a refuge of purity against the commitments and the obsessions of the fight for personal power that are characteristic of politics itself?[42] The specificity of politics would be sought, far from its own constitutive corruption, in the fact that "it is not limited to a bouquet or a sum of social accusations. It seeks to give a global answer to the impersonal systemic domination of Capital."[43] How can we bring into the field of TO the possibility of thinking about this global response if we keep our attention glued *only* to a multiplicity of social concerns? At the same time, how can we also be sure not to fall back on the old ways, an old Marxism where, in many parties, racism and many other oppressions were not allowed to be elaborated and fought against directly (indeed, a tendency to treat social issues as discrete has often arose precisely as a result of the exclusion of the voices of certain groups)? Avoiding the question of mediations leads to two problems: the first I will call, following Bensaïd, the "anarchist paradox"; the second is essentialism.[44]

The constitutive paradox of anarchism is that the rejection of any type of authority is logically extended to the rejection of majoritarian democracy in society, just as in a social movement. Here, instead of a substitution by the representatives for the represented, anyone has their own subjectivity as the only sovereign source of their own rules. The abolition of representation leads to the impossibility of creating a collective.

Within the world of TO, this is the paradox that constitutes the frequent practice of someone declaring in response to a scene, "I lived this situation, and this is how it was," asserting their individual personal experience as the supposedly unbeatable final word that automatically dismisses any criticism of the political orientation of a play's analysis of a system of oppression.

Not all oppressed people are the same, nor do they all feel the same in the face of their oppression. To deny that representation itself is separate from reality, but maintaining dialectical relations with reality, is also a way to reactivate the fantasy of a homogenous social world that is completely transparent to itself. One common social denominator does not mean the oppressed cannot suffer other specific oppressions.

A. Boal dedicated the French edition of *Theatre of the Oppressed* to the "oppressed classes and those oppressed within these classes," in a possible allusion to women workers. But it is not only important to recognize that, within a certain group of people, there are other groups. To suffer a certain oppression does not make one's interpretation of that oppression unambiguous. Not all the oppressed think the same way about their situation or about how to solve it, when they want to solve it. If the practice of Forum Theatre is, in a way, the practice of revealing and exposing the existing divisions in an audience—to whom the central question

For a Political History of Theatre of the Oppressed 21

could be summed up as whether it is possible for them to act collectively—we also find in the world of TO a certain essentialism that would make the oppressed the immediate repository of the truth about their own situation and an interchangeable *unit* of the oppressed group to which they belong.

Borrowing characters from the founding anecdote of TO, the question remains: If we understand that the representation of a peasant by the petit bourgeois is problematic, how can a peasant legitimately represent another peasant in theatre and politics?

The fetish of essentialism ends up providing the resources for a very curious criticism: theatre cannot be theatre in order not to betray the oppressed's truth. In the TO world, often theatrical mediation is seen as an extension of reality itself, since it is the oppressed who speak. This conception is what lays the groundwork for criticizing plays that would be "too" rehearsed, too "worked on." The attempt to create a language that is appropriate to reveal oppression is criticized as "artificial." The reproduction of the unaltered fact, of the "real," would then be the privileged access to the truth of oppression.

Oppression

It is interesting to note that oppression, a concept that should be at the heart of any TO practice, is what is truly absent from discussions between practitioners. The various processes of formation and learning in TO practice have as their main axes the following: techniques, games, and exercises. And then the most divergent interpretations of oppression (a concept that seems so fundamental to differentiate TO from other theatrical practices) circulate freely for lack of contradictory discussions, debates that would emphasize that different conceptions of oppression correspond to different conceptions of the world and of the struggles that would or would not be necessary to change it.

It is true that the lack of a clear definition of oppression on the part of the founder of TO allowed for a plurality of interpretations. Perhaps because A. Boal had an extremely dialectical spirit and was too aware of the processes that incessantly transform the world, he never desired to elaborate globalizing definitions of the Oppressed, the Oppressor, or Oppression itself. I do not find in his books any polished definitions of these terms, to which, however, he constantly refers. As a result, there is no *full portrait* but instead a painting made of successive brushstrokes across his writings.

Sometimes brief segments of his texts remind us that—if it is absolutely necessary for us to hold on to these terms—they cannot be reduced to a Manichean vision of the world. A worker oppressed by capitalist exploitation may also be an oppressor husband who beats his wife. The oppressed are not the bearers of the truth: "the heads of the oppressed are already so flooded with thoughts that do not belong to them,"[45] and they are also not faultless, positive heroes: "every oppressed person is a subjugated subversive."[46] The oppressed themselves are divided between those who wear a crown on their heads and those who have nothing to gain from exercising their oppression.[47] To say that there are oppressors and oppressed is not, as is often said, an oversimplification of the world. On the contrary, it is a means to problematize the world, to go beyond a simple moral juxtaposition that would divide it neatly into good beings and those with an evil essence. To acknowledge that there are oppressors and oppressed conveys that identities are not fixed but in constant movement, given that "the oppressed is not defined in relation to himself, but in relation to his oppressor."[48] One thing remains certain: "If Oppression exists, it must end!"[49]

These somewhat vague definitions can also be explained by the historical context in which A. Boal wrote them, when oppression was a hotly debated theme. Besides the obvious reference

22 _Criticizing a Critical Theatre_

to Paulo Freire's Pedagogy of the Oppressed, we must remember that, in what was certainly one of the most important texts for the Latin American Left in the 1970s, the _Manifesto of the Communist Party,_ the theme of oppression frequently comes up. Thus, the second paragraph of the first chapter of the Manifesto indicates the following:

> The history of all hitherto existing society is the history of class struggles. Freeman and [enslaved person], patrician and plebeian, lord and serf, guild-master and journeyman, in a word, oppressor and oppressed, stood in constant opposition to one another, carried on an uninterrupted, now hidden, now open fight, a fight that each time ended, either in a revolutionary reconstruction of society at large, or in the common ruin of the contending classes.[50]

Nowadays, when it is uncommon to talk about antagonism as constitutive of relations in our society—when politics as a space of struggle between divergent social interests seems to be disappearing, giving way to the strict definition of politics as the management of public affairs—have we reached the moment of the "ruin of the contending classes"?

To elucidate this question partially, it would be important to try to assemble a history of the transformations to which the word oppression has been subjected. If semantics really is a "war zone," then it is important to portray what the battles were—and who the enemies were—so that we can relaunch a new battle with better tools.[51]

A first "attack" on the word oppression was actually, at least in France, made by that which should have been its natural defender: the Communist Party. This extremely Stalinized party defended a concept of oppression as purely capitalist. No autonomy or specific dynamics were recognized for other oppressions that were not directly linked to the exploitation of workers. All oppression was ultimately linked to the production system and, according to this logic, did not need specific struggles against specific oppressions, since those, by themselves, would end with the end of capitalism. Patriarchy, racism, and homosexuals (not homophobia) were doomed to disappear under socialism. Every specific struggle was suspected of being petit bourgeois.[52]

Various movements had to rise against this authoritarian confiscation of the meaning of all struggles. French feminism is exemplary in this sense. The trajectory, both militant and theoretical, of Christine Delphy illustrates this need to try to find autonomy in relation to the confiscation that represented the conflict between Capital and Labor as presented by the French Communist Party. All of Delphy's work can be summed up as an attempt to constitute patriarchy as an absolutely distinct system of oppression: "I study the oppression of women. But women's oppression is specific not because women would be specific, but because it is a unique type of oppression. But is it a unique fact that an oppression is unique? It's not, it is banal: all oppressions are unique, as are individuals. The singularity is the best distributed thing in the world."[53]

The conceptualization of patriarchy as a mode of production where the fruit of women's work (historically defined as things like housework, taking care of children, etc.) is directly appropriated by men is undoubtedly of great interest. But by establishing that the patriarchal mode of production is parallel and distinct from the capitalist mode of production, this theory reveals itself incapable of analyzing why women are more affected by precarious jobs, why they earn less than men for the same jobs, and why they are generally relegated to less prestigious jobs. It is also unable to be used to analyze other aspects of the articulation between capitalism and women's oppression that represent the daily lives of millions of women around the world.

Other "attacks" on the concept of oppression were launched, including ones that this time not only rejected the idea of a plurality of semi-autonomous oppressions as central to our societies but also rejected the very fact that society is organized by the confrontation between

For a Political History of Theatre of the Oppressed 23

antagonistic social groups. One of the reasons offered to refute this conception is that it referred to totalizing systems, systems that would be the prelude to a totalitarian society.

In a world where having an analysis with a totalizing ambition was considered to be an objective alliance with Stalinism, only facts were left to support indignation and resistance. As Bensaïd tells us, the solution given by Foucault, after being "taken by the wrath of facts," proclaimed that it was urgent to "liberate political action from every form of unitary and totalizing paranoia."[54] But what are the facts? What is a reality based on no concept?

This immediacy of a self-explanatory reality is present in an imaginary built around a figure that competes with that of the oppressed: the victim. Campaigns against hunger in Africa carried out by large NGOs or by international institutions such as UNESCO, for example, always rely on images that are intended as an immediate presentation of a univocal and intolerable reality. Of course, the sight of a starving child is shocking, but what is the reaction demanded from the spectator of these images? Probably not of solidarity, but of pity. As Christiane Vollaire tells us, we should examine the political use of pity. Often, pity is used precisely as a way to depoliticize by "masking the criminal origin of economic power relationships, to make us focus our emotional attention only on the physical reality of their effects."[55]

In these representations, the victim is completely powerless in the face of suffering, suffering that will be more appealing if it appears to be inexplicable: the donations made to NGOs after the tsunami in Thailand, Indonesia, etc., were not comparable with others made in response to different tragedies with more easily identifiable political roots, such as in Darfur, for example. The *ideal* victims have no history; in fact, they are not fully human. They range between superhuman figures (when they evoke images of martyrdom, of humanity transcended by pain[56]) and subhuman ones: "This approach, reducing victims to the biological need (identified as animality) for nutrition and survival, also produces a form of dehumanization."[57]

There are other accepted usages for the term victim. When, for example, a woman is said to be a victim of domestic violence, what is emphasized is that this violence happens to her as an individual, so this violence is exceptional. In other words, it supposedly does not require the transformation of society as a whole in order to stop it.

This same individualization occurs with the term excluded. While it is widely used in European countries, the absence of its correlated term, "excluding," is notable. Given this absence, one might be led to understand that the person responsible for a situation of exclusion is none other than the excluded person herself. There is no longer any confrontation: "Two mechanisms are at work here: first, the perception of 'exclusion' as a replacement for 'vertical' class division and, consequently, of social 'cohesion' or 'integration' as a reading key (and a norm at the same time), successors of the places held by struggle and conflict."[58]

A broader study on oppression would be needed, one that would delve into several issues and questions. First could be an attempt to reposition the issues of conflict and interest (meaning that it is in the interest of the capitalist to make more money, while it is in the interest of the working class not to allow it) as central to the definition of oppression and to frame conflict as what defines camps facing each other against an essentialist vision of who is an oppressed or an oppressor. The second axis could be a study on what the notion of dialectical totality (in which every part is connected to every other part and the totality is bigger than the sum of its parts) can offer us against postmodern fragmentation and its two correlates, the abandonment of the perspective of overcoming capitalism (or any system of oppression) and the trend of micropolitics.

This enthusiasm for local action (with which we might, for example, plant a tree in our garden rather than helping out in the fight against deforestation in the Amazon) will have to be studied in all its contradictory aspects. Though it is often reduced to an adaptation of society as it is, or a contestation of its margins, this enthusiasm can also be seen as a refusal of both the

24 *Criticizing a Critical Theatre*

existing order and the prospect of waiting passively for horizons that today seem unattainable. Yonathan Shapiro, an Israeli member of Anarchists Against the Wall, states in the documentary *Rachel* that what separates his generation from the achieving generation is precisely the ability to fight without believing in victory.[59] What becomes of oppression, and especially the struggle for emancipation, when the strategic perspective escapes us?

Conclusion

The criticism of criticism has unfortunately become commonplace in our time. Often people pose a critique that the emancipatory forces that appeared in the last century have now become tools or props of domination. This commonplace notion is not entirely devoid of truth. The promises of emancipation brought by movements and ideas already seem far away, as they often turned into self-caricatures: a labor movement that globally renounced their struggle for another form of redistribution and production of wealth only to have a mere supporting role, accompanying the changes in the capitalist system; an instrumental form of feminism, which in some countries serves as a cover-up for racist discourses and practices; a mainstream LGBTQIA+ movement that mostly promotes an identity colonized by consumerist standardization; ecology, which was depoliticized to better become a commodity; and counterculture, which has also surrendered to become a commodity itself.

The list is long and has served, several times, as an argument for those who, between the bitterness of despair and the delights of accommodation, said that Capital was the unsurpassable horizon of our history and asked, like François Furet, that "we resign ourselves to living in the world we live in."

It is likely that we are living the end of this cycle. The (new) crisis of capitalism has already been met with demonstrations across Europe. In Spain, the best known case, struggles were waged through organizing and innovative slogans that won the support of most of the population. Dictatorships that seemed unbreakable in Tunisia and Egypt could not resist the winds of the Arab Spring, which continue to blow. Even in the United States, movements are opposing the dismantling of the few workers' rights that remain. This relative reawakening of struggles is accompanied by a relative reawakening of critical theory and even of a resumption of Marxist analyses. The present crisis has also affected the dominant ideas and their neoliberal matrix, with shifts away from postmodern philosophies that presented the construction of unprecedented micropolitics and the aestheticization of their own defeats and impotence as the only possible means of resistance. It is when a cycle closes that it is possible and necessary to analyze it, not only to be able to understand it in and of itself, but mainly to understand how it defines the terrain of the struggles to come.

Amid the rubble, we must identify what we have inherited that can be used to build our tomorrow. TO must also submit itself to an inventory, distinguishing between heterogeneity *across* its practice and divergence *from* it. We must investigate which of its presuppositions remain valid, and we must prevent A. Boal's proposals from becoming unquestionable dogmas. At the same time, we also must maintain his perspective of radical change, both in the world and in the theatre. To consider whether we will remain faithful to that perspective, perhaps we can turn to the initial lines of his first book for a criterion: "The elites consider theatre to be something that cannot and should not be popular. Contrary to this, we think that it is not only the theatre that can be popular; the rest must also become popular: in particular, Power and the State, food, factories, beaches, universities, life itself."[60]

Perhaps it is here—beyond questions of form and representation, contexts, or specific sociohistorical conjunctures—that we find the essential element to keep in mind as we consider whether or not we are doing TO: an attempt to ensure that the reclamation of the stage by all is inextricable from the reclamation, by all, of the world.

Notes

1 Augusto Boal, *L'Arc en Ciel du Désir: Du théâtre expérimental à la thérapie* (Paris: La Découverte, 2002), 8.
2 To learn more about A. Boal's experiences with literacy programs in Peru and Ecuador, see any of the published versions of the book *Theatre of the Oppressed.*
3 Augusto Boal, *Jeux pour acteurs et non-acteurs* (Paris: Éditions La Découverte, 2004), 11.
4 Michel Foucault, *Dits et écrits* (Paris: Gallimard, 2001), 364.
5 Augusto Boal, *Théâtre de l'opprimé* (Paris: La Découverte, 1996), 48.
6 Augusto Boal, *Jeux pour acteurs et non-acteurs* (Paris: Éditions La Découverte, 2004).
7 Paulo Freire, *Pédagogie des Opprimés* (Paris: Maspero, 1974).
8 Paulo Freire, *Pédagogie de l'Opprimé* (Paris: Maspero, 1980), 79.
9 Augusto Boal, *Théâtre de l'opprimé* (Paris: Librairie François Maspero ("Petite Collection Maspero"), 1997), 186.
10 Ibid., 14.
11 Theatre of the Oppressed Yellow Pages. Available at: http://theatreoftheoppressed.org. Accessed 14 Aug. 2011.
12 "Creative heresies" and "unforgivable betrayals" reflect my translation from Portuguese to English of how A. Boal wrote about these distinctions in the publication *Metaxis.*
13 In this book, "militant" connotes someone who works inside a social movement, making their decisions according to its collectively decided agenda. The phrase commonly used in English that is closest to capturing the sense of the Portuguese word "militante" would be "movement organizer." A militant is not precisely the same thing as an "activist," however, in the sense that sometimes "activist" can mean anyone who goes to a protest or two and holds a sign. A militant is someone who "militates" in an ongoing way for a specific movement.
14 See Roberto Schwarz, *Sequências Brasileiras* (São Paulo: Companhia das Letras, 1999).
15 With Invisible Theatre (one of the branches of the tree of Theatre of the Oppressed techniques), spectators are not made aware that what they are watching is a performance. This sort of theatre was used by Boal and collaborators as a strategy for, among other things, avoiding violent authoritarian repression. For more on the history of Invisible Theatre, see the chapter by Rafael Villas Bôas in Howe, Boal, Soeiro, eds., *The Routledge Companion to Theatre of the Oppressed* (London: Routledge, 2019), 162–167.
16 See Luc Boltanski and Eve Chiapello, *Le nouvel esprit du capitalisme* (Paris: Gallimard, 1999).
17 Jacques Rancière, *The Emancipated Spectator*, trans. Gregory Elliott (London: Verso, 2008), 2.
18 Peter Hallward, *Jacques Rancière et la théâtrocratie ou Les limites de l'égalité improvisée* (2006). Available at: http://1libertaire.free.fr/JRanciere42.html. Accessed 01 Dec. 2021.
19 Jacques Rancière, *The Emancipated Spectator*, trans. Gregory Elliott (London: Verso, 2008), 16.
20 Ibid., 16.
21 Jacques Rancière, *O Espectador Emancipado*, trans. Ivone C. Benedetti (São Paulo: WMF Martins Fontes, 2012), 58.
22 Walter Benjamin, *Obras Escolhidas: Magia e Técnica, Arte e Política* (São Paulo: editora brasiliense, 1983), 78.
23 Augusto Boal, *Teatro Legislativo* (Rio de Janeiro: Civilização Brasileira, 1996), 45.
24 Ibid., 46.
25 Augusto Boal, *Hamlet and the Baker's Son: My Life in Theatre and Politics*, trans. Adrian Jackson and Candida Blaker (London: Routledge, 2001), 320.
26 Karl Marx, *L'idéologie allemande* (Paris: Nathan, 1991), 53.
27 Antoine Artous, *Travail et émancipation sociale: Marx et le travail* (Paris: Syllepse, 2003), 84.
28 Roberto Schwarz, *Sequências Brasileiras* (São Paulo: Companhia das Letras, 1999), 124.
29 Ibid., 124.
30 Augusto Boal, *Teatro do Oprimido e Outras Poéticas Políticas* (São Paulo: Cosac Naify, 2013), 163.
31 Antoine Artous, *Travail et émancipation sociale: Marx et le travail* (Paris: Syllepse, 2003), 10.
32 Ibid., 19.
33 Augusto Boal, *Theatre of the Oppressed*, trans. Charles A. and Maria-Odilia Leal McBride (New York: TCG, 1985), 34.
34 This assertion deserves to be relativized given that, since their origins, the Soviets (organizations or councils that first emerged in 1905) were more comprehensive and had authorities over territories, the best known example being that of Saint Petersburg.

26 *Criticizing a Critical Theatre*

35 See Luc Boltanski and Eve Chiapello, *Le nouvel esprit du capitalisme* (Paris: Gallimard, 1999).

36 This scenario, valid for France, surely would also have a certain validity to be evaluated for other countries.

37 Isabelle Garo, "L'art comme activité: Marx et la critique de l'esthétique," *Revue Europe* 988–989 (Paris, 2011), 374.

38 Foucault & Deleuze, in Michel Foucault, *Microfísica do poder* (Rio de Janeiro: Editora Graal, 1984), 72.

39 Ibid.

40 Antonio "Toni" Negri in Daniel Bensaïd, *Penser/Agir* (Paris: Lignes, 2008), 281.

41 The Plural Manifesto is available at: http://www.esquerda.net/dossier/manifesto-plural. Accessed 12 Sept. 2021.

42 Daniel Bensaïd, *Éloge de la politique profane* (Paris: Albin Michel, 2008), 238.

43 Ibid., 248.

44 Daniel Bensaïd, *Penser/Agir* (Paris: Lignes, 2008), 220.

45 Augusto Boal, *Estética do Oprimido* (Rio de Janeiro: Garamond, 2010), 47.

46 Augusto Boal, *L'Arc en Ciel du Désir* (Paris: Éditions La Découverte, 2002), 49.

47 Augusto Boal, *Estética do Oprimido* (Rio de Janeiro: Garamond, 2010), 210.

48 Augusto Boal, *L'Arc en Ciel du Désir* (Paris: Éditions La Découverte, 2002), 293.

49 Ibid., 25.

50 Karl Marx and Friedrich Engels, *Manifesto of the Communist Party*, trans. Samuel Moore in co-operation with Engels, in *Marx/Engels Selected Works, Vol. One* (Moscow: Progress Publishers, 1969). Available via the Marx/Engels Internet Archive at: https://www.marxists.org/archive/marx/works/1848/communist-manifesto/index.htm

51 Augusto Boal, *Estética do Oprimido* (Rio de Janeiro: Garamond, 2010), 77.

52 Certain passages from Engels' *The Origin of the Family, Private Property and the State* legitimized the homophobia of many within the French Communist Party.

53 Christine Delphy, *L'Ennemi Principal, t.1, économie politique du patriarcat* (Paris: Syllepse, 2002), 46.

54 Michel Foucault qtd. in Daniel Bensaïd, *Une Lente Impatience* (Paris: Stock, 2004), 271.

55 Christiane Vollaire, *L'humanitaire, le coeur de la guerre* (Paris: éditions Les Insulaires, 2007), 18.

56 The declarations of Mother Teresa of Calcutta that depict dying lepers as "sublime" go in this direction.

57 Vollaire, 11.

58 Stathis Kouvélakis, *La France en révolte. Luttes sociales et cycles politiques* (Paris: Textuel, 2007), 25.

59 *Rachel* was directed by Simone Bitton in 2009.

60 Augusto Boal, *Técnicas Latinoamericanas de Teatro Popular: una revolución copernicana al revés* (Buenos Aires: Corregidor, 2015), 9.

2 Theatre of the Oppressed as a Formal Critique of the Brazilian Communist Party

Theatre of the Oppressed (TO) was born out of a specific context that, in my view, has as its main characteristic the dual collapse of democracies in Latin America and of the Left that fought to overcome those coups d'état, collapses that affected both the Left's organizations and their strategic hypotheses.[1] The largest organization of the Brazilian Left, the Brazilian Communist Party (Partido Comunista Brasileiro, or the PCB), earned enormous criticism for its inability to perceive and face the counterrevolution in progress. I hypothesize here that TO was born, at least in part, out of a critique of the core ideas inside the dominant theses of the Left at the time—about history, about alliances and the political subject, about the role of intellectuals—whose most important representative was the PCB.[2] The hypothesis is that the double collapse mentioned above and the attempt to overcome it not only constituted the conjuncture in which TO was born; but these factors also translated into an internal principle that ordered TO's formal devices. In other words, what I will try to establish here is that, though TO as a whole wanted to be an instrument in the fight against the dictatorship, it was also, through its own techniques, a critique of the PCB.

This possibility of transposing an external environment into a structuring factor of a form of work was put forward by Antônio Cândido in *On Literature and Society*: "We also know that the external (in this case, the social) matters not as a cause, nor as a meaning, but as an element that plays a certain role in the constitution of the structure, thus becoming internal."[3] This way of perceiving things, which seems highly fertile in its refusal of a strict separation between domains that would belong exclusively to historical research or aesthetic analysis, differs in one point from what I want to achieve here: for Schwarz, Cândido's research—or at least his analysis of the novel *O Cortiço (The Slum)*—tries to find the unreflective retranslation of ways of thinking that already exist in society: the migration of reflexes from the ruling class to the literary field, where they act as an ordering principle, playing their ideological role of presenting particular perspectives as general truths.[4] Though in Cândido's analysis, the external is *retranslated* into a principle of internal construction of a work by its author (as in the case of anti-Portuguese racism in *The Slum*), in this case it seems that Augusto Boal's driving element in the creation of his formal devices was the critique of the analysis and hegemonic practices of the Left.

Elements for a panorama of the Brazilian Communist Party

From 1954 onward, the PCB paradoxically managed to combine its aura of resistance to the Estado Novo (New State) with its image as the inheritors of the era of Getúlio Vargas. This rather peculiar combination was possible thanks to its position in favor of a great alliance of the nation's forces toward industrialization. Though the text of the fourth congress, written by Luís Carlos Prestes, declares that "the communists fight for the destruction of the current

DOI: 10.4324/9781003325048-4

28 *Criticizing a Critical Theatre*

regime in Brazil," this fight is presented as a process with several stages. At that moment, the enemies to be defeated were the landowners and the large-scale capitalists allied with imperialism, and the objective to be achieved was the independence of the national economy. In this struggle against imperialism and large estates, the number of allies was large and included everyone who was in favor of the development of Brazilian industrial forces. The alliance would only leave out big landowners and industrialists much too inclined to do business with North America.[5]

This vast alliance does not seem here to have major internal contradictions, with Prestes going so far as to declare that, in an industrially undeveloped nation like Brazil, "the proletariat suffers much less from capitalist exploitation than from the insufficiency of capitalist development and historical backwardness."[6]

The revolutionary subject—as conceived by the PCB—was not a particular social class, nor even a fraction of a class, at least not as the party understood that particular historical stage of the development of an independent Brazilian industry. One was not understood as an historical subject by occupying a certain position within the relations of production, but simply by adhering to nationalist-developmentalist discourse. In fact, this conceptualization automatically eliminated the landowners and the large-scale capitalists with interests linked to those of imperialism (the 1964 coup would prove that these big capitalists were far more numerous than the PCB had expected). But sizable parts of the working class might have also been left out of the scope of this subject if they were not convinced of their role in the process of making Brazil an independent country.

The PCB's understanding of the revolutionary subject gave intellectuals and artists various kinds of advantages. I will briefly mention two of them here. First, this conception made intellectuals and artists not have to question their privileges as a group compared to other groups or classes. Their belonging as part of the historical subject was guaranteed by their support for nationalist development. Because they were considered part of "the people," to question their own advantages within the process of the Brazilian revolution had lost all its meaning. The second advantage was the valorization of awareness, of the need to enlighten the masses about their historical role, a point of view that logically offered the specialists in intelligence and expression a privileged role in which they would play the part of tutors for the still-ignorant masses.

The 1964 coup made this set of theses appear to be completely out of touch with reality. Not only did the so-called national bourgeoisie prefer to cooperate with international capital, but also the coup d'etat actually did not keep Brazil in a backward position in relation to industrialization: "Following the conservative coup was a powerful industrial development which, however, failed to fulfill any of its political and civilizing promises that are usually associated with economic development."[7]

The *Partidão* (The Great Party, as it was called) was without a doubt the great interlocutor for the whole Brazilian Left. That is not to say that there was consensus within the Left, however. Though the PCB had the power to impose its agenda and make the discussions refer to their positions, there were other organizations, groups, and individuals that systematically criticized them. As Roberto Schwarz writes, the death of Stalin in 1953 helped the dissemination of the unacceptable realities of the Soviet Union and of the authoritarianism of the internal life of the communist parties: "The inconsistency with libertarian aspirations and the critical spirit of socialism were irrefutable."[8]

A friend of Schwarz, A. Boal, was also close to another great anti-Stalinist, the aforementioned Antônio Cândido, who was his best man in his first marriage. Even if two of the most important figures of Teatro de Arena—Gianfrancesco Guarnieri and Oduvaldo Vianna Filho—were PCB militants, there were also other people in the group—Nelson Xavier, for

Theatre of the Oppressed as a Formal Critique 29

instance—who were viscerally against the party's policies. It was possibly this plurality of political positions inside the Arena Theatre that enabled A. Boal to pose major critiques of the party in his play *Revolution in South America*, staged in 1960 in Rio de Janeiro. It was an ironic title, given that what the play presented was the counterrevolution in progress. Its main character, José da Silva, a worker fired in one of the first scenes, is driven by hunger; he is a passive spectator of all the mechanisms that perpetuate his domination throughout the play. In practically every scene, he is deceived—not only by his boss, by the politicians in power, but also by his former colleague, Zequinha Tapioca, now the leader of a revolution, whose allies are all young bourgeois. The so-called revolution will be the revolution of honesty, "in which everything remains as it is, everyone remains the same, but honest. José himself will become an 'honest hungry man'. One could not imagine a better caricature of the 'revolutionary' program of the Brazilian Communist Party, which supported a 'democratic' general for president."[9]

In this play, which was highly counterintuitive for the climate of the time and had little success, A. Boal had already shown that he did not believe in several of the central hypotheses put forward by the PCB: the inexorable march toward revolution, the possibility of class alliances, and the role of intellectuals as guides for the masses. Let's investigate how his critique put down roots inside the creation of TO.

Critique of historical determinism

Two logics intertwine in the book *Theatre of the Oppressed*, logics that appear to be juxtaposed rather than dialectically articulated. One of these logics is significantly teleological. A. Boal builds a history of theatre as born from the division between stage and audience imposed by the dominant classes:

> In the beginning the theater was the dithyrambic song: free people singing in the open air. The carnival. The feast.

> Later, the ruling classes took possession of the theater and built their dividing walls. First, they divided the people, separating actors from spectators: people who act and people who watch – the party is over! Secondly, among the actors, they separated the protagonists from the mass. The coercive indoctrination began![10]

> I will not get into the debate of whether or not the existence of art was possible without the individual figure of the artist, a hypothesis that is questioned by Cândido in *On Literature and Society*.[11] The premise that theatre is a creation of the ruling class is necessary for A. Boal to base his theatre history on a "primitive appropriation" of the means of theatrical production. The history of theatre would be that of its progressive reappropriation by the people, a history in which TO would be the imagined point of arrival.

> Brecht's poetics is that of the enlightened vanguard: the world is revealed as subject to change, and the change starts in the theater itself, for the spectator does not delegate power to the characters to think in his place, although he continues to delegate power to them to act in his place. [...]

> The *poetics of the oppressed* is essentially the poetics of liberation: the spectator no longer delegates power to the characters either to think or to act in his place.[12]

30 *Criticizing a Critical Theatre*

TO would be part of a necessary phase to "complete the cycle," together with other movements taking place in Latin America at the same time.[13] In this conception, theatre returns to its origins on a higher level, where representative mediation does not disappear in the face of dithyrambic singing. This narrative, which attributes a single goal to the history of theatre, is obviously more prescriptive than descriptive in the context of a continent ravaged by military coups. This teleology is parallel to that of a certain colloquial Marxist discourse. In it, we first find the archaic community, where the social division of labor does not exist but whose resources are highly scarce. Then, with the development of the means of production, society splits into antagonistic classes. In the third and last phase, humanity unites again, collectively taking possession of the means of production that, having been sufficiently developed, can finally provide for everyone.

This discourse on the origin of TO is opposed by another, without the contradiction between the two discourses ever being put into dialectical relation. In this other discourse, theatrical performance has to be entirely linked to a conjuncture that encompasses it and on which it depends. Thus, in an essay dedicated to retracing the history of Teatro de Arena, A. Boal states:

> It was a long period during which the Arena Theater closed its doors to European playwrights, regardless of their high quality, opening them to anyone who wished to talk about Brazil to a Brazilian audience. This phase coincided with political nationalism, with the flourishing of industry in São Paulo, with the foundation of Brasília, with the euphoria of prizing highly everything that is national.[14]

This coincidence is far from fortuitous for the author, who points out that both Bossa Nova and Cinema Novo were created in that same period. During his exile, in an interview in France, A. Boal continues to define TO as a theatrical practice that can only have a value if it is related to a certain conjuncture: "It is a theatre that finds its place in certain processes and that can intervene at certain moments, but not in others."[15]

But, in addition to A. Boal's positions on the historiography of theatre and the specific place that TO occupies in it, the forms he invented seem to contradict any deterministic vision of history.

> The bourgeoisie already knows what the world is like, *their* world, and is able to present images of this complete, finished world. The bourgeoisie presents the spectacle. On the other hand, the proletariat and the oppressed classes do not know yet what their world will be like; consequently their theater will be the rehearsal, not the finished spectacle.
>
> (…) Popular audiences are interested in experimenting, in rehearsing, and they abhor the "closed" spectacles.
>
> (…) All the methods that I have discussed are forms of a rehearsal-theater, and not a spectacle-theater. One knows how these experiments will begin but not how they will end …[16]

In fact, A. Boal said that Forum Theatre is the concrete analysis of a concrete situation, citing Lenin. A Forum Theatre performance is, or should be, a study of the real through theatre, a study in which a "homogeneous and smooth" whole is not constructed. Rather, Forum Theatre should explore how reality is constantly shaped by contradictory dynamics and tensions that intersect in ever new ways. We must always work on our own presence of mind to be able to perceive—within each new configuration of factors we face—what can be useful for us to transform reality.

Theatre of the Oppressed as a Formal Critique 31

We are far from the logic of the PCB here—for which, still following Pécaut, progress was the essence of historical time—and more in the vicinity of Benjamin: "What is decisive is that the dialectician cannot help but consider history as a constellation of dangers, which he—who follows its development with his thought—is always ready to deflect."[17]

Critique of the historical subject

The play *Arena Conta Tiradentes* (*Arena Tells the Story of Tiradentes*)—which was written by A. Boal and Guarnieri and premiered in São Paulo on April 21, 1967—managed to achieve a certain unanimity from left-wing critics, who were against it. The attempt—to use both Stanislavskian identification and Brechtian alienation to elaborate a national epic theatre, retelling the story of an aborted revolution to stimulate the current struggle—failed. Tiradentes' enemies use dramatic resources that show how cunning and intelligent they are, while the martyr (Tiradentes) tires the audience with his idealism, which borders on foolishness. According to Schwarz, however, the play's failure in this regard revealed a certain state of politics in 1967. For Schwarz, the incomplete critique of populism led to a formal impasse. Populism, rather than trying to understand the class composition of the popular movement and of its interests, tried to unify its diversity by using enthusiasm—leaving out of sight what would be the real material for a political theatre: alliances, organization, tactics, and strategy.

In the book *Theatre of the Oppressed*, A. Boal uses a long essay to defend his play—and the Joker system created within it—with great enthusiasm, to such an extent that his defense intrigued historian Iná Camargo Costa.[18] At the same time, other passages seem to demonstrate that a critique of the populism of *Tiradentes* as a play was already beginning to operate, dismantling both the idea of a homogeneous subject and the traditional functions attributed to theatre, those of educating and enthusing the masses.

Boal violently calls the unity between artists and their working-class audiences into question, describing it as a fallacy that would only concretely result in the demobilization of the popular strata of society. Artists, unable to free themselves from their class, would end up reproducing the imaginaries and discourses of their class on stage, only to pour them intransitively over their audience.[19] "And since those responsible for theatrical performances are in general people who belong directly or indirectly to the ruling classes, obviously their finished images will be reflections of themselves."[20]

But the classes themselves do not possess a flawless internal homogeneity, either. Thus, in an excerpt from the essay where he talks about his experience in Peru, A. Boal describes a street in a Lima favela that marked the border between those who had long been inhabitants of Lima, who felt their jobs threatened by their neighbors across the street, and precisely those newcomers, who had recently arrived from the countryside in search of work in the big city. The hostility and violence between the two groups were as real as their common misery and needs, which had to be reoriented so that these "equally exploited brothers" could fight their true enemies, those who live "in the posh neighborhoods."

In a rare text in which he attempts a theoretical definition of the oppressed, A. Boal states that TO could never be the theatre of a specific class because, in any given class, so many oppressors and oppressed coincide. In any group—we might take ones defined by gender, nation, race, etc. as examples—there are internal contradictions that constitute oppressions. "Therefore, the best definition for the theater of the oppressed would be that it is the theater of the oppressed classes and of all the oppressed, even within these classes."[21]

Here TO is then logically assigned the task of finding ways to build alliances between these different subjects in a common struggle against "the oppressive, authoritarian society, [which]

32 *Criticizing a Critical Theatre*

counts on the *oppressed-oppressor* to install and maintain itself." Curiously, though, the characterization of this oppressive society is what is missing. Only the *means* through which this society is oppressive (the division between those who can speak and those who can merely listen) is presented. A. Boal does not openly characterize the purpose of oppression in society. There is a clear gain that emerges as a result of this absence: the possibility of not ranking oppressions, of not subordinating one to another to the point of setting aside everything that does not highlight what would be considered the "main contradiction" of society.

> It is evident that there are oppressions fiercer than others; it is evident that there are oppressions which fall upon a greater number and with greater ferocity than others. But I believe that the fight against oppression is inseparable from the fight against all oppressions, however secondary they may seem. The struggle for national liberation in Algeria was inseparable from the struggle for the liberation of Algerian women. If not, which Algeria freed itself? Just a part.[22]

By abandoning the Communist Party's nationalist concept of People (half fetish, half puppet, but with an explosive charge arising precisely from the inclusion of categories that society usually separates), A. Boal opened himself to a possibly more nuanced analysis of the masses, an analysis supported by more dialectically opposed categories. However, the abandonment of any totalizing perspective was not free of impasses, either. Among those limitations are the abandonment of the questions of how oppressions are articulated and the correlative abandonment of the attempt to comprehend them from a systemic point of view, looking for what overdetermines them beyond a merely subjective perspective. Do these impasses—given that they encourage an infinite segmentation of oppressions—not run the risk of dismissing the prospect of an emancipation from the ensemble of all oppressions and from the system that organizes them? And, with such a dismissal, is it not the very idea of "revolution"—in the sense of altering the system and the structure of relationships in society—that is banned from TO, which intends to be precisely a "rehearsal for revolution"?

Critique of a hierarchy legitimized by knowledge

The position of the PCB in relation to the People was deeply ambiguous. If the People were valued as the historical subject called upon to carry out the nationalist stage of the Revolution, they could also be seen—at the same time—as an obstacle to that same stage when (for ideological reasons) they were unable to rise to the mission. Hence, as mentioned above, the role that the Party gave intellectuals was paramount. "Communist culture therefore satisfies the demands of many intellectuals. They are part of the people as well as their conscience. [...] They continue to distinguish themselves in what becomes an ideological hierarchy: they are not affected by the backwardness of which the popular masses remain prisoners."[23]

This conception that gave the intelligentsia a vanguard role was apparently also accepted by the left-wing intellectuals who were critical of the party. In an introduction written in 1977 to a text dating from 1968, Schwarz outlines a self-critique, describing the rather advantageous division this system encouraged, one that was beneficial for intellectuals: on one side, the holders of the scientific truth who have no material power; on the other side, the people who have the strength but need guidance. It is up to the people to change, which they will do thanks to the progressive intellectual "who, as a theorist, has the legitimacy of popular misery, and, as a leader, relies on the authority of science that his subordinates lack."[24] To other intellectuals, Schwarz suggests, the progressive intellectual theorist will speak as a political leader (and will then get a

Theatre of the Oppressed as a Formal Critique 33

kind of intellectual "pass" that allows them not to have to comply as much with academic rules), and, to the masses, that same theorist will speak as an intellectual who needs to enlighten them. A win-win game, for the intellectuals.

The inability of a large part of the intelligentsia to foresee the coup—and its complete inability to organize some kind of popular resistance to it—could only open up space to challenge this conception of the intelligentsia's role itself. In a way, such criticism had already begun even before the coup, by way of the Arena Theatre's modes of theatrical production, which tended toward collective creation and horizontal organization, as was the case with the structure of its famous dramaturgy seminar. In fact, criticism of the PCB can already be noted as an internally structuring factor for the Arena Theatre's production practices in 1965, when it premiered *Arena Conta Zumbi* (*Arena Tells the Story of Zumbi*). The production did not feature a more traditional model of lead actors playing leading roles opposite other performers portraying smaller characters. Instead, everyone played every role: "[T]he spectacle ceased to be realized from the point of view of each character and came to be narrated by a team, according to a collective criteria: 'We are Arena Theatre' and 'We, all together, are going to tell a story, what we all think about the subject.'"[25]

The criticism of the PCB expands within the design of TO itself, since in that case the innovation is no longer just about finding new forms to be used onstage. With TO, it is the very relationship between stage and audience that will be called into question as another figure of a founding division in our societies, a division that establishes an absolute separation between those who can legitimately act and those confined to silence and inaction. It is only when the oppressed are freed from their imposed passivity that we have a truly revolutionary process, and, because Goulart's government did not understand this, its transformation of Brazilian society was merely superficial.[26]

> The relationships of the peasants with the landlords were entirely different from those with the agent of the Institute of Agrarian Reform, but the ritual [that of the peasant lowering his gaze to talk to them] remained unchanged. The reason may lie in the fact that in both cases the peasant was the passive spectator: in the first case they took away his land, in the second he was given it. The same was certainly not the case in Cuba: there the peasants were the protagonists of the agrarian reform.[27]

This idea, which expands the Marxist hypothesis of trust ("the emancipation of the working class must be the act of the working class itself") to include all of the oppressed, not only demands that the oppressed occupy the stage and produce their own plays. (We have already seen how A. Boal rejected the theatre of artists and intellectuals, considering it incapable of doing anything other than serving as a conveyor belt for dominant ideology.) A. Boal also demands that this theatre be made by creating forms that break with the passivity of the audience, since "only the transformation of the spectator into a protagonist prevents theatre from having a cathartic function." With this spectator-now-protagonist, the action of the oppressed themselves is irreplaceable: "Let the oppressed express themselves because only they can show us where the oppression is. Let them discover their own paths to their liberation, let them rehearse the acts that will lead them to freedom."[28]

If there are, as it seems, advances made with this position that forcefully questions the pretension that intellectuals and artists are so-called natural leaders of social movements, it nevertheless seems equally open to criticism in terms of its definition of the oppressed and their possible emancipation. A. Boal states in several passages that only those suffering a specific type of oppression would have the legitimacy to stage a play about said oppression—or even to

34 Criticizing a Critical Theatre

go onstage to try to struggle against it. He writes, "If a spect-actor who does not suffer the same oppression tries to replace the oppressed protagonist, of course we will fall into the exemplary theatre: one person showing the other what he must do—the old evangelist theatre, the political theatre of yesteryear."[29]

These limitations cannot fail to raise several questions. I will list only some of them here, without trying to give them definitive answers, at least for now: How, then, can solidarity be organized across distinct oppressed groups? As just one example, would working black men have nothing to discuss with unemployed white women? Another question could be formulated as follows: If only those suffering a specific oppression have the right to speak up about it, what else would the oppressed have the legitimacy to speak about? Would they only be competent to speak about the oppression(s) particular to them? Wouldn't such an assumption be a severe limitation of their presumed capabilities? Furthermore, if the oppressions in the examples given are mainly related to the everyday lives of the subjects, who is responsible for talking about oppressions that operate beyond the scale of an individual's everyday life? Moreover, wouldn't this limitation precisely bypass one's capacity to create a sense of alterity, to be what one is not? And why not consider the possibility that precisely this capacity for alterity is one of the places where emancipatory potential could reside?

If, after this analysis, its initial hypothesis—which saw inside TO a critique of the Brazilian Communist Party—still seems well founded, that does not mean that other external factors have not also influenced the structuring of TO's devices. I am of course thinking here of what happened in the cultural sector in Brazil in the 1960s and 1970s. In my view, studies that try to see how TO incorporated the debates, solutions, and dilemmas of both protest culture and counterculture of the 1960s would be fruitful. The commodification of culture on the scale of mass media—and the impossibility for politicized artists of the time to stick to artisanal modes of production that had as their ultimate objective the expression of individual sensibilities—caused important contradictions that left their traces in TO as well. The debates provoked by the CPCs (Centros Populares de Cultura or Centers of Popular Culture)—about what was popular culture or culture for the people and about the role of culture in political struggle—are also present within TO, which has been regarded as both a criticism and a continuation of that movement.[30]

All of these areas of potential additional study would help make it possible for us to locate the broader history in which TO was born. TO is, as we have seen, sometimes conceived by its creator as the end point of the history of theatre, as the finally found form for liberating theatre. By historicizing TO, reinserting it into the context that fed it, we will be better able to answer the question that I believe is both disturbing and most important: What are the emancipatory potentials of this theatrical form now, since there are no guarantees that the critiques and the polemics of yesterday are good for today?

Notes

1 While the collapse was continental, only the Brazilian context is analyzed here.
2 I know that much of what will be criticized here is not exclusive to the PCB. There were certainly broad sectors of the Left who did not participate in the PCB and who shared several of the theses that will be presented here. If I focus on the "*Partidão*" (loosely translated as The Great Party), it is because of its hegemonic position within the Left that earned it this nickname. A more granular study would have to approach the conceptions of other components of the Left and see how they agreed and disagreed with the Party.
3 Antônio Cândido, *Literatura e Sociedade* (São Paulo: Companhia Editora Nacional, 1967), 4.
4 Roberto Schwarz, *Sequências Brasileiras* (São Paulo: Companhia das Letras, 1999), 38.
5 José Antonio Segatto, *Breve História do PCB* (São Paulo: Livraria Editoras Ciências Humanas, 1981), 71.

Theatre of the Oppressed as a Formal Critique 35

6 Daniel Pécaut, *Entre le Peuple et la Nation* (Paris: Éditions de la Maison des Sciences de l'Homme, 1989), 128.
7 Roberto Schwarz, *Sequências Brasileiras* (São Paulo: Companhia das Letras, 1999), 99.
8 Ibid., 88.
9 Iná Camargo Costa, *A hora do teatro épico no Brasil* (Rio de Janeiro: Paz e Terra, 1996), 64.
10 Augusto Boal, *Theatre of the Oppressed*, trans. Charles A. and Maria-Odilia Leal McBride (New York: TCG, 1985), 119. Translation copyright 1979.
11 Antônio Cândido, *Literatura e Sociedade* (São Paulo: Companhia Editora Nacional, 1967), 29–33.
12 Augusto Boal, *Theatre of the Oppressed*, trans. Charles A. and Maria-Odilia Leal McBride (New York: TCG, 1985), 156. Translation copyright 1979.
13 This idea may explain the frequent disinterest of Theatre of the Oppressed practitioners in other forms of theatre. After all, if TO overcomes all previous forms and is the culmination of theatre history, why seek other forms, which would—inside this logic—be necessarily outdated and/or smaller in impact?
14 Augusto Boal, *Theatre of the Oppressed*, trans. Charles A. and Maria-Odilia Leal McBride (New York: TCG, 1985), 162. Translation copyright 1979.
15 Ibid., 30.
16 Ibid., 141–142.
17 Walter Benjamin, *Passagens* (Belo Horizonte: UFMG, 2006), 511.
18 "Furthermore," writes Camargo Costa, "the conviction with which Boal defends theoretical amalgamations in his 'Joker' text suggests that he himself was unsure." See Iná Camargo Costa, *A hora do teatro épico no Brasil* (Rio de Janeiro: Paz e Terra, 1996), 134.
19 A. Boal, however, does not explain how it would have been possible for him to escape the very class determinism that he describes (which seems to give no room for exceptions), nor how the techniques systematized by him would not be somehow linked to the interests of his class.
20 Augusto Boal, *Theatre of the Oppressed*, trans. Charles A. and Maria-Odilia Leal McBride (New York: TCG, 1985), 155. Translation copyright 1979.
21 Augusto Boal, *Stop: C'est magique!* (Rio de Janeiro: Editora Civilização Brasileira, 1980), 25.
22 Ibid., 156.
23 Daniel Pécaut, *Entre le Peuple et la Nation* (Paris: Éditions de la Maison des Sciences de l'Homme, 1989), 132.
24 Roberto Schwarz, *O Pai de Família* (São Paulo: Companhia das Letras, 2008), 56.
25 Augusto Boal, *Theatre of the Oppressed*, trans. Charles A. and Maria-Odilia Leal McBride (New York: TCG, 1985), 170. Translation copyright 1979.
26 João Goulart, the 24th President of Brazil, was removed from office as part of the military coup d'état in 1964.
27 Augusto Boal, *Teatro do Oprimido* (São Paulo: Cosac Naify, 2013), 161.
28 Augusto Boal, *Duzentos e tal exercícios e jogos para o actor e o não actor com ganas de dizer algo através do Teatro* (Lisboa: Cooperativa de Ação Cultural SCARL, 1978), 16.
29 Augusto Boal, *Games for Actors and Non-Actors*, 2nd ed., trans. Adrian Jackson (London: Routledge, 2003), 268.
30 The CPC constituted the largest agit-prop movement to be created in Brazil. They operated between 1962 and 1964.

3 Theatre of the Oppressed and Epic Theatre

Notes on Two Attempts to Overcome the Bourgeois Drama

These days the presence of politics in theatre is often reduced to more or less radical content presented realistically—or to a form that diverges completely from the routine experiences of our subjectivities. This imagined binary, posed as inherently contradictory and unresolvable, is rarely dynamic, which only fuels "formalist" versus "content-oriented" debates. These controversies often pretend not to understand that form already has content, just as content requires an appropriate form to be represented.

The fact that Bertolt Brecht and Augusto Boal both conceived their work beyond this distinction is certainly one of the reasons why they are still relevant now. For both of them, it was imperative to try to situate theatre on the same plane as the contemporary events of their time, precisely in order to influence them. It seems to me that the two had a conviction in common, as formulated by Brecht, who writes, "We have to fully transform theatre, therefore not just the text, or the actor, or even the entire scenic space. We also have to include the spectator, whose attitude has to be changed."[1]

However, in this short essay whose objective is not to account for all the relationships between Theatre of the Oppressed (TO) and Epic Theatre, it will become clear that the solutions they found were not always similar—quite the contrary.

A common enemy: Aristotelian theatre

Moments of social crisis are often accompanied by crises of political representation, in which both the institutions of such representation and their possible translations into theatrical forms are questioned. It was from these sorts of crises that Epic Theatre and TO were born, theoretically built on a rejection of a theatre their creators knew and that they, in both cases, called Aristotelian.

Brecht's critique is composed of several arguments. In articulating the first of those, he wrote that "[t]he truth is that the old form of drama is fucked."[2] It was "fucked" because it no longer corresponded to the lived experiences of the population, whose problems could only be solved on a much higher level than that of relations between individuals. Such drama also failed, in Brecht's view, to see individuals as they are: members of classes. Insisting on a conception of art that would try to unite individuals through an aesthetic pleasure—a sensation completely indifferent to the interests of those feeling this very pleasure—would lead only to two options: failure or audience alienation.[3] The audience would be submitted—through identification with the catharsis—to a process that would make them more appeased.

The reasoning is the same for A. Boal.[4] "Aristotle's coercive system of tragedy" can no longer portray anything current but "survives to this day, thanks to its great efficacy. It is, in effect, a powerful system of intimidation."[5] It does not matter so much whether that system is outdated (or not) in relation to the way people exist. Such a system is functional for the ruling

DOI: 10.4324/9781003325048-5

Theatre of the Oppressed and Epic Theatre   37

classes in the sense that it is one of the elements bent toward guaranteeing social peace, eliminating room for contestation by those who watch plays, films, or soap operas that are built with its formal processes. To create another form of society, another form of sociality, it is necessary to invent other theatrical forms, other ways of producing theatre.

Beyond discourses: how production dominates the producer

After the unexpected success of *The Threepenny Opera*, Brecht worked diligently to build a failure or, rather, a scandal. The opera *The Rise and Fall of the City of Mahagonny* is such an exaggerated parody of bourgeois society that no bourgeois spectator can be carried away by the fable. Screams and whistles welcomed the premiere in Leipzig. The rupture between Brecht and traditional theatre had already happened by the time he wrote *Notes on Mahagonny*.

In those notes, he developed the theory that the artist, usually presented as the emancipated being *par excellence*, is in fact a victim of an ideology associated with their working conditions: "Convinced that they possess what really possesses them, they defend a machine they no longer control; an apparatus that no longer exists, as they believe, in service of creators, but which, on the contrary, has turned against them and therefore against their own creation."[6] The device gains autonomy in relation to its producers and imposes its demands, often in spite of the producers. It is evident that Brecht, by this point, had already read Marx: "To them, their own social action takes the form of the action of objects, which rule the producers instead of being ruled by them."[7]

The ideology of the theatrical apparatus is, according to Brecht, determined by social order: therefore, only what contributes to the maintenance of order is good. "Artistic freedom" will be strictly limited, and only innovations that lead to the perpetuation of that apparatus will be accepted. Brecht's interlocutors in *Notes on Mahagonny* are creators of art (who seem to be more assimilated to the world of authors of dramatic texts than to that of technicians, directors, or actors) who think they have the theatrical apparatus at their service when it is indeed the opposite. But this constraint on individual freedom is not in itself negative, since the historical moment demands more than individuals expressing themselves. It demands people committing, with each other, to transform the world.

In this text, what Brecht criticizes is that the theatrical apparatus does not belong to the community, and that this work is subject, like others, to "the general laws of commodity." In another text probably written in 1928, "On the Current Way of Philosophizing," Brecht's criticism is more forceful.[8] A philosophy that is content with trying out "all the ways of handling thought" presupposes the division of labor, a division that does not make philosophers more free, only more unconcerned with what is being done in other sectors of society. This lack of concern makes them even more dependent on those other sectors, since this dependency is uncontrolled. (When you don't reflect on that upon which you depend, you become even more dependent on it.) The conclusion logically imposes itself: in order to truly be able to philosophize freely, we must try to control this dependency: we must fight against the division of labor.

The social division of labor is a central problem for A. Boal, to the point of him giving all his theatrical exercises a "de-mechanizing" function so that participants can perform actions beyond those for which they have been programmed.

This is an ideal image of society, where all people can do everything, even run that society! *And this ideal is dangerous!* That is why society protects itself – that is, people in privileged positions necessarily defend these privileges, they protect themselves! And the way to protect yourself is through the consolidation of a status quo, through specialization [...][9]

38 *Criticizing a Critical Theatre*

And theatre-making does not escape this logic. The professional actor necessarily becomes dependent on those who can pay for their work, the bourgeoisie. But beyond that, the actor's craft as a specialization is just another tool used to intimidate the oppressed, making them believe that they do not possess the necessary qualities to be able to take the stage. The fact that there are specialists in theatrical expression delegitimizes the expressiveness of everyone else, just as the existence of specialists in politics relegates the rest of the population to the position of spectators: "Theatre reaches its most revolutionary level when the people themselves practice it, when the people stop being just the inspirer and the consumer to become the producer."[10]

New forms of making theatre: didactic plays and Forum Theatre

This play [The Decision] *was not meant to be read.*

This play was not meant to be seen.

Bertolt Brecht, in the magazine *Europe*

If our thoughts and ideas are not pure spiritual products and instead originate from our historical life processes ... if ideology is only capable of a partial representation of itself, a representation with its origins in the relations of domination and exploitation (that in turn justifies those relations) ... then the critique of ideology cannot happen solely in the field of representation. It is necessary to find other ideas, but mainly other ways of producing them. The opposite of ideology cannot be a system of thought located at exactly the same social coordinates. It must be the actual anticipation of another relationship between theory and practice, a struggle at least tending against the division of labor, which poses individuals against each other while also structuring them.

Brecht took very hard stances against the contemporary spectator who would seek in theatre "a kind of massage for lazy souls who lack exercise in their daily lives."[11] When he started writing didactic plays in 1928, he wanted not only to dispense with the bourgeois audience but also to dispense with the audience itself.

In that historical moment, when the struggle "between socialism and barbarie"—to borrow the famous phrase of Rosa Luxemburg—was at one of its most acute periods, Brecht began to leave the places where the theatrical devices produced their managed images.[12] He tried to gain ground with a new use of culture, created not *for* a new audience but *with* new users: youth, the labor movement—in other words, the living forces interested in social transformation, those who did not think without reason or consequence. "[I]n reality," he writes, "the politicians should be philosophers and the philosophers politicians. [...] It's based on this constatation that the one who reflects proposes to educate youth through theatrical practice, in other words to transform them into active and contemplative people at the same time."[13]

The Lehrstücke or didactic plays, according to Brecht himself (who wanted to mark the Lehrstück's specificity), are more to be acted than witnessed. But this performance no longer had the same function as in bourgeois productions. The actor was no longer an instrument that solely acted as a spokesperson for the imagined genius of the author and/or director. It was a matter of replacing a necessarily closed or finished performance with a collective experimentation, which presupposes both a model and free improvisations based on that model. It was no longer a question of presenting a final product to be consumed en masse by isolated individuals, but of transforming the spectator into a producer, one actively involved in the process of collective production. Personal inventions were not only accepted; they were encouraged.

Theatre of the Oppressed and Epic Theatre 39

The principle of the best known dramaturgical form invented by A. Boal, Forum Theatre, is precisely to allow for these "personal inventions" through the direct intervention of spect-actors. The idea is not only that the oppressed themselves seize the means of theatrical production, but that this seizure takes place in such a way that it cannot constitute them into a new vanguard, one that pours knowledge from above to a passive audience below. Unlike Lehrstücke, Forum Theatre has an audience. However, it is in the incessant back-and-forth between the audience and the scene that power is activated. The spect-actors have the task of discovering alternatives to a problem depicted by the scene, which does not impose on them with any kind of slogan or position. It is helpful to remember that A. Boal was left with an ambivalent impression from his experiences with the CPCs (Popular Culture Centers, Centros Populares de Cultura). On the one hand, he admired their attempts to break with the mercantilization of theatre, to approach a population that never frequented theatres, and to wholly subordinate art to politics. On the other hand, he did not appreciate their dogmatism, which reduced plays to a schematic teaching of the doctrine of the PCB (Partido Comunista Brasileiro, the Brazilian Communist Party).

Brecht's anti-schematism could not fail to intrigue A. Boal, who went so far as to declare that Forum Theatre was "a logical and more or less inevitable development of a Brechtian restlessness."[14] The search for a more open pedagogy was driven not only by ethical motives, but also by the fact that the two authors believed that those not subjected to a "banking pedagogy," to use Freire's vocabulary, would be more militant: "'I have noticed,' said Mr. K., 'that we put many people off of our teaching because we have an answer to everything. Could we not, in the interests of propaganda, draw up a list of the questions that appear to us completely unsolved?'"[15]

Narrative interruption as a resource against the bourgeois drama

Interruption of the dramatic narrative is one of the strategies used most often by Brecht, specifically to ensure that the spectator is no longer harnessed and then carried away by their emotions. With this form of interruption, there is no longer an implacable logic that drags the characters from scene to scene until the end. The sequence of scenes no longer corresponds to an absolute causality that would transpose a kind of fatalism onto the characters on the stage. On the contrary, the juxtaposition of a scene with the one that follows it has to be shocking—just as it is when, for example, the character of Mother Courage curses the war at the end of one scene and then begins the next scene precisely by forbidding that one speak ill of it. The interruption of the drama can occur in different ways: songs, film or slide projections, speeches addressed directly to the audience. All of these tactics have the same purpose: to make identification difficult and to make the spectator start to reflect about what is happening onstage. In contrast, the continuous flow of the action would lead the audience to identify with the characters; the spectators' relationship with the characters would happen via an empathy that would prevent them from thinking.

Without A. Boal having explicitly formulated anything about it as a strategy, narrative interruption is also a resource used frequently by Forum Theatre. Though the first time the scene is shown it develops with no interruption, at the moment the forum itself starts, the thread of the story is completely disarticulated. Each spectator has—*a priori*—the right to fast-forward or rewind the narrative, and each scene can be chosen to repeat as many times as the audience wishes, for as many interventions as are desired. The demand made by bourgeois drama that the actors onstage should evolve chronologically is completely disregarded by the very rules of Forum Theatre. The effect of these interruptions could also be, in theory, a way to create a distance. No alternative offered through an onstage intervention would be "an answer" in the full sense of the word. (If one person alone manages to resolve

40 Criticizing a Critical Theatre

an oppression, then the situation presented is not, in fact, oppressive.) These "answers" or "responses" to the question framed by the Forum Theatre play are actually perspectives that, collectivized in the room through mediation, reveal aspects of a situation. And if the audience is an organization itself, they can then prepare for a next phase, which no longer happens within the space of theatre itself.

However, as we will later see with Bernard Dort's critique of TO, this process, even with its narrative interruptions, does not interrupt identification. Neither does it prevent the belief that it is possible for alternatives proposed by spect-actors to be individualistic and/or moralistic. Spect-actor intervention after spect-actor intervention, we often see individual accountability shown as the solution to all ills. Later I will also expand on how this tendency can reveal the nature of our contemporary subjectivities. Here I just want to sketch a hypothesis mirrored in Herbert Marcuse's criticism of the Living Theatre.[16] The philosopher argued that the inspiration that the Living Theatre sought from Antonin Artaud's Theatre of Cruelty was no longer of great use. If Artaud wanted his theatre to be cruel to its spectators, enacting violence against their senses to destroy their complacency of conscience, the audience of the 1970s—accustomed to images of massacres and genocides—would not experience this violence as an exception but as something already present in their daily lives. In the same way, the explosion of stunning sounds that Artaud advocated in his shows would only be redundant for a spectator accustomed to the intense traffic of our metropolitan areas. Similarly, we can ask ourselves: In our time—when various media forms compete for our attention, when the great attraction of cable television is the ability to change channels incessantly, and when stability seems not to be promised in any aspect of our lives—does narrative interruption in itself still contain such great demystifying power? Or is it merely a scenic transposition of the uneven rhythm of our very routines?

The hero and its interpretations: The general and the particular

Much more could be said about the similarities between Epic Theatre and TO. After his exile, Brecht never wrote didactic plays again. I do not know whether it was because of an evolution that made him understand that what he called the "big pedagogy" of the Lehrstücke was no more valuable than the "small" pedagogy of his other plays—or if it was simply because he would never again have found a truly revolutionary, organized movement capable of making use of these exercises, which he considered stretches for athletes of dialectics who are militants. However, Brecht continued writing plays that demanded that his spectators not surrender to the logic of the scene; those in the room had to take a position in the face of what unfolded on stage, not passively accepting what was shown but questioning and imagining other ways of narrating. All these concerns evidenced in Brechtian theatre can also easily be located within TO.

There are, however, profound differences between the two methods, one difference being their distinct conceptions of heroism. Brecht's fierce criticism of heroes is well known. The myth of the hero places him above classes. An exceptional man, he is completely free and can shape the world to his will. In contrast, Brecht's plays judge or ridicule heroes, showing them as mere instruments of the ruling class.

The few positive heroic figures that appear in Brechtian dramaturgy are far from fitting into the classic imagery of the hero. In *The Horatians and the Curiatians*, the Third Horace doesn't even have a name; he is only the personification of astuteness, with his victory possible thanks only to what the first two Horaces achieved. Pelagea Vlassova, the central character of *The Mother*, is a little ant, her greatest virtue being her determination in a routine fight without any decisive deeds. And if the "temptation of kindness" is terrible in a world that doesn't allow room for kindness, the temptation of heroism can have disastrous consequences, as in the case of the Young Militant in *The Decision*.

Arena Tells the Story of Tiradentes, which A. Boal considered in 1974 to be the culmination of his dramaturgy, was widely criticized precisely for giving in to the myth of the hero. Among others, critic Anatol Rosenfeld pointed out that this myth was a fatal mystification that prevented the analysis of reality in concrete, historical terms. A. Boal's answer inverted Brecht's terms: if "unhappy was the country that needed heroes," Brazil would need them precisely because it was unhappy.

This appreciation for heroism, which will be further discussed later, carries with it the belief that the individual can do anything. Such an overvaluation of the subjective element of experience can be explained by the fact that A. Boal does not seem to recognize any specificity between the general and the particular; the only difference between the two would be one of scale. Therefore, there is no difficulty in trying to represent the mechanisms of society since they are contained in every interaction: "In the smallest cells of social organization [...] are contained all the moral and political values of society, all its structures of domination and power, all its mechanisms of oppression."[17]

This undialectical vision—in which different levels of human organization (for example, family being the particular and society being the general) would only reflect each other without any mediation introducing specific determinations—in fact opens space for the reduction of the social to the personal. This is not how Brecht works. For him, the proper representation of society needs many ruses, since it cannot be directly provided by the raw material of theatre: the interaction between individuals. In a note as brief as it is valuable on the use of dialectics and detachment, Brecht writes of "*[t]he particular in general* (the event in its singularity, its uniqueness, and yet typical)."[18] It is only in an articulation of all these elements that the real can be represented without limiting it with a kind of formalist straitjacket that would restrict its movement. But for this kind of representation, it is necessary to be counterintuitive, to go against the grain of the audience's expectations. Therefore, the great capitalists will not be presented as evil beings full of perversity. On the contrary, they will be full of sensitivity and good intentions, their personal impulses always clashing with their class positions in a contradiction that for them is both painful and useful. Those exceptional figures only better demonstrate the rule.

Given this examination, it seems difficult to agree with Richard Schechner's statement that "Boal managed to do what Brecht only dreamed of and wrote about."[19] Their dreams might have been similar, but there were substantial differences. TO has spread across the world at a rate that is rare and probably unmatched by any other theatrical theory or form. The invention of simple, quickly replicable techniques responded to the urgency of mobilizing against authoritarian regimes. In fact, the haste that facilitated multiplication was perhaps the enemy of a more rigorous system. And even if Epic Theatre had more systematization, that did not make it an invincible fortress, either, as I had the opportunity to witness in Porto Alegre, Brazil, at an International Brecht Society symposium in May 2013. There I heard the most respected contemporary critic, Hans-Thies Lehmann, gave a conference presentation in which Brecht was presented as a rationalist positivist who—when faced with an obstacle in his didactic plays—would glimpse beyond the omnipotent Reason at another Almighty force, God.

At the moment when the entire arsenal we have inherited falls to the ground—or is absorbed with disconcerting ease by people who transform it into mere commercial adornment or academic paraphernalia—the temptation is to focus on a kind of museological conservation. But to fall into this easy trap would be to go against the great attempt of these two authors: to try to represent and intervene in the contemporary world.

42 *Criticizing a Critical Theatre*

Notes

1 Bertolt Brecht, *Écrits sur le théâtre* (Paris: L'Arche, 1999), 163.
2 Bertolt Brecht, *Écrits sur le Théâtre* (Paris: L'Arche, 1972), 168.
3 Ibid., 93.
4 A more honed study could determine precisely how much specific information A. Boal had about Brecht—and the sources of that information. For the moment, I can only hypothesize that Boal encountered similar problems, leading him to develop theories and resources similar to the German playwright, rather than a real knowledge of his work.
5 Augusto Boal, *Theatre of the Oppressed*, trans. Charles A. and Maria-Odilia Leal McBride (New York: TCG, 1985), 46. Translation copyright 1979.
6 Bertolt Brecht, *Estudos sobre Teatro* (Lisboa: Portugália Editora, 1957), 17.
7 Karl Marx, *Capital: A Critique of Political Economy.* Available at: https://www.marxists.org/archive/marx/works/1867-c1/ch01.htm#S1. Accessed 22 Aug. 2022.
8 Brecht, Bertolt, *Escritos Políticos y sociales* (Mexico D.F.: Editorial Grijalbo, 1978).
9 Augusto Boal, *Stop: C'est magique!* (Rio de Janeiro: Editora Civilização Brasileira, 1980), 29.
10 Augusto Boal, *Duzentos e tal exercícios e jogos para o actor e o não actor com ganas de dizer algo através do Teatro* (Lisboa: Cooperativa de Ação Cultural SCARL, 1978), 180.
11 Bertolt Brecht, *Théâtre épique, Théâtre dialectique* (Paris: L'Arche, 1999), 102.
12 Rosa Luxemburg was not using "barbarie" in the sense of projecting certain primitivist ideas but instead to refer to the possibility of what could happen if Western civilization continued on the imperialist path, leading to an eternal war and permanent destruction of other civilizations.
13 Bertolt Brecht, *Théâtre épique, Théâtre dialectique* (Paris: L'Arche, 1999), 50.
14 Augusto Boal, *Depoimento em Brecht no Brasil* (Rio de Janeiro: Editora Paz e Terra, 1987), 253.
15 Bertolt Brecht, *Stories of Mr. Keuner*, trans. Martin Chalmers (San Francisco: City Light Books, 2001), 18.
16 I learned about this criticism through Olivier Neveux's excellent book *Politiques du Spectateur* (Paris: éditions la Découverte, 2013) 58; here I summarize aspects of Neveux's argument.
17 Augusto Boal, *L'Arc en Ciel du Désir* (Paris: Éditions La Découverte, 2002), 53.
18 Bertolt Brecht, *Écrits sur le théâtre* (Paris: L'Arche, 1999), 167.
19 See the back cover of the 2005 edition of *Theatre of the Oppressed* published by Civilização Brasileira.

4   Critiques of Theatre of the Oppressed

This chapter is not an attempt to outline all of the critiques that have been launched toward Theatre of the Oppressed (TO). Here I merely try to tackle some of them, particularly those that are put forward most frequently or that seem to me to be most relevant. As I have noted previously, however, it is worth pointing out that all of them seem insufficient, either because their admonitions of TO have been weakly argued or because they are incomplete to the point of only raising partial defenses from those who may want to "protect" TO in some way. As a result, it feels necessary to outline some critiques that I think are more comprehensive, which I do at the end of this chapter.

Critiques of oppression

One of the most common critiques of TO, which unfortunately seems to be the least elaborate, is the criticism of the term oppression itself.

The gist of this criticism has often been that oppression is a concept no longer suited to our times and/or that it would be a sin to project onto so-called first-world countries methods that are supposedly only valid in the "third world."

> In the context of the 1970s, marked in Latin America by movements to fight against military dictatorships and by pedagogies of liberation, Augusto Boal proposed an approach to reality using the concept of oppression, *which he imported[1]* [emphasis mine] to Europe at the time of his exile. [...] Too univocal, the term of oppression proved to be of little relevance to identify the problematic situations experienced under our democratic latitudes.[2]

This perceived inability of the concept of oppression to explain reality is also suggested by Kennedy C. Chinyowa. In a "post-conflict" South Africa, where, the author notes, black people "were now in control," insisting on the vocabulary of oppression would only serve as a "repressive myth," creating binary categories, a barrier to our infinite capacity to autonomously reinvent ourselves.[3]

> Taking gender as a case in point, Judith Butler (1988) points out that gender is not a biological given, but rather a social construct instituted through performative acts such as language, gesture, movement and other symbolic activity. Butler further argues that if gender identity is instituted through performative acts, then the possibility of gender transformation can be found in the deconstruction of such acts. By extension, one can also argue that if gender identity is capable of being reconstituted differently, the same can apply to more or less similar constructions of otherness, such as race, class and ethnicity.[4]

DOI: 10.4324/9781003325048-6

44   *Criticizing a Critical Theatre*

While I do not disagree with the baseline idea that gender and many other categories of identity are, at their roots, constructed socially and that we can, as a result, act with some agency in relation to those categories, Chinyowa appears to interpret our possibility and agency as being ample to a degree that drastically downplays the material force of oppression itself. Oppression seems here to be uniquely located in our thoughts and beliefs.

The notion of an autonomy of choice that is independent of any social dynamic grounds the theory and practice of Theatre of the Oppressor created by Marc Weinblatt, in which members of privileged groups will have the opportunity to reflect critically on their privileges and think about ways that they could become better allies. Recalling an image of oppression that he remembers being used by Augusto Boal, one of a man with his foot on the chest of another man, Weinblatt writes:

> I kept returning to the classic image of oppression that Boal describes–of the man lying on the ground with another man's foot on his chest. [...] While the self-empowerment of the oppressed is indeed critical work, how much easier might it be if the oppressor removed his own foot from the man's chest? Sometimes the one standing is not even aware that his foot is figuratively on the other's chest. However well-intentioned that person may be, he may still be inadvertently "oppressing." [...] Those with more power have the ability, access, and perhaps the duty to be a part of the solution.[5]

Here the idea that oppression has an essential link with how power is structured in our society is absent. Weinblatt seems to be interpreting oppression as an accident, a surplus easily avoided by some awareness generated through an interactive theatre class, since power and oppression are not presented as intertwined in the very fabric of social life as we know it.

On the other side of the Atlantic, in France, a former collaborator of A. Boal sees in the category of oppression an easy way to blame our adversities on an external guilty party: "Instead of designating the 'other' as the oppressor and solely responsible for our ills, I proposed to the spectator a work of analysis of shared responsibilities. [...] What is the social environment part of responsibility? **What is the part of personal responsibility** [emphasis theirs] in what does not work as desired?"[6] Here the interests that would motivate and/or oblige people or groups to act are logically put outside this exaltation of the free will, a free will that would be, in this conception, unfairly hampered by the concept of oppression.

For David Diamond, the creator of Theatre for Living, oppression belongs to a "mechanistic" model of understanding, per Descartes, a model that separates everything: mind from body, nature from society, oppressor from oppressed. He writes, "If we want to end cycles of oppression, the empowerment of the oppressed is only one necessary step along a path of numerous steps that lead to a healing of the larger network or organism. Empowerment cannot be an end unto itself without working to change the patterns of behaviour that create structure."[7]

In another passage, the author begs us to "note that it is the *pattern of relationships that creates the structure*, not the other way around. The *structure* is the *material embodiment* of the *pattern.*"[8] But if this were true, we would only need to change our patterns for the structures to change and for us to live in communities that are finally healed. It would, it seems, be enough for police officers not to systematically search young black people for the Brazilian State to no longer be racist.

Critiques of oppression as a concept tend to have several things in common. Besides perceiving oppression as outdated or relevant to certain geographical areas only, critics tend to particularize conflict, rejecting any social dynamics that constrain an individual's decisions and make them something other than free will. Conflict is not seen as the founding structure of our society,

Critiques of Theatre of the Oppressed   45

and it is similarly not recognized as precisely what *constitutes* categories themselves, with categories existing *through* conflict. In other words, within the logic of these critiques, it would be possible to have other arrangements of these same groups in which there would no longer be any oppression or conflict.[9] Oppression is not conceived as a cornerstone of our societies, but as a peripheral and occasional disorder to be resolved through negotiation between non-antagonistic members of a community whose harmony must be restored. This restoration, which happens mainly through dialogue, dissolves neither the reason for the conflict nor its actors. The distinct groups will continue to exist as before, but now without friction between one another. After all— if, as Weinblatt says, "racism is racial prejudice + power, sexism is gender prejudice + power, classism is class prejudice + power" (never explaining to what extent prejudice is functional to power)—perhaps it is possible, according to that perspective, to purge power of its prejudices to make it just.[10] The parodic scene written by A. Boal in *Revolution in South America*—where the hungry are promised that after the revolution they will continue to starve, but at least they will be *honest* hungry people—is unexpectedly resonant here. Later I will explore how obscuring the ideas of relationship and conflict cannot simply be dismissed as intentional concealment on the part of groups doing TO, even if doing so is useful for them when it comes to seeking resources. In fact, such an eclipse of these concepts only reflects a much broader movement, one that here in this book is seen only through the lens of theatre groups inspired by A. Boal's work. Bernard Grosjean limits this movement to a particular period when he states that, if TO surfed "the wave of the social movements of the 70s" in France, that dynamic was largely replaced "in the late 80s by the work of AIDS prevention."[11] What this author very briefly suggests seems to raise many questions. Keeping those questions to the field of TO, we could ask: This change in dynamics would not necessarily invert the meaning of TO? When supported by social movements, TO served groups of oppressed people denouncing an injustice, with society as a whole as its potential audience and the state as interlocutor and opponent to this denunciation. The logic of much prevention work (like, for example, with anti-tobacco campaigns) originates with the state, who designates a specific target group/segment of the population with whom the work will unfold. If, then, TO is used as part of such prevention work, it is no longer the population that seizes TO to accuse the state; it's often the state that implements TO within the populations that the state chooses. The population framed as problematic and imagined as the object of interventions using "TO techniques" would—according to this logic—have all the capacity to solve their problems without any sort of structural change.[12]

Criticism of a moralism manifested in dramatic form

In a way, the next critique of TO that I will explore here is diametrically opposed to the preceding one. In the previous scenario, the critics of oppression were almost entirely theatre people who appreciated the technique of Forum Theatre and were just anxious to free it from the Manichaeism imposed by the concept of oppression. Now we turn to a critique in which the existence of oppression is not questioned. In this case, what is harshly examined is the capacity of Forum Theatre to cope with systems of oppression. This critique is one that Bernard Dort advances with immense effectiveness.

Of all the critiques of TO that I have encountered, Dort's operates at a different level. This acuity results from several factors, one of them certainly being Dort himself. This French critic was, along with Roland Barthes, one of the staunchest supporters of Brecht in France. His participation in the magazines *Théâtre Populaire* and *Travail Théâtral* facilitated an affirmation of the political responsibility of form and the development of a new generation of playwrights, critics, and theatre directors in France.[13] Another factor is that the subject of Dort's criticism

46 *Criticizing a Critical Theatre*

is not only A. Boal's writing but also a Forum Theatre performance made by Boal himself in 1983; generally, other critiques tend to refer only to A. Boal's books or to plays performed by third parties. Dort also points out problems that seem to me to recur in Forum Theatre practice in many distinct parts of the world. To my mind, that potentially broad relevance of Dort's critique makes it particularly piercing.

The first thrust of his critique is that the picture painted by a Forum Theatre performance would create spectacular tension. The possibility of intervening in the scene, Dort argues, would produce pressure to make each intervention more inventive and more fun than the previous one. So, far from speaking in the first person, doesn't the spectator-actor invest even more in the third person, and, instead of being themselves, don't they become, on the contrary, a comedian and often a mediocre comedian? Instead of opening up about the real, doesn't the anti-model still add fiction?[14]

If there is often a certain excitement or a demand for spectacle on the part of the audience in many Forum Theatre sessions, it does not seem to be A. Boal's main objective to satisfy it. In a text he wrote years before the presentation watched by Dort, A. Boal considers the following:

> [...] as far as spectator interventions are concerned, a spectator often yells "Stop" when the preceding spectator has not yet finished his action—the Joker [the Forum Theatre facilitator] must make him wait for the first spectator to finish what was proposed, but he must also be sensitive to the audience's desire, which may have already understood the proposed action, preferring to pass it on.[15]

A little further on in the same passage, A. Boal raises the question of whether Forum Theatre should privilege theatricality or reflection. The opposition posed—between a "good show" and a scene as a space for developing a deeper reflection—seems somewhat reductive. What gives the opposition consistency is, according to A. Boal, the use of technical resources in a "good show" only to guarantee the public's attention and the sustained rhythm of the interventions ... Boal does not offer any definitive answer to his own question, only indicating that it is necessary to try to avoid the excesses of exhibitionist spectators and a tendency toward the burlesque. Reflection can be more fruitful when the group is watching the show for reasons beyond aesthetic enjoyment.

Dort's critique seems to me only partially relevant, given that Forum Theatre itself could easily avoid falling into mere entertainment if it makes use of resources that are readily at hand. In other words, to address Dort's concern that spect-actors go onstage and try to "entertain" so that the joker/facilitator doesn't just move on to the next intervention, all that would need to happen would be for the joker not to place tight time limits on each intervention and instead allow sufficient time for each person to express themselves so that the pressure to entertain is less a part of the experience. Such adjustment would be sufficient for Forum Theatre not to operate as the futile and possibly manipulative entertainment that Dort describes.

Another critique of TO that Dort formulated appears to be of greater relevance, however. The Forum Theatre session that Dort attended used a text by Brecht, *The Jewish Wife* (which is a scene from the play *Fear and Misery in the Third Reich*) as its dramaturgical model. In the spectator interventions at that Forum Theatre event, Dort notices a return of morals and psychologism: "[I]t was a social system that was questioned by Brecht, here there are only characters left. Psychology returns to gallop. For a little while, instead of anti-Semitism and Nazism, the culprits would be Judith and her friends or people who are close to her. Change the characters, change their behavior and everything will change!"[16]

Dort suggests that Forum Theatre's interactivity could only lead to an intersubjective drama. The structure of the performance puts the weight on the back of the protagonist, who is regarded as always able to change the course of action, either through cunning or through the force of their convictions. In this dramaturgical scenario, everything is reduced to the scale of the individual. Dort writes, "In *The Jewish Wife*, for example, where Brecht described, through an individual situation, a political situation, A. Boal shifts the center of gravity: now it is Judith's and her neighbors' ability to tell the truth and behave accordingly that constitutes the central question of representation. Thus, he replaces morality with politics."[17]

If Dort's criticism here seems to me to be more on point than others I have discussed so far, it is because I have witnessed many Forum Theatre presentations in which the responsibility for the oppression falls solely on the oppressed character. For example, I have watched the same scene performed—by groups who did not know each other—in numerous TO festivals in various countries (Austria, India, Guatemala, among others): a husband raises his hand to a wife; the joker freezes the scene and invites participants to change the situation. The interventions conform to the structure of the scene. Invariably the range of interventions involves the woman making her husband's favorite dish, hiding whatever object "caused" the dispute, begging him to calm down, etc. The award for contemptible abasement probably goes to a group who attended a festival in Guatemala in 2012; their scene asked spect-actors to intervene and take the place of a protagonist precisely at the moment when she was about to be sexually assaulted by a group of assailants.[18]

These groups—who do not necessarily present themselves as critics of the concept of oppression—nevertheless fall into the easy representation of the world as composed solely of fully autonomous and all-mighty individuals exercising their wills. The oppressors, in this context, can only fall into two categories: the morally perverse, who consciously decide to use their will for evil, and the unsuspecting, who do not know what they are doing and will presumably stop oppressing if the unjust nature of their actions can only be illuminated for them. From the oppressed (and, more to the point, from the whole audience invited to act through the oppressed protagonist), exemplary behavior is expected: bravery, wit, and even purity of heart are considered sufficient, as a principle, for the struggle against the oppressor. And that struggle frequently takes place without any mediation: the will of the oppressed clashing directly with the power of the oppressor. Forum Theatre therefore becomes the place where we turn into the attentive evaluators of the capacities of individual spect-actors[19]: Will they be canny enough to escape the traps set by the oppressor? Will our dear friends, with their eloquent words, be able to touch the hardened hearts of such cold enemies?

Though it may seem obvious that Dort's critique of moralism in TO is more pertinent and better articulated than the critiques of the concept of oppression, it is still not entirely satisfactory, either. It lacks radicality in two senses; the first is that this criticism demands an answer that lies almost solely within the field of dramaturgical structure. To address it, using parts of A. Boal's legacy and refusing others, practitioners could construct a dramaturgical approach that is capable of both dealing with systems of oppression and carving out space for interventions by spect-actors in a way that does not make them autonomous subjects. Materials for developing this approach could be found, for example, in Epic Theatre theory or in the concrete experiences of the MST (Landless Movement) culture brigades, as well as in relevant dramaturgy of groups who do TO.

The other issue is that this criticism does not account for the fact of the extraordinary success of TO. In other words, it does not try to perceive—precisely within the flaws pointed out—the factors that lead to TO's massive popularity with practitioners around the world. What does the fact that so many people have so much interest in this interactive and intersubjective theatre tell

48   *Criticizing a Critical Theatre*

us about our situation? What expectations does this form answer, and how did it come about? As we try to understand the popularity of TO, we must tap into the same kind of astonishment that Brecht had at "the surprising availability of the audience" for the bourgeois drama,[20] yet we must do so in such a way that, after accounting for the disposition of the audience toward TO, their openness to it no longer seems so inconceivable to us.[21]

Forum Theatre dramaturgy

First, here it is important to speak to the extent to which the question of a particular form of dramaturgy for TO practices is addressed (or not) within the book *Theatre of the Oppressed*. Two of the most important essays in the book aim to demonstrate how Aristotelian and Hegelian dramaturgies have reactionary effects, and in one essay, Brecht is even hailed, through countless examples from his plays, as the creator of a "Marxist poetics." But the question of the architecture of a play's structure—of the dramaturgical means or formal resources that should be deployed—does not receive any particular attention after that. From 1974 to 1996, this issue never went away entirely for A. Boal (and a few brief passages across his books from this period are particularly illuminating on this score), but overall it is clear that his efforts to create new dramaturgical models did not correspond in intensity to his rejection of other theatrical forms.

This apparent contradiction actually is resolved easily: if A. Boal's efforts do not focus on the objective of creating a new anti-Aristotelian dramaturgy capable of genuinely mobilizing the masses, it is because, for him, that is no longer the crux of the matter. Over time, what happens on the stage becomes less important than the organization of the transgression of the stage by the spectators. Questioning what is said by people onstage evolves into an incomparably smaller task than trying to provide the largest number of people the possibility to speak and act.

> What is insufficient in Brecht is the lack of spectator action. His theatre is also cathartic, because it is not enough for the spectator to think: it is also necessary for him to act, activate, perform, do. Brecht's mistake was not realizing the indissoluble character of ethos and dianoia, action and thought. He proposes to dissociate and even oppose the spectator's thinking to the character's thinking, but the dramatic action continues to be independent of the spectator, who remains in a spectator's condition.

> [...] The important thing is that the spectator enters the scene and takes back his right to lead [...] [22]

What needs to be explained is not so much why the dramaturgical question disappeared but why it returns in the 1996 book *Legislative Theatre*. Was it that having the spectator on the stage was not a philosopher's stone capable of solving all the problems linked to theatrical oppression itself? A. Boal clearly states the objective of the text: to give Legislative Theatre groups, who have often not done theatre before, "a well-structured, reliable scheme" before they eventually try "other paths."[23]

Without delving so much into this topic as to veer off the road, it is undeniable that the dramaturgical schema/method of Legislative Theatre represents a setback in relation to the more critical positions of A. Boal himself. Aristotle, once scolded for inventing the reactionary tragic-coercive system, is now valued as the author of Laws that "are useful, (...) as general rules, guidelines, suggestions."[24] Hegel's aesthetic becomes the model to be followed or further developed. Brecht, cited only once, is in fact forgotten. The drama of free wills opposing each other is now, A. Boal suggests, the model to be followed: "If we are going to write a play on racial prejudice the nucleus of the conflict must treat precisely that: a victim of prejudice struggling against the prejudiced discriminator."[25]

Tracing the history of these changes in A. Boal's work and personal life (where, theoretically, the different positions seem to exist separately and alongside one another, rather than in relation to each other) does not seem a very promising task. A more interesting perspective would be gleaned from finding out whether social movements faced this question of how to use Forum Theatre without turning their characters into pure subjects (meaning people with full autonomy over their actions)—and what solutions, if any, were found. Knowledge of Epic Theatre will also have to be factored into this work, since, for Brecht, aiming for the scene to offer modifiable images of the world to its spectators—making them recognize their capacities for intervention—was never incompatible with overcoming the dramatic form; on the contrary, one was intended to motivate the other.[26] For now, however, let us deal only with the heart of the matter: the task of overcoming bourgeois drama (while still retaining the capacity for intervention onstage) would entail trying to outline a dramaturgy capable of dealing with oppression as a central issue of our society.

On February 16, 2022, the first São Paulo Anthropophagic Fair of Opinion was held, and 16 São Paulo theatre groups performed, always responding to the same question: "What do you think of the Brazil of today?"[27] This question was the same as in the 1968 São Paulo Fair of Opinion directed by A. Boal. At the time, he wrote a text detailing the multiple goals of the fair. The intention was to bring together the various tendencies of left-wing art so that each one of them could be analyzed as moments that needed to be overcome, as they were all produced by and for an outdated conjuncture. The text also called for new ways to continue the struggle during the time of the dictatorship. In addition to these specific programmatic aspects, the fair has been recorded in history as an act of defiance against the Brazilian dictatorship. The theatrical class organized and fought for the show to exist. The artists opposed the authoritarian government with the tactic of expressing opinions freely in the face of censorship.

Restaging a Fair of Opinion today undoubtedly has a critical connotation in terms of equating today's democracy with yesterday's dictatorship, but are we really evolving in the same conjuncture now? Can this resource—the expression of opinions—have the same strength against our current system of domination? Have we not entered a world in which democracy and dictatorship would precisely name regimes that are not entirely mutually exclusive?

It is only through a fine-tuned analysis of our reality and of the configurations it imprints even on our subjectivities that we can determine whether or not any dramaturgical/formal device has any potential for criticizing the dominant order. An analysis that considers the relationship between the present conjuncture and the techniques and dramaturgical structures of TO has not yet, as far as I know, been carried out, and it has only been outlined here. A lot of work remains to be done before being able to conclude what TO still has to offer the struggle against this world.

Notes

1 It's really too bad that French customs officers were not more careful.
2 Bernard Grosjean, *Du Théâtre interactif pour (dé)jouer le réel* (Paris: Lansman Editeur, 2013), 44.
3 Kennedy C. Chinyowa, "Interrogating Spaces of Otherness: Towards a Post-critical Pedagogy for Applied Drama and Theatre," *Applied Theatre Research* 1, no. 1 (2013): 10.
4 Ibid., 8. Would it then be enough for me to adopt the "symbolic activities" of capitalists to become the owner of the means of production?
5 Marc Weinblatt with contributions from Cheryl Harrison, "Theatre of the Oppressor: Working with Privilege Toward Social Justice," in Toby Emert and Ellie Friedland, eds. *'Come Closer': Critical*

50 *Criticizing a Critical Theatre*

    Perspectives on Theatre of the Oppressed (New York: Peter Lang, 2011), 24. Weinblatt is the speaker in the quoted section.

6 Lorette Cordrie, *10 théâtres-forums – Education à la santé et au vivre ensemble* (Paris: Chronique Sociale, 2013), 25.

7 David Diamond, *Theatre for Living: The Art and Science of Community-Based Dialogue* (Victoria, BC: Trafford Publishing, 2007), 63–64.

8 Ibid., 46.

9 Such critiques fail to acknowledge that it's the very oppression that *creates* the groups in conflict. As an example, the capitalist relations of production *create* capitalists and workers. The class conflict only ends when those relations end.

10 Marc Weinblatt with contributions from Cheryl Harrison, "Theatre of the Oppressor: Working with Privilege Toward Social Justice," in Toby Emert and Ellie Friedland, eds. *'Come Closer': Critical Perspectives on Theatre of the Oppressed* (New York: Peter Lang, 2011), 23. Weinblatt is the speaker in the quoted section.

11 Bernard Grosjean, *Du Théâtre interactif pour (dé)jouer le réel* (Paris: Lansman Editeur, 2013), 172.

12 In this section, I am of course not arguing against the material importance of certain prevention measures in and of themselves, like many of those against HIV/AIDS, for example. Rather, I am pointing to the complexity of how some of the logics behind certain prevention initiatives can have the effect of localizing and circumscribing problems that are systemic and stretch far beyond the populations identified as in need of prevention measures themselves.

13 Dort's importance is also evidenced by the fact that he became a character in the play *Improvisation* by Eugène Ionesco, in which the playwright criticizes Dort, Barthes, and Gautier, turning them into censors who are as pedantic as they are ignorant.

14 Bernard Dort, *Le Spectateur en Dialogue* (Paris: P.O.L. Éditeur, 1995), 95.

15 Augusto Boal, *Stop: C'est magique!* (Rio de Janeiro: Editora Civilização Brasileira, 1980), 149.

16 Bernard Dort, *Le Spectateur en Dialogue* (Paris: P.O.L. Éditeur, 1995), 94.

17 Ibid., 95–96.

18 To be honest, the contest for deplorable uses of TO should also include groups who deploy it as a tool for human resources; the only reason those groups are not officially part of the competition is that the author of these lines has not yet witnessed their work.

19 I use here the neologism created (and so often used) by A. Boal to designate the participants in a Forum Theatre session.

20 Bertolt Brecht, *Théâtre épique, Théâtre dialectique* (Paris: L'Arche, 1999), 59.

21 In a way, Dort implies the assumption that this form better adapts to the dominant vision of society, which explains both its success and its inability to overcome the individualistic vision of action and social conflicts. But this implication is never fully developed.

22 Augusto Boal, *Stop: C'est magique!* (Rio de Janeiro: Editora Civilização Brasileira, 1980), 83–84.

23 Augusto Boal, *Teatro Legislativo* (Rio de Janeiro: Civilização Brasileira, 1996), 79.

24 Augusto Boal, *Legislative Theatre: Using Theatre to Make Politics*, trans. Adrian Jackson (Abingdon and New York: Routledge, 1998), 55.

25 Ibid., 63.

26 I will not develop these reflections more here in this chapter; rather, I do so later in this book.

27 In its specific use in the title of the Fair of Opinion, "anthropophagic" draws on Oswald de Andrade's concept of how what is "foreign" should be devoured to become our own, incorporated without being copied.

5 Theatre of the Oppressed in Neoliberal Times

From Che Guevara to the Uber Driver

There is a fundamental paradox inside Theatre of the Oppressed (TO).[1] This "rehearsal for revolution"—which was created to serve as a tool in the struggles that sought to take on capital or at least imperialism headfirst—did not suffer from the ebb of politics; rather, TO experienced dizzying expansion. These days there is virtually no country or political issue untouched by TO. How can this paradox be explained? Generally, it has been explained by the fact that TO contemplates what are often considered universal aspects of experience (the will to act, the desire to transform one's life, etc.). I don't deny that this explanation is partially true, but I don't believe that it exhausts the reasons for this expansion because it does not fully account for the innumerable uses of TO which can in no way be called emancipatory. Another explanation, also equally partial but less explored, is that the success of TO is not due to its critical disposition in relation to the dominant way of life, but rather to the fact that TO *reproduces* significant traits of dominant subjectivity. To use the capacious expression of Portuguese sociologist, Member of Parliament, and TO practitioner José Soeiro, TO is perhaps less the opposite of this world than its shadow. I explore that hypothesis here—knowing, of course, just how limited it may be in some respects.

Regarding the impermanence of politics

What was political in the past is not necessarily political today. The capacity for concrete criticism that any slogan, campaign, or mode of organization may have cannot be rooted in faithfulness to some principle or dogma that lies outside of history. This capacity can only be judged, case by case, if taken in relation to a certain moment, a certain configuration of the forces that oppress us. This configuration is always capable of transforming itself so that even goals as respected as the union of the working class can become slogans in favor of maintaining order. Thus, in an editorial from *Senza Tregua*, the most important newspaper of Italian autonomy, one could read a call for the end of the unity of all workers: "It is this unity that the Trade Unions and the new authoritarian social democracy (the P.C.I.) invoke as they wage war against the revolutionary network in the factories where all the blows are allowed. […] Today, the 'unity of the workers' is claimed by the bosses themselves […]."[2]

This principle—that only what is oriented critically toward its time can be considered political—is often forgotten in the field of art, even in what is referred to precisely as political art. Many of us very often forget that what makes art political is not that it addresses certain themes or uses certain procedures, but, rather, how certain forms, themes, and modes of artistic production relate with a certain political, social, and economic conjuncture, as well as a certain conjuncture of feelings. These relations occur within history and are constantly changing. Ignorance of this principle—that of the necessary relation between political art and its moment—means that often forms and procedures of one era are used in other eras, provoking effects contrary to what is desired.

DOI: 10.4324/9781003325048-7

52 *Criticizing a Critical Theatre*

According to my father, Richard Schechner once staged a happening with students [an event I would later learn was called *Bringing the War Back Home*, an adaptation of another performance created by HED (Bob Head)].[3] In *Bringing the War Back Home*, three of the performers were tied together: a member of the National Liberation Front of South Vietnam a "black militant," and a "white Communist." The three were marched down the streets of New York City near New York University, and the street audience was offered the chance to shoot them. The common thread between both the original piece by HED and the adaptation was the invitation to kill a character who was represented as Vietnamese. The implication with the Vietnamese characters was that people were already participating in the genocide of the Vietnamese people since they did nothing to oppose it. The actors asked the audience (many of them likely students) to—instead of delegating murder to third parties by paying taxes and joining US imperialist society—have the courage to kill the supposed "enemies" of the American Way of Life with their own hands.

The idea that theoretically gave force to this invitation is that US Americans in the campus audience were lethargic petty bourgeois, living in a world without any violence or risk, and that this violence had to be introduced to shake them so that they would become active in the fight against imperialism. This idea—of a necessary violence that art should inflict on its public to awaken it—is today an extremely common and perhaps even dominant form of discourse and practice. Jan Fabre, a choreographer and director renowned to the point of being the co-director of the 2009 Avignon Festival—which is one of the most important theatre festivals in the world—stated, "I want my actors and my audience to learn through suffering. My theatre is a purifying ritual," and La Fura dels Baus, an extremely well-known Catalan group, states, "[W]e do not do political theatre, we just want to mess with spectators who do not feel anything, spread out in front of the TV."[4] But this discourse—which values suffering against the soft complacency that operates as the new opium of the people—presents two fundamental problems. First, it is a recurrent figure of speech of capitalists. Within that capitalist logic, all the rights won by workers would actually be anaesthetizing us by keeping us under the state's dependence, which would prevent us from fully living the ideal life of the entrepreneur, who is always alert, always confronting risk, and always recreating themselves. In this sense, the statement of the then-President of the Union of French Employers, Laurence Parisot, is particularly emblematic: "Life, love, and health are precarious. Why not work?" Second, we may wonder how such discourse—the kind that advocates for performance that jolts the audience through suffering—actually opposes today's reality. Though in the 1970s many students from the United States may have perhaps had their lives secured from the moment they entered college, this is not the case at all nowadays, as the majority leave universities with many thousands of dollars of debt, which they will have to pay off by trying to sell their labor in an increasingly unpredictable and precarious market. The precarity has become so standard, so commonplace, that to want to make our existence less cozy and more exposed to risk is in fact totally tautological in relation to our daily life. Therefore, now this artistic approach—of doing theatre that shocks people out of stasis—does not condemn or criticize reality. Rather, it just repeats reality in a new way.

This was the criticism addressed by Herbert Marcuse to the groups who, in the 1970s, sought to realize the theatre conceived by Antonin Artaud:

And if Artaud wants "constant sound reinforcement"— sounds, noises and shouts, first for their quality of vibration, then for what they represent, we wonder: hasn't the public, including the "natural" public of the streets, already familiarized itself long ago with violent noises, shouts, and screams which are commonplace in mass media, crowd sports, on the roads, in places of recreation, etc.?[5]

Theatre of the Oppressed in Neoliberal Times 53

The uncritical use of certain artistic forms that reproduce in their works essential characteristics of precisely the reality that they wish to combat is unfortunately not limited to the field of happenings or to theatre whose foundational points of reference are Artaud and Grotowski.

Though in Brecht's era a stage light may have been exposed rather than hidden under a fake sun—or actors may have been asked to change costumes on stage and not in dressing rooms—the effect would have been one of estrangement to allow the public to think. Witnessing the means of production of the scene, perhaps audience members would think about the hidden means of production in their daily lives and maybe imagine how to produce a different life for themselves. However, today such disclosure of the means of artistic production would be redundant. For example, James Cameron, the writer and director of *Titanic* and *Avatar*, seems to have become a specialist in directing films whose main attraction is to offer special effects "never before seen," special effects whose "behind-the-scenes" functional description seems to be one of the essential bonuses that accompany any blockbuster DVD. The unveiling of the means of production does not seem to impel any critical consciousness in relation to our society today, but only to feed the fetish of technique. Thus, as Roberto Schwarz argues: "The distancing not only stopped creating distance, but on the contrary vivifies and makes palatable our semi-capitulation, the awareness that among the competing brands of household cleaners, for example, there may be no major difference and yet we are still 'choosing.'"[6]

Whoever repeats artistic formulas and approaches without asking how our subjectivities function in the present moment runs the risk—as noted by the publication of the National Collective of Culture of the MST [*Movimento Sem Terra* or Landless Movement]—of "doing the enemy's work for free." I don't believe that TO is an exception. All art intended as political is necessarily linked to the conjuncture from which it knows it arises and in which it wishes to intervene. It is an intervention within a precise historical moment. For this reason, the goal of artists making political art was often not focused on creating "eternal" works to be placed within the pantheon of world literature, but rather on creating routes of dialogue with the public, taken not as an abstraction but as consisting of real people, involved in concrete processes, whom one should oppose or with whom one should ally—"theatre to be burned" said Dario Fo, regarding his works from his most militant period.

Regarding the "bad uses" of Theatre of the Oppressed

In a broad sense, there is nothing new about criticism of the commercial co-optation of the aesthetic resources invented by the Left. Generated by artists and revolutionary militants as forms of struggle against society, Leftist art techniques would later be seized and deployed by artists only concerned with personal success and the sale of their productions.

Such criticism also arises in the world of TO today. According to such critiques, the primary pitfall from which contemporary TO suffers is that its practitioners deviate from the initial goals for which these forms were specifically invented. The Left of the TO world thus—more or less openly—calls for a return to a certain orthodoxy that could easily be found in the texts of Augusto Boal.

Alongside those perceived as sinning by forgetting the principles of the founders—and who therefore end up misusing TO or creating unnecessary inventions of new forms inspired by it—would be those who voluntarily emptied TO of its political content. The objective of such deliberate emptying would be to more easily access the benefits of state funding for endeavors such as smoking prevention or citizenship education, which are hardly compatible with A. Boal's revolutionary objectives established in his early writings. However, many TO groups depend—to greater or lesser degrees—on state funding in order to survive, and this arrangement is not regarded as

54 *Criticizing a Critical Theatre*

very serious by many TO practitioners, including those further to the Left in the field of TO. And in terms of the most commonly agreed-upon critiques of certain uses of TO, the peak of "bad faith" would be achieved by those who intentionally depoliticize TO by working with the human resources offices of companies and other employers. To object to the use of TO for the recruitment and domestication of workers seems to be the critique of practice that most easily unites the vast majority of those who do—or are interested in—the theatrical techniques invented by A. Boal.

Indeed, it is absolutely not my intention here to defend such uses, which I condemn. And I definitely do not deny that there are people who have "forgotten" the principles of the founder of TO.[7] It just seems quite reductive, however, to fully explain the current and profound depoliticization of TO as only a sort of amnesia shared internationally or as a large-scale betrayal by money-hungry parties. I do not refuse the realities that such phenomena exist. I only reject the idea that they can—in and of themselves—explain the uses of TO that I have witnessed (an unfortunately high number of times) that clearly revealed, whether deliberate or not on the part of the practitioners, a deep acquiescence to the current and deplorable state of affairs.

To think that the problems of TO come only from a lack of respect for some kind of "orthodoxy," either due to innocence or bad faith, precludes several other hypotheses on the important issue of the lessening of the political potential of TO. This rather simplistic logic brings with it an easy solution: the good uses of TO must overlap with its bad uses. I mean that, if the problem were merely about "bad" uses, then it would be solved by having the groups without a "correct" understanding be trained by—and do workshops with—groups with "good" interpretation (we see in this case, as probably in many others, how the guardians of the temple are actually also its merchants). And in such an imagined scenario, theoretically then the groups of "traitors"—those unwilling to learn the "correct" ways—would be expelled so that we can return to truly emancipatory achievements. Exempted from this line of criticism, however, are (1) the groups who supposedly use TO "correctly" and (2) more fundamentally, the methods of TO itself. These things often pass unscathed, as if for many people it is unthinkable—despite TO being around five decades old now—to evaluate what it concretely produced or its possible inadequacies today. I will add here that such "orthodoxy" does not seem to have ever been defended by A. Boal himself. The book *Theatre of the Oppressed*'s extremely ambitious history of a kind of universal theatre defines TO—as well as politicized Latin American theatre—as the movement that "completes the cycle" in terms of being a point of arrival and overcoming of this history. The rest of his writing never seems to reach that degree of ambition. As Fernando Peixoto rightly points out in his introduction to A. Boal's book, *Stop, c'est magique!*, the text oscillates between "a pretentious but healthy theoretical exposition" and an entirely different style: "The book becomes a kind of attentive and carefree journal aboard a contradictory voyage through seas of theatrical expression never before navigated."[8]

In one of A. Boal's most famous books, *The Rainbow of Desire*, there is a long section in which he describes theatrical techniques. These descriptions are repeatedly followed by elaborations of precise occasions on which the techniques were used. During such occasions, the technique in question regularly fails, and what A. Boal recounts is how he can draw meaning from his own "mistakes." In other words, the concrete case is almost never the confirmation of the rule, and the meaning does not derive from the technique but remains to be discovered by the one who uses it.

To believe that the only problems of TO are those arising from the intentions of its practitioners is to leave no room for what Gilda de Mello e Souza called "the uncontrollable autonomy of forms."[9] In an article about this author, Schwarz writes:

If it were just one element among others, the artist's intention does not have the last word, which belongs to the configuration, more substantial than the intention itself.

Theatre of the Oppressed in Neoliberal Times   55

The discussion shifts from what the artist did or did not want to say to what was effectively established and is only made explicit through formal analysis. It is an advanced critical position, which conceives the artwork as a process of knowledge that escapes the intentions of the creator.[10]

There is thus a distance between "project and realization," and to think that this distance is only an error or deviation does not allow us to ponder the involuntary political truth contained in the hundreds of Forum Theatre works carried out all over the world today. It does not allow us to think about why these "non-conforming" ways of doing TO (those thought of as diverging from the goals of "original" TO) are exactly what is seen as emancipatory by those who enact them, nor does it allow us to analyze what this "non-conformity" contains that specifically makes it conform to our present subjective configurations, themselves in connection with the broader configuration of society. I will not linger too much on the somewhat unpleasant task of "verifying" whether—or to what extent—works of third parties follow the original plan of the creator. Such an approach will never cease to give off a certain odor of policing. Instead, I prefer to try to follow a path opened by an intuition of Marx.

It is true, for example, that the three unities, as interpreted by the dramatic authors at the time of Louis XIV, are based on misunderstood Greek drama (and on Aristotle, who exposed them). On the other hand, it is also true that they understood the Greeks in a way that responded precisely to their own aesthetic needs.[11]

What would our own "aesthetic needs" be that make it almost unnecessary to rely on the study of the books and theory of Augusto Boal to immediately find an "interest" in presenting a work of Forum Theatre? What were the changes in the world that made the books' slogans, loaded with controversy in the 1970s, become today perfectly acceptable phrases, ones almost automatically met with consensus? In addition to the question of misunderstanding the concepts of A. Boal, it is particularly interesting to grasp how this new understanding was made, materially and subjectively, possible. It is certainly necessary to forcefully denounce the blatantly commercial practices of TO, a denunciation that will require the most rigorous possible reasoning. However, what seems much more disturbing to investigate is *why* so many games, exercises, and forms of TO have been so ripe for recruitment by countless human resources services worldwide. Such research would undoubtedly reveal unwanted affinities between TO—this method of critical theatre—and the present state of our subjugation.

On guerrillas and micro-entrepreneurs

This paradoxical destiny—the combination of the successful geographic and thematic expansion of TO and the relative dilution of its critical capacity—will be analyzed in the following pages as, to a great extent, not due to the "errors" of its creator nor to the "deviations" of practitioners today. The problems of TO, in my hypothesis, are due to the fact that A. Boal was able to transform the emancipatory hypotheses of the Left into theatrical practices. Today those hypotheses are mostly realized but in a perverse manner. What I have called emancipatory hypotheses were: the abolition of the social division of labor, the critique of the autonomy of art, confidence in the capacity of self-emancipation of the oppressed, and a strategic bet on individual heroism.[12] It is this last one that I will analyze more in depth now to see how, in a time of lowered expectations, the call to heroism—which had the goal of arousing guerrilla inclinations—fits perfectly, without criticism, with a contemporary micro-entrepreneur imperative.

56 Criticizing a Critical Theatre

In order to understand how a notion of heroism within a guerilla context may have transmuted to function in particular ways in the context of contemporary TO, let us turn to the mythology constructed by the Cuban Revolution. According to that mythology, in the beginning, there was the individual. The inflexible will of a small group knew how to arouse the dissatisfaction of the peasant masses and direct them to its true target, the confrontation, and the victory against the apparatus of the repressive state of the dictator Batista. These are the ideas we can easily identify in one of Che Guevara's most famous essays, "Socialism and Man in Cuba"[13]: In the beginning, when there existed only the "germs of socialism, man was a fundamental factor. In him lay the trust, as a specific individual, with a name and surname, and the failure or triumph of the actions he was assigned depended on his capacity of action." These men, with exceptional qualities and a sense of sacrifice, organized themselves into the vanguard of armed struggle. It was their heroic acts that confirmed their status as leaders, revealing the greater importance of personal courage and military ability over any other militant attribute. In front of these, guerrillas were "the people, the still dormant mass we had to mobilize." Though not a "meek herd," they nevertheless follow their leaders—and especially Fidel Castro—without hesitation because those leaders are able to give voice to their deep aspirations and because they fight with sincerity so that they—the masses—can realize them. Though the people are not presented as an absolutely uniform mass, and the vanguard lacks a "more structured connection with the masses," these contradictions do not seem to have much consistency, and they disappear when the two elements are confronted in an almost carnal fusion in the Maximum Leader's speech. Per Guevara:

> In large public gatherings one can observe something like the dialogue of two tuning forks whose vibrations provoke new ones in their interlocutor. Fidel and the masses begin to vibrate in a dialogue of increasing intensity until reaching the climax, in an abrupt end, crowned by our cry of struggle and victory.[14]

However, the group of men led by Fidel Castro was not relying only on the heroism of the individuals who composed it to generate the revolution. According to Vânia Bambirra, who engages some passages from Guevara himself, the warm welcome given by the peasants to the crew of the Granma already demonstrates the previous existence of mobilization against the Batista regime.[15] Moreover, Bambirra suggests, the Cuban example tends to show the impossibility of sticking to a single form of fighting to defeat the state.

> Such an absolute priority [of the rural guerrilla] did not really manifest. Contrary to what may erroneously support a simplistic analysis, the Cuban experience demonstrates how in a revolutionary war various forms of combat combine; how there is no absolute predominance of one form over the other at every point in the process; how forms of combat are related to political situations, and thus how one mode of fighting that may be predominant at one moment might no longer be so in the next, giving way to a more adequate form in light of the conditions of the period.[16]

As Jacob Gorender argues, this mythology was built by the guerrillas to accentuate their role in the revolution, erasing the participation of other actors (such as trade unions, parties, student movements, among others) in order to better be able to establish their power over the new state apparatus that arose.[17] Regardless of which internal interests in Cuba gave rise to this mythology, the fact is that it was very well received by the Brazilian social groups interested in the armed struggle.

Theatre of the Oppressed in Neoliberal Times 57

The Cuban Revolution—and the analyses made by Guevara—moved Latin America from the periphery to the center, placing the continent under the sign of imminent revolution. The "backwardness" of Brazilian underdevelopment and its low industrialization became a benefit. The workers, too integrated into capitalist society, were replaced by the peasantry, whose pre-capitalist sociability would facilitate their conversion into a revolutionary subject. "Focalism"[18] favored the idea that there was no need for mediations, in the sense that not having a party, a union, or any other kind of organization was not seen as a problem because contact between the masses and the leader was viewed as sufficient for the masses to be prepared to rise up. This political perspective also asserted the preponderance of a small group over the party, "liberating" intellectuals from the need for prior discipline as militants. The lack of a strong, structured social movement seemed not so much an obstacle but an advantage—and a guarantee against bureaucracy. The guerrillas, who claimed that the material conditions (the means of production) for the revolution were somehow already realized and that only the subjective spirit of the masses was lacking, seemed to confirm the importance of ideology and to place intellectuals and all involved in the ideological production in the natural leadership role, even if such production now had to be that of armed actions. This eternal availability of the masses for armed struggle also offered the advantage of being able to conjure up the ghost of inaction in the coup d'état of 1964. According to Gorender, armed struggle had a sense of "delayed violence": "[...] the fundamental mistake [of the Left] was not preparing itself or the organized mass movements for the armed struggle against the conservative and pro-imperialist bloc of forces."[19] There was perhaps yet another reason that could more specifically entice the artists to the guerrillas: their "performative logic."

> The armed groups, lulled by the sensationalist echoes of their activities, considered themselves to be greater: they believed in the ghost of an advertising image [...]. From the most tragic moments of defeat, the most important thing was to show a demonstrable performance, as well as a "rebound action" that "established a presence", rather than portraying a continuous and solid political movement. The "action," in this performative logic, became an immediate intervention, gradually ceasing to be part of a revolutionary movement.[20]

This harsh analysis, made after the armed struggle, criticizes what it perceives as a formalism in the strategic choice that underlies many guerrilla organizations, namely that of the activism of a small group whose exemplary actions—due to their violence, intransigence, and audacity—would be able to gather together the masses in a struggle against the dictatorship. Such a choice can be found in the slogans coined by Carlos Marighella: "Action makes the vanguard" and "whoever gives the first shot pulls in the people."

Augusto Boal was a fervent defender of the armed struggle. He wrote no less than four pieces where it is presented as the best option for fighting, one of them being an adaptation of Che Guevara's diary in Bolivia, a play that was presented at the São Paulo Fair of Opinion that A. Boal later described as a "theatrical guerrilla." Additionally, A. Boal was a member of the ALN (Ação Libertadora Nacional or National Liberation Action). Though he never participated in armed actions, he participated in meetings, lent his house for various activities to be held there, and went to Cuba to bring confidential information for the movement.[21] It is because of that affiliation that I will briefly pause to describe ALN, a paradigmatic organization for the Brazilian guerrilla.

Much of the configuration of the ALN can be better understood through the rejection of its leader, Marighella, for the principles that had guided his previous actions within the Brazilian Communist Party. Thus, according to Marcelo Ridenti: "The work of this revolutionary never

58 *Criticizing a Critical Theatre*

failed to emphasize the bureaucratic character of the party structure of the PCB, which would tend to make the organization politically inoperative in terms of revolutionary action."[22] Also part of this struggle against debilitating bureaucracy was the option for a networked organization made up of small armed focal points that possessed the "tactical autonomy" to conduct various actions as soon as they entered the fight against dictatorship and imperialism. The primacy given to action unfolded in two other conceptions. The first consisted of a certain anti-intellectualism, a "reaction to the practice of long theoretical discussions within the PCB [...]." Every theoretical discussion was suspected of unrealistic abstraction, and the only valid revolutionary practice was done by hand. Second, and as a result, leadership within the organization could only be enacted on the basis of direct participation in the armed struggle:

> The leaders of our organization cannot come from elections. Leaders arise from the action and confidence they arouse through their personal participation in various actions. We are all guerrillas, terrorists, and assailants, not men who depend on the votes of other revolutionaries or anyone else to carry out the duties of revolution.[23]

The idea in this case was that not only must the organization be exemplary, but each of its members must have a visible degree of heroism that manifests in armed propaganda. Here a certain heroism is required, which necessarily implies, according to some commentators, a dose of mythology.

> The history of the international communist movement is replete with the construction of myths [...] The worst was the systematic encouragement of the functionality of myths by communist parties and socialist states. Though [myths] facilitate the leading of the masses, myths discourage them from the perspective of the formation of socialist ideology and make it difficult to correct the errors in direction.[24]

This appreciation for heroism, to be linked to the ideology of armed struggle[25] that seemed to prove the immense force of personal engagement, *appears to have passed into TO itself.* Thus, analyzing the differences between Forum Theatre and the play *The Enemy of the People* by Henrik Ibsen, A. Boal writes:

> Who exactly is taking an heroic stance? The character, the fiction. What I want is for the spect-actor to take an heroic stance, not the character … Stockman has an heroic attitude and demands of me that I sympathise with his heroic attitude. He drains me of my desire to behave like a hero myself.
>
> In Forum Theatre, the reverse mechanism is at work. The character gives in and I am called upon to correct him, to show him a possible right, to rectify his action.[26]

In this passage, it seems that the only reason for defeat in a struggle would be a lack of will or a refusal to continue. The character in the model presented fails because he yields, and the spectator corrects his error by being inflexible. By not having linked the idea of intervention onstage with a dramaturgy that escaped the drama, A. Boal ends up making Forum Theatre an ambiguous object. On the one hand, he suggested in many moments that Forum Theatre's purpose is a concrete analysis of a concrete situation. These moments—which certainly echoed Lenin arguing for precisely that—a "concrete analysis of the concrete situation"—indicate the ambition that Forum Theatre may participate to some extent in the revolution, since this

Theatre of the Oppressed in Neoliberal Times 59

Leninist "method" had the function of understanding the "concrete situation" with the aim of transforming it by revealing its hidden contradictions, the movement of the whole, and the ways of influencing it. On the other hand, by focusing on a way in which social mediations cannot be adequately represented, A. Boal not only seems to exaggeratedly inflate the potentialities of the subject and his decision-making capacity, but also to proportionately reduce the strength of systems of oppression. In an excerpt explaining why Forum Theatre cannot be reduced to the moment of physical violence, A. Boal takes as examples a woman attacked by her husband and another woman abused in the subway. Nothing can be done at the height of violence, so he argues that Forum Theatre should look for other moments for possible interventions:

> And in situations like this I believe it is best to go back, pick up the story again at an earlier point in time and find out at what point the oppressed still had a choice of several solutions (before the scenario wends its way to an aggressive end).
>
> Take, for instance, the girl who went into the underground on her own—what might she have done *before* the point she found herself alone on the platform? Why was she alone? Could she not have awaited the arrival of the train near the station master (if there was such)? Could she not have insisted on being accompanied by a friend? Or why hadn't she bought one of those tear-gas canisters designed for handbags? Or even, why didn't she stay over at her friend's place?
>
> Similarly, the woman attacked by her husband, physically incapable of defending herself— why hadn't she left him earlier? Why had she stayed at home that night? Why didn't she call someone?
>
> As for the man picked up by the police, what tactical errors had he committed to let himself be taken by surprise? What precautions should he have taken?[27]

As A. Boal is insisting on the supposed ability of the protagonists to decide without seeing what concrete options were (or were not) offered to these two women, they inevitably are constructed here in this excerpt as co-responsible for the violence they suffer. My point here is not at all about pondering what a woman can or cannot do when confronted with violence from her partner or any other person. However, what seems extremely damaging in my opinion is to reduce the issue of combating violence against women to a series of tips and advice that they should follow when confronted with aggression, as if society as a whole should not instead be transformed so that such violence will no longer occur.

Besides the dramaturgical conceptions of A. Boal himself, the question remains as to why so many people around the world are genuinely interested in TO if it fails to account for systemic oppression, which goes far beyond individual choices. What is the appeal? How does this form correspond to the damaged yearnings of so many people? With these questions in mind, I will examine how the tenacious attachment to the dramatic forms in which the free wills of various individuals collide cannot be seen as mere deception or false speech. In fact, these dramatic forms correspond to a horizon of expectation of our subjectivities, one that is created by the current moment of the systems of oppression. In other words, I will explore here the hypothesis—which I do not consider to be the only one that could explain Forum Theatre's success— that TO is nowadays often used not as a tool for struggle, but rather as a minor helpmate in the reinforcement of the systems that dominate us.[28]

60 *Criticizing a Critical Theatre*

Here I will address a few brief points regarding the relation between theatrical form and society by turning mainly to the work of Iná Camargo Costa. She summarizes the drama by stating that "the autonomous individual (free, in the Kantian sense) [is] the historical presupposition of the drama, its axis is the *action* that always results from a *conflict* of wills […], whose main vehicle is dialogue."[29] And, according to Camargo Costa, that drama began to enter into crisis when the historical conditions that gave rise to it began to collapse, around 1870, with the Paris Commune and the crash of the German stock exchange.

> On the business front, one of the solutions to the problem of "free competition" was the concentration of "free enterprise" in a few hands, with its corollary, the merger of industrial and banking capital that Hilferding called financial capital [...] The social experience of these new realities is the new content that the form of drama *no longer had a way to represent*.[30]

But if the reality that shaped the bourgeois drama disappears, and if the individual disappears, individualism remains. The subject, within a developed capitalist society—increasingly needing to go through the mediation of money to satisfy their basic needs, to sell the goods they have to offer at the highest possible price (even if this includes their own labor force), and to buy what they need at the lowest price—necessarily contrasts with others as an autonomous producer and one in competition with those others. The audacity and intelligence needed by the early capitalists for their business have now been socialized in a certain way for the majority, not with the prospect of building great businesses or with the ambition of enrichment without measure, but to ensure the survival of each one submitted to the cruel laws of supply and demand, which insist that all the characteristics of the subject be put into play. In 1940, Brecht could already make one of his characters exclaim that "[t]o get a lunch it is necessary to have the hardness of an empire founder,"[31] and this excerpt has not lost any of its acuity in these days marked by the crisis in which we have found ourselves since the restructuring of the labor force in the 1980s.

In the labor market, that crisis creates the favorable environment for a development of individualistic behaviors, behaviors that are well received, as they correspond to the practices and speeches of the new management of human resources under neoliberalism. For Pierre Dardot and Christian Laval, "[t]he great principle of this new work ethic is the idea that there is only a possible conjunction of the individual aspirations and the company's excellence goals, personal projects and the company's projects, under the condition that each becomes a small company."[32]

Under this principle, wage labor no longer occurs in a necessary subjection to the will of another but becomes the privileged field where we fully develop our potential. We seek at all times to enhance it, given that—according to entrepreneurial logic—nothing is guaranteed beforehand and everything could require conquering or defending. Instability and risk are perceived as the engines that lead us to constantly outdo ourselves and as the elements necessary to update our capabilities. This logic, which constructs each person as a small company always exposing itself to new challenges, is incorporated through the increasingly frequent use of evaluations where the performances of each person are always measured and compared. As Dardot and Laval argue:

> Everything changes when we no longer want to prejudge the effectiveness of the subject through his titles, his diplomas, his status, his accumulated experience, in other words his place in a classification, because we refer to the finer and more regular evaluation of his competencies effectively exercised at all times. The subject is no longer worth the qualities recognized by statutes, but by the directly measurable use value.[33]

Theatre of the Oppressed in Neoliberal Times 61

This self-measurement is far from being restricted to the labor market, imposing itself equally on the unemployed in European government systems to increase their employability. It also extends beyond this dimension to increasingly encompass all dimensions of existence. The fascination with breaking sports records and the staggering number of tests to measure the inherently immeasurable (love, happiness, etc.) found in so-called women's magazines can be interpreted as stemming from our urge to evaluate everything. "Such a subject places their truth in the verdict of success, they submit to 'a game of truth' in which they prove their worth and being."[34]

Perhaps this is what explains the appeal of Forum Theatre for our subjectivities: that evaluation and competition have been inextricably integrated into our routine. Perhaps this form can now be used as one of those "truth games" where each spectator, through their intervention, would use all of their resources to enact, within a framework seen as not capable of intentional changes, the best possible insertion, without a critical questioning of this framework. This dynamic would explain the excitement and competition perceived by Bernard Dort in the development of a work of Forum Theatre,[35] since such a form of theatre would be the place where each person could evaluate both their own strengths and those of the other members of the audience, with each new person trying to outdo those who came before. Because the quality of our individual calculating capacity is our greatest guarantee of access to a certain level of well-being, Forum Theatre can become a suitable stage for us to exhibit that capacity in a non-offensive and playful transposition of the much more aggressively competitive behaviors of our routine.[36] The need to transpose this painful reality, demanding of so many self-sacrifices, to our playful activities may seem paradoxical at first glance. However, it seems to be a fairly common necessity to metamorphose our pain into a pain that burns less. Franco Moretti offers:

Thus, Marxism and psychoanalysis converge in defining the function of this literature [*Dracula* in this case]: taking on certain fears in order to present them *differently from their real form*; to turn them into *other* fears, so that readers do not have to face what may really scare them. It is a "negative" function: it distorts reality. It's a work of "achievement". Yet it's also a work of "production". The more these great symbols of mass culture depart from reality, the more they must necessarily expand and enrich the structures of false consciousness, which is no more than the dominant culture.[37]

Taking these ideas into account, one could argue—as I am arguing here, to a degree—that the planetary success of Forum Theatre could be linked not to its capacity to challenge, but, on the contrary, to its function as a theatrical device in which the need for testing and competition is constantly affirmed and self-affirmed. It is akin to a therapy that would invariably reinsert the patient into the very framework of the symptom. The stage would become the equivalent of the exhausting routine of the incessant calculation of probabilities in order to succeed in any of our endeavors, a calculation that paradoxically traps us in the most complete impotence in relation to a world imagined as unchangeable. The feverish activity of workers to "get on well" is indissolubly linked to an unmitigated passivity. The various answers to the question posed by a piece of Forum Theatre would no longer be seen as a necessary and preliminary stage to the elaboration of a collective point of view, nor as several tactical proposals prepared by militants of the same organization, proposals from which one should choose. The interventions would only be demonstrations of the aptitudes of each intervener in solving the problem on their own. Such individualistic heroism is in fact one of the few options left over for the shape of our existence in a world perceived to be ever-changing and uncontrollable.

62 *Criticizing a Critical Theatre*

This text is intended to account for the so-frequent neoliberal uses of TO, and especially Forum Theatre, noting how these uses cannot be explained away as mere treason and that they instead reveal something of the present conservative potential of TO. At the same time, I also know that such uses do not exhaust the whole of TO's potential. There are numerous examples of the highest beauty created by those who use TO to resist the people-grinding machine that is our current society; the reader will find exploration of those joys in some of the sections in Part III of this book. It is for such joys to last that we need to engage in the hardest criticism. This form of theatre, created as an instrument of struggle, has also become a battlefield. The present text only has the ambition to help us better probe the terrain where this struggle takes place. My goal in writing it is that the critique it contains will resonate for a few readers not as a chant of despair, but as a call for action.

Notes

1 This text was translated from Portuguese by MendWord Translations, Los Angeles, California, USA, originally for publication in *The Routledge Companion to Theatre of the Oppressed* (2019). The translation was revised by the author and the other editors of that volume, with the permission of the translation service, and then revised additionally for inclusion in this book.
2 Editorial from *Senza Tregua*, in Marcello Tarí, *Autonomie!* (Paris: La Fabrique, 2011), 106. P.C.I. refers to the Partito Comunista Italiano, the Italian Communist Party.
3 For more information on these performances, one could read HED, "Kill Viet Cong," *The Tulane Drama Review* 10, no. 4 (1966), 153, and Richard Schechner, "Guerilla Theatre," *The Drama Review: TDR* 14, no. 3 (1970), 163–168.
4 In this section, my argument is much influenced by an excellent book by Olivier Neveux, *Politiques du Spectateur* (Paris: La Découverte, 2013, 57), as well as much of the author's reasoning about art forms that reproduce the reality that they claim to fight.
5 Herbert Marcuse, *Contra-Revolução e Revolta* (Rio de Janeiro: Zahar Editores, 1973), 111.
6 Roberto Schwarz, "The Relevance of Brecht: Highs and Lows," *Mediations* 23, no. 1 (2007), 130.
7 This "oblivion" can often be the result of a pure ignorance of these principles. Upon the launch of the book *Theatre of the Oppressed* in Buenos Aires on 07/10/2015, the various groups present commented one after another just how superficial or non-existent their knowledge of this book was. Everyone had started with practice, through workshops. Few people there seemed really determined to finally read the book. This was not, in itself, an impediment to making their work very good sometimes.
8 Fernando Peixoto, in Augusto Boal, *Stop: C'est magique!* (Rio de Janeiro: Editora Civilização Brasileira, 1980), 17.
9 Gilda de Mello e Souza, *A ideia e o figurado* (São Paulo: Duas Cidades/34 Letras, 2005), 170.
10 Roberto Schwarz, *Martinha versus Lucrécia,* (São Paulo: Companhia das Letras, 2012), 188.
11 Karl Marx, *Cultura, arte e literatura, textos escolhidos* (São Paulo: Expressão Popular, 2010), 126.
12 For brief explanations/explorations of the concept of the social division of labor, see the appendix of selected key terms in *The Routledge Companion to Theatre of the Oppressed* as well as the chapter "Facilitation/Mechanization" in this text.
13 Che Guevara, "El Socialismo y el Hombre en Cuba," 1965. Available at: https://www.marxists.org/espanol/guevara/65-socyh.htm. Last Accessed on 11 Jan. 2016, author's translation from Spanish to Portuguese, translation service's translation to English.
14 Ibid.
15 Granma is the name of the yacht that was used to transport Che Guevara and Fidel Castro, among other fighters of the Cuban Revolution, from Mexico to Cuba.
16 Vânia Bambirra, *La Revolución Cubana, una reinterpretacion* (Santiago, Chile: Editorial Prensa de Chile, 1973), 47.
17 Jacob Gorender, *Combate nas trevas* (São Paulo: Editora Ática, 1987).
18 Focos was Guevara's armed struggle strategy as portrayed by Régis Debray.
19 Jacob Gorender, *Combate nas trevas* (São Paulo: Editora Ática, 1987), 249.
20 Herbert Daniel, *apud* Marcelo Ridenti, *O fantasma da revolução brasileira* (São Paulo: Editora Unesp, 2010), 53.

Theatre of the Oppressed in Neoliberal Times 63

21 All this information, which I obtained through personal conversations with Augusto Boal, is also confirmed in the following book: Mario Magalhães, *Marighella, the soldier who set the world on fire* (São Paulo: Companhia das Letras, 2012), 366 and 509.

22 Marcelo Ridenti, *O fantasma da revolução brasileira* (São Paulo: Editora Unesp, 2010), 41.

23 Carlos Marighella, *apud* Marcelo Ridenti, *O fantasma da revolução brasileira* (São Paulo: Editora Unesp, 2010), 54.

24 Jacob Gorender, *Combate nas trevas* (São Paulo: Editora Ática, 1987), 27.

25 This influence in the field of the arts seems to precede *Arena Tells of Tiradentes* and to not be restricted to the theatre, as the following criticism by Maurice Capovilla of the movie *The Given Word* of 1962 shows: "According to this view of the world, the main revolutionary force is the 'people,' still an abstract idea, built around a mythical hero whose actions are developed by irrational and uncontrollable impulses. It is not the classes, nor class struggles, which solve contradictions, but rather just the 'people' unified by sacrifice or the example of an individual, the 'hero,' capable of catalyzing this popular, dangerous, and explosive force which tends to overflow the limits of rational plans of action. With this, one does not think of revolution but of simple revolt by unified people … not through an awareness of their needs but by admiration and belief in the power of an unusual personality who presents himself as the Messiah from antiquity here to offer salvation." *In* Marcelo Ridenti, *Em busca do Povo Brasileiro* (Rio de Janeiro: Record, 2000), 88.

26 Augusto Boal, *Games for Actors and Non-Actors*, 2nd. ed., trans. Adrian Jackson (London: Routledge, 2002), 251.

27 Ibid., 254–255.

28 This interest in TO, sometimes counterproductive from the point of view of emancipation, is not limited to the dramaturgy of Forum Theatre only.

29 Iná Camargo Costa, *Sinta o drama* (Petrópolis: Vozes, 1998), 15.

30 Ibid., 19.

31 Bertolt Brecht, *A Alma Boa de Setsuan*, in *Teatro v. 2* (Rio de Janeiro: Editora Civilização Brasileira, 1977), 69.

32 Pierre Dardot and Christian Laval, *La Nouvelle Raison du Monde* (Paris: La Découverte, 2010), 415.

33 Ibid., 432.

34 Ibid., 442.

35 Bernard Dort, *Le Spectateur en Dialogue* (Paris: P.O.L. éditeur, 1995).

36 As a concrete example, I remember a Forum Theatre session, organized by a group in which I participated, on racism in the workplace—in which the interventions followed on stage to show, one after another, how the labor of an Arab worker was as or more competent than that of a white worker, in addition to being cheaper.

37 Franco Moretti, *Signos e Estilos da Modernidade* (Rio de Janeiro: Civilização Brasileira, 1988), 128.

6 Notes on Oppression

It's not my intention here to give a final or implacable definition of oppression.[1] Rather, I want to pose points of departure for a debate. I hope the conversation will be as open and contradictory as possible. Oppression is a term that is hard to define. It can unite positions or identities that don't inherently have many things in common: workers and LGBTQIA+ people, women and colonized people; people with disabilities and people of color. The list of positions from which one might experience oppression is long, and those positions don't always have an obvious common denominator.

A first possible definition could be to say that oppression is what is felt by each person who experiences themselves as oppressed or is said to be oppressed. This definition can be problematic in some cases. For example, once, in a workshop I facilitated with my father in Switzerland, a woman proposed her own experience as the content for a Forum Theatre scene: she felt oppressed by people asking her for money in the street. She may have felt uncomfortable or even attacked as a result of the situation, but I believe that we can all agree that the experience she described does not constitute oppression.

During a workshop that Jana Sanskriti gave for women from Indian villages, Sanjoy Ganguly asked (as he later relayed the exchange), "Do any of you suffer from domestic violence—or know someone who does?" One woman replied, "I don't suffer from domestic violence—my husband only beats me when he has to." But is a woman who is beaten by her husband only oppressed if she thinks she is?

Thinking that self-definition is sufficient where oppression is concerned could dangerously lead us on a path where we would fight against people who are asking for money on the street and would not do anything to engage with people who have accepted the domestic violence that they experience as somehow necessary. To say that self-definition is enough supposes that society is absolutely transparent to us, that we have a total consciousness of the social processes of which we are a part. And we know that it is not that simple.

Another possible (and maybe appealing) definition of oppression would suggest that, at its root, it is a set of actions that occur between individuals. For example, within the logic of this definition, violence would be an oppressive act in itself. Any victim of violence would be oppressed; anyone who enacted violence would be an oppressor.

Yet I believe that Chen Alon (of the bi-national movement of Palestinians and Israelis known as Combatants for Peace) and Edward Muallem and Iman Aoun (of the Palestinian group Ashtar Theatre) would agree with me when I say that a Palestinian boy is not oppressing an Israeli soldier when he throws a stone at them. And I ask Europeans living in countries where there was armed resistance against the Nazi occupation if they would have preferred that their ancestors had not taken up arms to fight such extreme brutality. Was my father an oppressor when

DOI: 10.4324/9781003325048-8

Notes on Oppression 65

he joined the guerrillas against the Brazilian dictatorship? To essentialize a particular action, violent or not, as intrinsically belonging to the oppressors or the oppressed tends to obscure its reasons and motivations in the first place.

The definition of oppression that I prefer is the following: oppression is a concrete relationship between individual people who belong to distinct social groups, a relationship that benefits one group in a way that is to the detriment of another. In this attempt at a definition, oppression pushes beyond individual relationships; it is not reduced to what is often described in English as a "one-to-one relationship"—it always contains something more than that.

Imagine beings who come to Earth in a UFO to try to understand how a city works. In order to do so, they install cameras everywhere, including at traffic lights. After watching the footage several times, the aliens understand that cars stop at a red light and go on green, that pedestrians cross the street when cars stop, that cars drive on one side of the road and pass on the other. Their footage shows what the rules are, but it doesn't reveal the essential: Who designates that lights should go on the streets and physically puts them there? Who makes the traffic laws and enforces them? Who grants drivers' licenses? The state. The state, which is absolutely necessary for understanding this reality, remains invisible in the context of this scene. The same occurs with situations of oppression: relationships between individuals can only be understood within systems—often invisible systems—that determine them.

One cannot understand a relationship between a worker and a boss without trying to understand capitalism. Neither can they understand a relationship between a white person and a black person without taking racism into account, nor a relationship between a man and a woman without considering patriarchy.

On the other hand, there are social groups to which we do not choose to belong and from which it is difficult, or even sometimes impossible, to extract ourselves. I could use myself as an example. I am a man, and I live in France,[2] which, like virtually every society in the world, is patriarchal. In France, in general, women make 25% less on average than men. In the same profession, with the same workload, same experience, they earn 10% less. For example, in the context of a relationship with a woman, statistically speaking, I would be likely to make more than she does. But … I'm kind and generous. I'll invite her out for dinner, pay more toward vacations and house bills, etc. I am an extremely kind and generous man.[3] But here we are talking about how I use the power society gives me as a man; we are not dealing with equality within my relationship. And how far is this "gentle" use of power from being condescending or patronizing?

Patriarchy—even if I try hard not to replicate it—will undoubtedly infiltrate my relationship with my partner in some way. To be an oppressor or an oppressed is not a matter of mere individual choice; it is not, fundamentally, a moral issue. Neither is it a question of essentialism: oppressors/oppressed do not exist as such in their essence or as a result of their nature; instead, they belong to social groups in relation to one another. Oppression is an historical issue. For me, a question that should be asked about slavery is not whether a slaver was, is, or could have ever been "good" or not, but, rather, why does slavery exist? Paraphrasing Brecht in *Round Heads and Pointed Heads*, we could say that many people worry too much about the abuse of power and too little about power in and of itself.

As we each belong to various social groups, all of us can be oppressors and oppressed. My father always posed the example of a Chilean worker, an active union member who simultaneously was a violent husband at home. In his relationship with his boss, he was—without a doubt—oppressed (my father said he met this man before Pinochet's regime and that he was probably killed by it); but we can also say—again without any room for doubt—that, in relation to his wife, he was an oppressor.

66   *Criticizing a Critical Theatre*

To talk of oppression is not to imply a Manichean construction of the world. Systems of oppression are not, at their core, about good facing off with evil. My father dedicates the French edition of *Games for Actors and Non-Actors* to the oppressed classes and the oppressed within those classes. Recognizing class oppression—that is: capitalist oppression—was never an attempt by my father to deny or diminish other forms of oppression.

Oppression was a much-used term in the 1970s. Today, we encounter an abundance of other terms and expressions: victim, excluded, etc. What do these terms mean? A victim tends to be presented as a person without the resources to confront the fate that knocks at their door, as an object we should pity, as someone toward whom we should feel guilt or remorse. A victim does not tend to be represented as someone with whom we must establish solidarity or position ourselves as siblings in a common fight.

A piano falling onto someone by accident certainly does make that person a victim. A shark attack on a crowded beach makes victims. But is it possible that an unemployed person is the victim of the economic crisis in the same way that someone might be the victim of lightning that strikes her on the head? The word *victim*, when used without specificity and intention, can privilege the irrational aspect of social life and avoid holding oppressive groups accountable.

This is also how the word "excluded" often works. Its use frequently results in the perception that there are not oppressors and oppressed, but only people who are included or excluded. "Excluded" hides the causal relationship that exists between the privileges experienced by one group and the oppression lived by another. No one would be to blame for the exclusion, and no one would benefit from it. Perhaps, inside this kind of logic, the only ones to blame for the exclusion are the excluded people themselves; for instance, in France, we glimpse the emergence of increasingly more complex, humiliating, and even authoritarian approaches to help the excluded "include" themselves. The National Employment Agency (ANPE), as just one example, offers unemployed women courses in changing their appearances, in which they learn how to dress and put on make-up for their next job interviews. In other words, for ANPE, there is no unemployment problem in France; instead, the problem would supposedly be "unattractive" self-presentation. Society does not have to question itself, this program would seem to imply; rather, those who are excluded must make more of an effort.

Another characteristic of these two terms (victim and excluded) is that they insist that injustice is peripheral and intermittent. In comparison, the word oppression insists on the central place of injustice in the foundations of our societies.

We must recognize that there is no revolutionary romanticism in the use of the word *oppressed*. Being oppressed is a social position and not a political strategy. Within the same larger oppressed group, many strategies (and, more broadly speaking, reactions) will likely coexist. For example, Malcolm X—in "Message to the Grass Roots," a famous speech on Black revolutionary strategy in 1963—spoke of a conception of two groups among black people enslaved in the US: those in the field and those in the house. According to X, the first group, identifying with the perspective shaped by life in the fields, was more ready to rebel, to try to rebel. The second—who, in X's categorization, lived nearer to the slaver (literally and figuratively), sometimes would have likely eaten his leftovers, and was envisioned as more likely to identify with him, etc.—would, when asked to run away, respond: "Where is there a better house than this?" Both of the groups in this scenario are oppressed by the violent institution of slavery, but they are perceived as having different responses, even different strategies for survival, that result in part from distinct material realities. If these differences can be explained by the social diversity that exists within a group of people who have been enslaved, there are also sometimes differences that are of a political nature. Not all people who are part of a specific oppressed group are guaranteed to have the same strategy to fight against oppression.

Notes on Oppression 67

What else is there to say about strategy? Or about how to defeat and overcome oppression? At this very general level at which I am speaking, I am not sure. It's only in front of the concrete conditions framed by a specific struggle that we can determine our means. The only thing I know for sure in a general sense is that this fight will have to be a collective one. Alone, left merely to our own devices, we can evade oppression, route around it, negotiate with it—but we can never overcome it. One black man can become president of the United States without the end of racism; one woman can become the prime minister of England without the end of patriarchy; one factory worker can become the president of Brazil without the end of exploitation. Defeating oppression is no task for a hero or a messiah; it is the task for collectives, groups, and organizations, the task of the masses. And theatre can be a huge help in this task, but it cannot do it all. The actor has to become an activist, leave the stage, and take on the streets and other spaces. As my father used to say, Forum Theatre is a *rehearsal* for revolution or transformation, which means that it is not *itself* transformation or revolution.

Much remains that could also be said here about the links between different systems of oppression: how racism helps capitalism, how patriarchy and homophobia are intertwined and reinforce each other, etc.[4] There is also the necessity of refining the definitions of oppressor and oppressed. For example, is any individual who benefits in some way from patriarchy necessarily an oppressor on the same level as a capitalist or a dictator?

Whenever someone asked my father about a technical issue, about a specific aspect of Theatre of the Oppressed (TO) as a methodology, what would work in a given situation, which technique should be used, he usually replied that the methods had been developed for the people and not the people for the methods. But for which people? Oppressed people, always. How, then, do we define who is the oppressed and who is the oppressor? How do we build strategies to bring about the opposite of oppression, which is emancipation? We can never abandon these questions. They are what allows us to distinguish TO from mere cultural diversion or interactive training toward subjugation.

As we answer these questions, understanding my father's legacy is pivotal but not sufficient. It was never sufficient. My father continually supported what he called creative heresies, always distinguishing them from unforgivable betrayals. From here on out, we have the difficult task of reconciling fidelity with creativity.

Notes

1　This text is an edited, newly expanded and translated version of a speech I delivered at the First International Conference of Theatre of the Oppressed, hosted in Rio de Janeiro in July, 2009, two months after the passing away of my father. The people referenced with a tone of familiarity during my talk were there in the room: Sanjoy Ganguly, Chen Alon, etc.

2　That was true in 2009.

3　I hope that the reader will understand and forgive the use of an irony that is perhaps better understood when the text is delivered in front of an audience, not in its written form.

4　On the topic of how oppressions overlap and intensify each other, Black feminists have inspired important analysis; the Combahee River Collective and Keeanga-Yamahtta Taylor are just two examples of many in this regard.

7   Facilitation/Mechanization

I would like to start my talk with a quotation from my father that I have understood only recently: "Everybody can do theatre, even the actors."[1] Before, my understanding of this sentence was quite simple: everybody can do theatre because, even if I think that my voice is not good enough, that I don't know how to move my body in a certain way, theatre is a human capacity that every human can and should use. All well. But that was not at all accounting for the second part of the sentence, "even the actors."

It's a rather counterintuitive sentence, in fact, when you really think about it. It means, if my English is correct (but it *is* the meaning of the sentence in Portuguese), that, "[f]or those who are actors it will be more difficult to do theatre than it will be for any other person." It's quite bizarre, isn't it? If someone chooses to be an actor, studies theatre, learns how to use their voice, their body, becomes familiar with the playwrights and acting methods many consider to be the best, has experience, makes a living from it, it is precisely that person for whom it will be the most difficult to make theatre. Strange.

Does this idea apply to other professions? I've tried with some; most of the time it doesn't work. Sometimes, it fails miserably. If, for example, I were to break my leg leaving this stage and one of you were to come to me saying, "Everybody can do medicine, even the doctors," I would presumably shout out loud, "I don't care! Get away! Help! Bring me to the hospital!"

Actually, I have found only one profession to which it applies perfectly almost all the time: the professional politician. If you make a living from professional politics, if you engage in the process of running for something, spend your time trying to convince donors that you will benefit them, making laws, lobbying, deciding which war your country will engage in next, you are very unlikely to do politics. What you will do is not politics; it is the administration of the routine of oppression. Politics is not that. Politics is the concrete manifestation of the complete equality of all human beings. It is the equal sign inserted between one person and any other person. I believe that anyone who has slept even just one night in one of the encampments of the Occupy Movement has very likely done more politics than the vast majority of politicians do in their entire lives. Of course, this general rule is not always true. For example, we have here José Soeiro, who, for three years, was a Member of Parliament in Portugal and who passed a law against transphobia.[2] But I am sure José will agree with me: Even with this extremely important sparkle of equality, how many oppressive laws were made by the majority of Parliament during your mandate?

Let's go back to theatre. Why can't actors do theatre as easily as anyone else? There can't be any other reason except that it's not *in spite of* their specialization that they cannot do theatre as well as the non-specialists can, but instead it is precisely *because* of their specialization that they cannot. Their specialization becomes the obstacle to them being able to perform.

DOI: 10.4324/9781003325048-9

Facilitation/Mechanization 69

Why is that? Because specialization is an image of the mechanization that my father wrote about. Mechanization is when, out of the millions of possible ways to interact with your surroundings, you are obliged to choose one. It is when a particular and limited set of activities becomes the main vehicle through which you relate with the outside world, to the point that you can't see anything else of the world other than that which you see through this set of activities. A classic slapstick image of this situation of mechanization is one from the 1936 movie *Modern Times*. After hours of repetitively tightening bolts on an assembly line, Chaplin cannot stop. He runs around wielding wrenches in both hands, trying to tighten every "bolt" in sight: the noses and chests of fellow workers, the buttons on skirts and dresses, the valves on the fire hydrant outside the factory doors. But mechanization doesn't occur only with workers on a factory line. I was talking about doctors .... All of us have experiences of doctors who are no longer able to see the patient, just the disease. They diagnose a kid with anemia: "Here, take three tablets of iron, three times a day, for three months." They don't ask if the kid is eating properly, they don't ask if the kid is eating enough spinach, beans, meat, they don't ask if the kid is eating enough food, they don't ask if the parents can afford food: "Three tablets of iron."

My father was pointing out that this limitation of the specialized being could also occur with actors themselves, that art wasn't an invulnerable shield against the limitations to which specialization can lead.

Very well then:

Specialization, even in acting, can be a limitation, can be—and this is actually the real word for it—an alienation.

Okay.

But then ... There was a kind of specialist who didn't yet exist by the time Paulo Freire or Augusto Boal started their experiments, their reflections, their praxis: the specialists of Theatre of the Oppressed (TO) and Pedagogy of the Oppressed (PO). And here we are. We, the specialists/facilitators of TO and PO.

So ... Let's ask the question, let's make the parallel. Can the very fact that we became specialists in TO become an obstacle in our practice? Is it possible that everybody can do TO, even the facilitators? Will it be easier to do TO for everyone else than it will be for a facilitator?

A difficult question, and even more difficult to answer it.

We all know how some aspects of our specialization have brought us many good things, the works that were achieved all over the world, the impacts we had, the advancement within the techniques, the very good books and articles that were written, the excellent programs .... We, here in this room, know all this, so I won't repeat it. It is very important to say those things out loud, to say them to the governor of Arizona, for instance, and to stand for them.[3]

But not here, not now.

Let me explore with you some of the not-so-positive aspects of this specialization.

The first aspect that I consider to be particularly negative is the very way that we can get support for our work: the funding systems. I guess that in the United States it works more or less the same as in any other place. Let's imagine a young facilitator who starts to work inside their own community with people they know. The project goes well, they get some funding, they make some performances, everything works fine. Then the funding ends. When this facilitator starts fundraising again, the funders' policies have changed. They don't finance any more projects on X, only on Z. So the facilitator will have to change their project a bit. Now, because of the success of the former project, they are also invited, by the funders or city hall, to go to another place, to do something different. Little by little, the facilitator has less and less of an organic link, neither with the community in which they used to work nor with a certain issue. And this is not because the facilitator is evil or corrupted, but instead it is occurring by the very rules of the

70 *Criticizing a Critical Theatre*

funding game. Let's take a counterexample, one of the hidden jewels of the world of TO, Muriel Naessens. Muriel started working with TO 30 years ago.[4] She learned it with my dad when he was in France. Since then, Muriel has worked on one set of issues only: women's rights. That is because, before anything else, Muriel is an extremely strong feminist activist. You will find her at every march, her name on every petition. She will be known by almost all feminist organizations. But, for every example of a Muriel, how many of us simply cannot afford to work on just one set of issues?

The funding systems as they exist in most countries create facilitators who need to jump from community to community, from issue to issue. As a result, the facilitator begins to be an outsider within the community, with no heart link with the issue the facilitator is working on. So what justifies their presence? What legitimates their work? The specific knowledge that they have of techniques—and I am talking here about popular education in general and community art in general, not only about TO—and that the other participants don't. And I think that it's strange. I am not sure that this is healthy. The very motor that helped fuel what some called the new social movements (which included movements of women, black people, LGBTQ people, among many others) was the fact that everybody could legitimately speak because everybody had shared experiences of oppression. The model of the facilitator being legitimated by their specific knowledge of a technique might be a brake to that motor. The sentence "Everybody can become an actor, even the actors" is being interpreted in a new way: "All of you can become actors, as long as you have me as a facilitator."

There is another problem with this specialization. As I said earlier, specialization reduces our possible actions to a certain routine, to a certain utilization of a certain set of activities, tools, concepts. And those become the whole world to us. We can see reality only through them, as with the example of the doctor incapable of seeing the patient beyond the disease. We make a whole out of a fragment. We take a slice of reality and start believing it is reality itself. Does that occur with us, the facilitators? I believe that, yes, it does. And, paradoxically enough, precisely in the moments in which we are the most genuine, the most generous. When faced with a problem, we absolutely want to make it fit within the techniques we hold. We cannot admit that the problem is part of a bigger process and that we won't be able to solve it with the techniques alone. How many times I heard my father being questioned, especially about Rainbow of Desire, especially by drama therapists, especially in the United States: "How come your techniques have no closure? How come there is no solution? How come they don't have an ending?" (And I must say that I couldn't help but hear, behind their need for an "ending," the desire for a happy ending.)

How many times I heard my father answering back that it was simply impossible to close within the four walls of the workshop room something that didn't start there, something that was bigger than the space between those walls and would continue until somehow brought to an end somewhere outside of that space. In how many places did my father write that the techniques were not an end in themselves? From the first book on TO until the last, I can't even count the moments in which it was made clear that the Tree of TO culminates with concrete actions. Something that isn't TO itself—concrete action—is in fact the highest branch of the tree. But, as specialists, we can tend to believe that our technique is not just a moment in the long march toward emancipation. We believe, wrongly, that TO, PO, or any technique can provide emancipation in and of itself.

Is this impairment of ours—this restriction of ours—a curse, a fatality? I don't think so. Will it be easy to find solutions so that we are no longer in this very bizarre position of being specialists of a method that demands despecialization? I don't think it will be easy, not in society as it is. The Brazilian dictatorship had a slogan: "Workers have to work, students have to study."

Facilitation/Mechanization 71

Well, in the 70s here, things got interesting when students went to learn and organize in communities and you could see Panthers walking around campus.[5] The most interesting things happen when people run away from the places and roles in which they are supposed to stay and start to occupy some others. Sanjoy says that TO is complete when the actor becomes an activist.[6] In order for that to happen, I would add, it's time for us to understand that, if a facilitator works with oppressed people, it is not because the facilitator owns a specific technique. If a facilitator works with oppressed people, it is because the facilitator is just one oppressed person more.

Notes

1 This talk, revised slightly here for a print context, was given in English as part of a keynote panel at the 18th Annual Pedagogy and Theatre of the Oppressed Conference in Berkeley, California, USA, on June 1, 2012.
2 José Soeiro, Portuguese sociologist, TO practitioner, and Member of Parliament (2005–2011, 2015–present), was present at the conference session where I gave this talk.
3 During the conference where I gave this talk, much conversation focused on the attacks on ethnic studies and critical pedagogy happening in the United States (including, as I understood it, especially vehement attacks in Arizona).
4 Now 40-plus years ago. Muriel Naessens passed away in February of 2016.
5 By "here," I refer both to the United States but also specifically to Berkeley, CA, the site of this conference talk.
6 Sanjoy Ganguly and Sima Ganguly of Jana Sanskriti (discussed elsewhere in this book) in West Bengal, India, were also speakers on the keynote panel on which this talk was given.

Part II

Small Screws, Big Twists

8 What Can Art Do in the Anti-Capitalist Struggle?

This text emerges from my impressions of the 2020 electoral campaigns for mayor and city councilors in Brazil. Here, however, I will not tackle the good and bad surprises, the campaigns that impressed with their dynamism, or how those campaigns changed the terrain of our daily struggles. What they revealed about the Brazilian conjuncture—which those campaigns helped to change—is a discussion of great importance that I will not take on here.

Instead, here I wish to shed light on one specific issue, which seems to be a symptom of a greater evil: the relationship between candidates and artists and, even beyond that, the relationship of candidates with art and culture in general. In these pages, I will not cite anyone in particular, since it is not a question of denouncing this or that candidate. In fact, of the candidates I have witnessed, the overwhelming majority repeats the same discourse, whose limits I want to debate.

When asked what they will do for cultural work on the social and geographical margins of the city (referred to in Brazil as the *periferia* or periphery), Candidate X—who has original and bold positions in other policy areas—proudly says: "It is not about promoting culture on the periphery but promoting the culture OF the periphery. The periphery has a vibrant, rich, and diverse culture that we have to help; we have to find the resources so that artists can continue doing their work that is so essential to the social fabric, work without which life is meaningless …." Another candidate will speak of the need to repair and create new facilities, to which a third candidate will not fail to add that the uneven geographical distribution of these same facilities—which are so concentrated in the central and wealthy areas of the city—is absolutely unfair. Finally, the most radical of all will bring to the table the oh-so-radical idea that we should have special public calls for support of cultural work done by specific groups or segments of the population; after all, the distribution of resources and equipment has to favor the underprivileged so that "other voices" can be heard.

And that's it.

Nothing more.

Here, summarized above, are almost all of the Left's proposals for the arts in Brazil.

These proposals are right; they are absolutely right. It is more than obvious that all cultural workers should be entitled to certain rights—and that these rights are many and that they should guarantee a dignified life, as it should be for all workers. It is also of course necessary to discuss the ridiculously low budget allocated to culture, to do everything to increase it, and to ensure that its distribution within the city and its population obeys the principles of justice. This is all undeniable.

But is that it? That's all there is to be said? I don't deny that discussing money is important, but does the debate end with only that? Isn't it kind of strange that this is the entire scope of

DOI: 10.4324/9781003325048-11

discussion about an activity and a sector that are hailed as being of such vital importance to society? Isn't there room for even a little discussion about what art is? About how it is made from day to day, about how sometimes it helps maintain the cruelty of the times we are living, about how sometimes it also helps to build a different, freer tomorrow? Nothing?

What do these candidates tell us when they limit the debate in such a way? That culture is intrinsically good, that it helps humanity at every step of the way (help with what is not so clear), that everything that is produced today is positive, with no shadows. Logically, then, the only possible discussion is quantitative, since the qualitative aspect of art was already awarded a seal of excellence. "We will have More of the Same!" candidates enthusiastically say to the cultural workers. "You are dealing with the Same, keep doing the same as before, but now with More, and let me take care of that. Bring me your audience, your followers, tell them who to vote for so that soon your interests will be at the forefront of the institutional struggle." As a friend who probably prefers not to be mentioned by name pointed out to me, the number of artists among the first signatories on any petition is the clearest sign of this somewhat shady negotiation in which politicians take advantage of the prestige of art professionals, who are much more represented than any other professional category on political petitions in Brazil.

The kind of candidate discourse I am addressing in this text also reveals a division of tasks: art is left strictly to artists, and the administration of public affairs is left solely to politicians. What nonsense it would be if artists thought politically … poor things, they don't know how to do that! They are just people blessed with a gift, but that gift is a burden! They are eternal innocents who don't think like the rest of humanity! And, moreover, they are absolutely incapable of thinking WITH the rest of humanity! Let's leave them to their craft, which means that, even if they are living on the outskirts of society, they are still in ivory towers! An even greater dislocation would be to ask politicians to think about art! You already know where this ends! TOTALITARIANISM! Just talking about it, I can already smell the gulags! No, it is safer to leave politicians as managers for the state.

Here I allow myself a moment in parentheses to consider whether in education this is also how the debate goes, only in quantitative terms: better pay for professionals, better career plans, schools with more resources. It is obviously noble to fight for these things, especially in a country like Brazil. But isn't it also possible to think more capaciously? It can never be merely a question of democratizing access to education since, in a capitalist regime, education is partially determined by capital and its practices are also functional *for* capital. Is trying to have both reflection and action—simultaneously defending and criticizing the school—an impossible task today? Wouldn't the maintenance of that productive tension, however, be precisely at the heart of Paulo Freire's teachings?

I return here to the previous point, in my view the most important, about this distribution of tasks (politicians do politics; artists make art) that means that no one is surpassing the bounds of the places that society created for them, a distribution that leaves all stones unturned. Yes, we can—why not?—leave the artists to art. But what are we actually saying if we say that politicians are only responsible for managing public resources? When we say that politicians should not have a vision of the totality of reality because to do so risks totalitarianism?[1] In other words, here I am concerned with the problem of politicians who merely consider society an assemblage of disconnected relationships and who are not interested in changing the totality: society itself. With these kinds of logics and divisions, we are creating a limit: "You will be nothing but a servant of social democracy! It is up to you only to administrate the state as it already exists, distributing its resources responsibly, but never thinking about the part you play!" This division of the world is problematic because it helps to keep the world as it is.

What Can Art Do in the Anti-Capitalist Struggle?   77

The extreme difficulty of thinking about the relationship between art and politics has an understandable cause: the more than disastrous experience of Stalinism, a totalitarian regime that killed the Soviet revolution and used art in a purely utilitarian form, forcing artists to serve the regime. However, failing to face this issue is precisely what makes Stalinism win once again. Thus, all questions linked to what many have called this "revolution in reverse" that was Stalinism must be faced, and attempts to overcome it must be debated and put into practice. Otherwise, we will mortgage something infinitely more important than art or culture: radical transformation itself. Political art cannot be reduced to an instrument at the service of bureaucracy, with its bad taste, aesthetic authoritarianism, and the sole purpose of strengthening a deplorable power. Political art, on the contrary, serves to question the crystallizations of power, even of power born from a revolution.

The lack of a real policy for the arts that goes beyond the question of its funding is a serious symptom of the badly frayed debate on strategy. When I say strategy in this case, I mean plans to gain and maintain power against the state and capital. If this debate were to be taken seriously, we would not settle for addressing funding issues and nothing else. We would have to ask ourselves what roles art and artists can play, we would have to consider what would be the criteria for winning artists over so that they are willing to do these tasks that serve larger movements, and we would have to confront ourselves with all the experiences of the past— sifting them through the filter of an analysis of our conjuncture—to determine which strategies or approaches from the past could still be used today.

I am not saying here that a revolutionary program for the arts would be enough to generate a revolution. I am saying the opposite: that the lack of such a plan shows us how much the strategic debate is not taking into account all necessary dimensions, perhaps because it does not even exist with the acuity that the present situation demands.

And, without this debate, what do we have left? The prospect of gaining—gradually—more and more spaces within institutional frameworks? Forcing the revolution forward by gaining more city representatives for the Left in each election? Who knows: mayors, even governors? Will we dream of having presidents? What these scenarios would leave untouched is what was previously the main strategic enemy: the state. This gradual institutional advancement is compatible with the mildest identity agenda policies, those for which it is enough to have "one of our own inside" without actually *questioning* at all what is the inside itself—and without seeing that the division between inside and outside is precisely the root of the problem.

This bet on a slow accumulation of institutional strength, on a revolution at the polls, feels like a redux of old bets, wagers made when there was faith in progress, when many people thought tomorrow would be better. How to understand such bets when today we don't even know if there will be a tomorrow? It is clear that the transformation of the world involves the seizure of state power and that elections can be an important step in this process. But this transformation demands a radical transformation of the state itself. Its structure and functioning cannot remain untouched if we aim to concretize real democracy.

We cannot be satisfied with a merely quantitative cultural policy because we cannot be satisfied with the state.

Perhaps a Theatre of the Oppressed (TO) of the 21st century—one that is indeed up to the tasks of those who do not want to despair—cannot be defined as an arsenal of games, exercises, and specific techniques. This fixation on forms always carries with it the tendency to believe that emancipation in its entirety could fit on a stage. Perhaps it is better to define TO as an attempt—always using the most critical forms of dramaturgy—to contribute to the construction of modes of organizing that ensure that popular demands are not merely heard or recognized by the state. Such organization would instead insist that the state can only bow before a population

78 *Small Screws, Big Twists*

that recognizes itself for what it actually is: the true source of all power. To think about this kind of organization today requires an almost superhuman imagination, but isn't that what art is for?

As a result of the concerns arising from the electoral campaigns I have mentioned, others were born. The first had me wanting to return to the problem of the state. What makes it necessarily an instrument of oppression? Why is it not enough to have reforms or victories in terms of its scope? With this discussion, other questions crop up: What is strategy? What sorts of thought and action would be implied by the task of overcoming this state? And, returning to the initial question of this essay, does art have a role in this struggle?

Notes on the capitalist state AND its necessary overcoming

The modern state, the one arising from the Bourgeois Revolutions through which capitalism became the dominant system, presents itself as an enigma. It is the first to give consistency to the assumption of equality between people. In elections, for example—the moments of greatest importance when this political form takes on the traits of a democracy—one vote is strictly equal to another. However, this form of equality leads precisely back to inequality. It equalizes differences, but, at the same time, it does so in a way that makes it a necessary element for the identical reproduction of power relations in the capitalist sphere. The conundrum to be deciphered is exactly this: How is this type of equality the means by which the state guarantees that capitalism has the conditions to reproduce itself?

Before capitalism there was a merging of the economic and political (and, to a certain extent, religious) structures. The economically dominant class was immediately also the ruling class of the state. The ruling class was such because it dominated both the economy and the state. In the feudal state, the monarch was the main figure of the nobility and straightforwardly the head of a state, in a world order validated by religion.

Each individual had their place in society, per their status, which guaranteed them specific political-legal rights as well as access to specific means of production. Therefore, only nobles could have access to large estates, just as only a large-scale landowner could be a nobleman, thus having access to certain privileges. Privilege has to be understood here in its etymological sense of private law. These private laws existed not only for the nobility; every statute had them.[2] Statutes were organized hierarchically in society. A peasant during the feudal era could be relatively economically autonomous in relation to the lord (owning his own lands, producing what was necessary for his survival). However, his status meant that he had duties to his lord (fees, tithes on the harvest, unpaid labor …). The latter had rights over those who were constructed as "his" peasants as a result of personal dependence relationships.

In the modern state, everything changes. The citizen is theoretically, as a citizen, absolutely equal to any other citizen. Social differences, apparently, do not at all affect the constitution of the state. All are equal before the law and its guarantor, the state. It is a state that is not the property of someone or a specific group, but a "public power" (a formula found in the Manifesto of the Communist Party) whose administration would be based on an organized dispute through elections. In other words, those who govern are not chosen and validated by a higher religious power.

While this political form was a great advancement in some senses, the fact that the abstract individual is the starting point for the modern state's judicial-political constructions conceals the division of society produced through existing structures of domination and exploitation (class division, hierarchy that results from patriarchy, forms of domination provoked by colonialism and its racism, etc.). This concealment produces an imaginary community with very real effects. (As Anatole France said, "the law is equal for all, it prohibits the rich and the poor from stealing bread alike.") Themes which supposedly concern the people as sovereign and the general will of the nation create an illusion with consistent rationality and concrete practices that treat individuals as if they were not inserted in antagonistic social groups.

In addition to "guaranteeing peace" between opposing classes, the notion of legal equality is necessary for the exploitative relations inherent to capitalism. The state considers as equals both those who represent capital and only aim to increase value, and those who, having only their labor power to sell, have to accept that their ability to act is determined by others. Contracts, protected by the courts and the state, treat deals of purchase and sale—as well as employment contracts—as exchanges of the same nature. Contracts provide a formal legal framework for the exchange of equivalent goods that, in effect, allows for unequal practices of ownership of goods and activities. The law is both the overcoming of violence and its maintenance, given that it makes some have to submit to others and sustains social inequalities, repressing those who have nothing left. The state, which guarantees the application of the law, is a power that is necessarily external to the agents who sell and buy goods. And this externality is necessary so that capitalist exploitation can operate through the exchange of supposed equivalents and not by the simple imposition of brute force. For there to be capitalism, there must be a state that guarantees that agents are subjects of rights. Thus, the state is capitalist not because of the dominant classes, but because of the type of relationships it allows by framing individuals as citizens with rights and bearers of equivalent trading goods.

Perhaps it is important to introduce a nuance here. The introduction of labor laws in the 20th century involved precisely the creation of an autonomous field of law that emancipated labor law from civil law. This distinction was based on the fact that, unlike in the latter, in labor law there is no so-called freedom of parties and the function of the law would be to protect the weakest part in a relationship marked by dependency and inequality. In this sense, the state and the legal apparatus incorporated political processes in which the strength of labor, trade unions, and movements was noted. However, it is worth observing that—while labor law mitigates the violence of exploitation—it also helps maintain exploitation by creating norms that regulate the nucleus of the unique commodity that is the workforce. The state limits itself to recognizing an inequality between the parties of the contract, without extinguishing the inequality within the work relationship.

Let's return for a moment to the political abstraction of the modern concept of citizenship. In pre-capitalist societies, belonging to an estate was also the expression of a certain relationship with the means of production. A person was a peasant both because they had to obey certain laws and because they owned land. The process of separating direct producers from their means of production is completed in the creation of this political abstraction that is the modern citizen, whose figure emerges in the destabilization of pre-capitalist societies.

This separation of the abstract citizen, supposedly equal to all others in their rights, from the concrete individual—immersed in the needs and constraints of capitalist modes of production—corresponds to the separation of the state from society. Thus, for Marx, elections are not the moment in which society delegates its sovereignty to its representatives. On the contrary, elections are what establish the state as a separate political form: "The separation of the political state from civil society appears as the separation of the deputies from their mandators," writes Marx in *Critique of Hegel's Philosophy of Right*.[3] In fact, after the election, there is no formal device that requires representatives to be constrained by their constituents during their term of office. No procedure is legally recognized in a way that forces representatives to stick to what was indicated to them by voters: "They are supposed to be delegates, and they are not." For Marx, elections are not the way in which society constructs its representation, but the way of accessing the world separate from the state. He also regards the examination to enter the state bureaucracy

80 *Small Screws, Big Twists*

(to fill positions like those of judges, teachers, police officers, etc.) as a mark of the separation between the state and society. The exam, like elections, is a democratic right of access to the separate order of the state: "Every Catholic has the chance to become a priest (i.e., to separate himself from the laity as well as the world) [...] bureaucracy is *la république prêtre.*"[4] As I noted earlier, multiplying the devices so that the population can be closer to their elected representatives and officials does not fundamentally change this separation, since it reproduces within the institutions the necessary separation of the state from the market agents who exchange goods.

This separation is not only functional because it creates a real illusion of a community of equals distinct from the concrete conditions of individuals. In parallel, the Christian religion consoles its followers from their daily earthly oppressions by speaking of a kingdom of heaven, one of equality, justice, and calm. The relative independence of the state is necessary to impose an organization on the bourgeoisie as a class. The implacable selfishness imposed by the capitalist system on each individual bourgeois makes the consolidation of bourgeois class hegemony impossible without state intervention. The infinite greed—the systematic individualism that each capitalist has to develop to maintain their social position—would render any agreement inoperative if it were not imposed from the outside by an institution endowed with considerable power of constraint. Without the bourgeois state, there would be no power of the bourgeoisie: "The bourgeois state is nothing more than a mutual insurance pact of the bourgeois class against its individual members as well as against the exploited classes."[5] The modern state, thanks to its separation from society, manages to impose a cohesion on the capitalist class that assures that class's domination: "the bourgeoisie is not made to rule directly."[6]

Of course, there is room within the state to fight against its dominant logic that serves to reproduce capitalism and the society that derives from it. There are countless rights that have been won and that have allowed the majority of the population and specific groups to have access to a better life. These realities are not to be denied. Nor do I deny that the state, which is absolutely necessary for capitalist sociability, can sometimes act against the reproduction of capital. Here, however, I will pay attention to the limits of these struggles and victories. Citizenship, as I have noted, presents itself as an overcoming of individuality by the public sphere, supposedly responsible for representing the general well-being. This idea, however, does not prevent concrete citizens from being part of specific social groups in economic competition with one another— or from suffering specific forms of discrimination. The struggle to improve the lives of these groups generally involves recognition—often through parliamentary representation—of their interests as legitimate and compatible with—and integrated with—the interest of the general population and the preservation of the fundamental elements of a social balance by the state. The problem is precisely that. We should not wish for a balance of this social order, one whose main feature is to subordinate most human activities to a greater generation of value. Arguably this issue is especially notable now, as this order reveals itself to be capable of integrating fewer and fewer people each day.

Though in the Fordist era the economic model meant that large portions of the population could expect a salary capable of satisfying their needs—if organized labor allowed for political groups who demanded public policies from the state to improve the concrete lives of millions of people—today the situation is no longer the same.

We are not confronting the same enemy as Lenin, who saw in the tsarist state nothing but a great repressive apparatus. However, there is an undeniable worldwide upsurge in the repression exercised by states: the police violence of the Spanish state against the referendum organized in Catalonia and the silence that followed from the European governments; the systematic use of non-lethal weapons to mutilate protesters in Chile and France; the Global Security Law bill that intended to prohibit protesters from filming police officers in acts of violence in France; the extermination of the black population in Brazil; black and brown people killed in the US by an over-armed, racist police force whose functions also include financing the state through fines.[7] In fact, here in Brazil, the massive presence of military officers in the high ranks of power and the multiplication of uniform candidacies leave no doubt about this colonization of the state by repressive forces. These examples are just some of many.

To what does this international increase in authoritarianism correspond? What follows is only a hypothesis (one among many) as to why even bourgeois democracy seems to be a burden for capitalism.

Historically, the right to vote was never conceived as a right without counterparts. Depending on the period, it could be the paying of taxes, which guaranteed that those who voted were specifically those who had possessions—in other words, things to defend, things that they were imagined to possess because they were supposedly smarter and therefore allegedly better at understanding the mysteries of public life. At one point, military service was also a counterpart; a "blood tax" opened up space to those who paid for their right to participate in decisions about the common good and about whether the state should go to war with others. More fundamentally, with the development of capitalism and wage relations, that counterpart became labor. Often those who presented themselves in the market with equal rights to other merchants, even if the good in question was their working strength, would have the right to be treated as an equal by the state. As a result, in many countries, there is a correlation between women's entry into the labor market and their right to vote. The "coincidence" that exists in many nations—between the age that people are allowed to enter the labor market and the age at which they are allowed to vote—is another indication that appears to corroborate this hypothesis that labor is the counterpart to the right to vote.

Today we are perhaps facing the end of the link between employment and the right to vote. Employment is increasingly more flexible, precarious, and rare. That situation has led to the ongoing emergence, at least in some countries, of masses and masses of people without the slightest prospect of integrating themselves into capitalist relations of production. This population is far beyond a reserve army of labor; they are no longer functional for a system of surplus-value creation. They are, in such a context, an excess population. Perhaps this is the reason for the emergence of an authoritarian neoliberalism, creating a new contradiction between capital and bourgeois democracy.

The state, this ancient enemy with new traits—an enemy against which we can have significant victories, albeit always under the sign of its domination—is what we must urgently defeat, if only because it keeps alive this all-consuming vampire that converts everything into value and that today puts at risk the possibility of life itself on this planet. There will be no possibility of ending the separation between workers and the means of production without also ending the separation between citizens and the state. To end these separations also entails dissolving their dividing poles. To dissolve the latter separation, for example, would require the dissolution of both the state itself and the category of citizens. What will have to emerge are other means of production, other producers, as well as another society and another way of governing it, radically different from what has been witnessed so far.

Strategy

As Daniel Bensaïd has pointed out, for so long now we have been living in the times of the eclipse of strategic reasoning. I don't refer here to an electoral strategy (perhaps the most common usage of the term today), one that tries to find the right niche for—or the right construction of—a public figure to invite the greatest number of votes. Neither is strategy an opinion poll to

82 *Small Screws, Big Twists*

find out what voters want, as if they were consumers of public affairs. When political strategy is watered down to the elaboration of programs subject to electoral calendars, to communication techniques, and to electoral tactics, it contributes to depoliticization. Generally, this debasement of strategy leads to a debasement of parties, which no longer attempt to transform the whole but act as the representative—inside the state—of the interests of particular groups. The party's own mission—to think about the totality and act to transform it—breaks down. We find in its place something closer to unionism, in the sense of partial representation of the population for what are also partial demands, economic or not. This similarity, however, cannot erase the numerous differences between parties and unions—one of them being that unions can legally interrupt the very process of capital reproduction, something that parliamentarians cannot do.

Strategy is, in its most elevated political sense, the collective construction by the oppressed of a project of transformation that is both radical and complete—and that allows for the mobilization of the masses to conquer state power. At the same time, strategy wants to invent ways to go beyond conquering the state: it wants to foster popular participation. Without that participation, insurrection is only a moment of redemptive beauty, one condemned solely to instituting a new sequence of exploitation and bureaucratization.

Here I will address strategy as a project aimed toward the seizure of bourgeois power, a project necessarily linked to the *destruction* of that same power.

If the state as we know it today is indeed, as I explored above, a kind of conjoined twin of the capitalist system, the prospect of winning elections—of progressively integrating ourselves into the state apparatus—can never be the only strategy. In the same way that a car cannot run under water, it stands to reason that the state—regardless of who runs it—cannot achieve the equality and freedom for which we yearn.

The first current of socialist tradition to think the opposite was that of German social democracy at the beginning of the last century. This conception—that a transformation within the state was possible—was supported for several reasons. As the economy grew, so did unions and the number of newspapers of popular organizations, and all sorts of organizations linked to social democracy continued to develop. It seemed to many at that time that there was an unstoppable march of Reason and Science. This march was paralleled by a belief in the continuous progress of the working class: cultural, organizational, political, and numerical progress. It was thought that, under such conditions, the seizure of power should take place automatically. The workers would become the majority of the population and would understand their interests with complete clarity, since the party would have already done its work as a great educator—with workers voting for "their" parties to take power. The state was not seen as an instrument that serves one class in order to oppress another, but as a conquest of civilization, a purely empty form that could be filled up by either the bourgeoisie or the proletariat. As Walter Benjamin famously declared, "There is nothing which has corrupted the German working-class so much as the opinion that they were swimming with the tide."[8] This corruption led to a nationalism so deeply rooted that the social democratic deputies voted with enthusiasm for the war budgets that would lead to the massacres of the First World War. They voted in such a way because the German state needed to be preserved, not destroyed. Millions of workers from many nationalities died as a result of this tragic betrayal.

What I explore here is not the question or option of completely abandoning the electoral route, but of how to complete electoral politics with something that goes beyond it. I want to try to unfold and develop upon all the political intelligence contained in the Argentinian slogan, "one foot inside the institution, a thousand feet outside it."

There is a simplistic double trap to be considered: the notion that we can take the state as it already exists or we can act at an absolute distance from its power. Each of these opposing

What Can Art Do in the Anti-Capitalist Struggle? 83

orientations has a line that ends up complementing the other in a belief that the state cannot or should not be transformed.

Those who think that politics can only exist away from the state—those who take refuge within social movements or alternative spaces so as not to be corrupted by power—may be doing (and many are!) invaluable popular organizing work through which some basic needs of the population are being met: food, housing, etc. However, they condemn themselves to eternally resisting an evil that in fact they do not fight at its root.

In a similar way, those who abandon the perspective of revolution and are content with the electoral route as an insurmountable horizon cannot go beyond the limits of an organization that sets as its main task the resistance of capitalism without ever questioning how to overcome it. The abandonment of this perspective can only bring with it an endless urgency in which all struggles have the same acuity. After all, if no political route can lead to victory, then what differentiates one tactic from another? This urgency is usually accompanied by realistic accommodations—which, starting from the imperative of avoiding the worst, at best manage to delay it.

Brazil experienced an attempt of mediation between these two poles with the so-called tweezer strategy (it was perhaps more of a tactic than a strategy, since it did not contain the prospect of state abolition). It is not within the scope of this text to analyze that strategy at length, but, according to the hypothesis at its root, the party's institutionality should act as a way of strengthening the development of popular power (trade unions, occupations, grassroots organizations …), which, in turn, would have to be the strong arm of this tweezer. This participation would, according to this approach, theoretically have the capacity to split the state from within, hindering the reproduction of capital as well as state repression. The abandonment of this political strategy was one of the countless markers of the transformation of the Workers Party (PT) into the managing party of the monstrous Brazilian society.

A social transformation that reaches down to the roots of oppression requires the seizure of power. It cannot, however, be limited to that. Instead, such a shift would involve a collective process that extends over time with the aim of transforming the institution so that it becomes its opposite. If the modern state is about distancing the majority of the population from the decisions that affect them, we have to find forms of popular self-organization that can tend to reverse this separation, making politics something tangible that can be understood in a practical sense. By that I mean politics in the sense of getting one's hands dirty in such a way that local actions can influence decisions that involve society as a whole.

Strategic thinking holds a couple of fundamental principles. The first one is the actuality of revolution. We start from the principle that revolution is possible, that the contradictions posed by the dynamics of capital reproduction open up cracks to overcome it. The second is that, though revolution is possible, it is far from inevitable. These dynamics I am describing—these contradictions—will not themselves be the gravediggers of capital. History does nothing by itself. The contradictions of capital offer us a range of possibilities. Few of them are revolutionary and, to a certain extent, it is up to conscious action to make concrete what was previously only hypothetical or virtual. Strategy therefore demands reflection: What can be done today? How do we explore the maximum number of possibilities hidden everywhere we turn? But to do so demands urgent action, where reflections can be elaborated as well as tested and verified. But for reflection and action, individuals are necessary: Who will enact the revolution? Discussion of the revolutionary agent has often been lost in a confusion between sociology and politics—as if occupying a certain social position necessarily led to greater knowledge that, in turn, would necessarily trigger revolutionary action. It seems to me that not even the great Lukács escaped this mistake. He thought that workers—by constantly transforming nature with tools and procedures—would be more able to transform themselves, too. He supposed that they

84 *Small Screws, Big Twists*

would be more apt to understand dialectics and a global vision of the whole, and he concluded that, from the living conditions of a specific group, this same group would acquire a capacity for the critical understanding of those conditions. For others, notably the Stalinists, the bearer of a vision of totality would be the Working Class Party. The error here is reversed: the political element thinks it can immediately express the social sphere, as if that sphere were not too rich and contradictory to be captured by a single political mediation/representation. The will of the masses, on the contrary, can only be expressed through the confrontation of different factions that compose the social, a conflict that also has to unfold between the different political expressions of those factions (for example, only in the confrontation between different kinds of groups—feminist groups, theorists, etc.—can women be understood *as* a group). Political totalization is not a given that comes as a result of a stable mediation; it is always a transitory result of a constitutively unfinished process.

The debate on who would constitute the revolutionary agent seems to have finally given up on the idea that it is a question of finding a single subject capable of leading the masses throughout the process toward communism. There is not one subject; instead, there exists a plurality of revolutionary subjects whose specificities must be respected. Hegemony cannot mean the flattening of autonomies in the face of a struggle that would have the magical ability to resolve all others in itself. Revolutionary organizations no longer think that patriarchy and racism—to name just two of the most important systems of domination as examples—will magically disappear with the victory of the working class. However, the recognition of a multiplicity of subjects brings the question of how to articulate them, an issue that does not seem resolved today. For instance, what axes can bring together in practice the environmental struggle and the disability rights struggle? The multiplication of subjects can also lead to an infinite dispersion in which each individual group can only see the state as an interlocutor for satisfying their unique demands. We have to understand how to weave together the demands of each group, and that is precisely why we need a strategy.

The former prominence given to the working class cannot be attributed to a notion that it suffered the most, had the most miserable existence, or was the largest in numbers (that was not the case in Russia, for example). The special prominence of the working class in the strategic thinking that lasted until the 1970s was due to an assessment of its special insertion within the capitalist mode of production—an insertion that is of the greatest importance when it comes to blocking this same production. When we try to organize this or that sector of society today, do we have a broader understanding of what place they occupy in the reproduction of the conditions necessary to maintain the system? And how would they be able to block that very system, given their characteristics? What possibilities do we open up when we try to organize such agents?

The two great strategic hypotheses of the last century, whose relevance to the present day seems problematic, had specific agents. The prolonged revolutionary war had as indispensable elements, according to Mao, a weak and poorly centralized bourgeois state and large territories with an acute agrarian contradiction. This long-lasting war would have the help of the peasantry in the progressive liberation of parts of the territory where the red power would establish itself, creating the necessary means for the population to meet its needs. This liberation requires both self-management and at least a partially autonomous economy. And for the process to start and have continuity, it is necessary to have great popular support and participation. The other major strategic hypothesis, the general strike, is based on a certain type of confrontation between the state and the labor movement in an urban space. This confrontation, in its decisive phase, is brief. A newborn revolutionary power cannot live long with a bourgeois state, even if a weakened one. The fact that there is an intense, brief moment of confrontation after the rising of a

What Can Art Do in the Anti-Capitalist Struggle? 85

new revolutionary power does not stop the labor movement from—before reaching the moment of the confrontation—going through many intermediate stages in order to gain support and legitimacy among the population. The organization determined to radically confront the state must be able to show all segments of the oppressed population that it is capable of solving each of their problems in a superior way. In other words, it has to become hegemonic.

In both cases, therefore, it is necessary for the party to be able to develop ways of approaching the population that go beyond parliamentary mandates and propaganda (if propaganda is solely reduced to speeches). The ideas that help maintain bourgeois society are strong not because they are better than the ideas that support the fight against it. Dominant ideas do not spring out of thin air; they are rooted in materiality. Let us take the example of gender. As many gender theorists have explained, gender is historical rather than "natural"; it is constructed rather than an implacable biological reality. That does not mean that the *effects* of gender ideology are not *materially* real, however. In fact, it can be very difficult to convince people *through arguments* that gender is constructed—that it does not rest on any biological law—precisely *because* gender is experienced materially by the population in a way that happens almost prior to comprehension itself. We live in a world objectively shaped by gender, from the clothes we wear to the bathrooms we use. Therefore—and gender is only one example here of so many—to simply oppose the *materiality* that determines our worldviews with mere *arguments* is to greatly limit our power to convince. To try to change the world with opinions, with arguments, is not effective. We have to shape reality itself differently to change the world.

By materiality I mean all the relationships that are experienced by individuals in their attempt to reproduce their living conditions. In that sense, materiality refers both to things that are absolutely essential to human metabolism (obtaining food, housing, healthcare, etc.) as well as experiences of sociability (sharing values with others, bonds of affection). Absurd ideas can circulate more easily when everyday life is already absurd. It becomes easier to think that only individual violence solves problems when we live in a world where violence reigns. On the other hand, it is easier to believe in something that is legitimized by a circuit of strong sociability. Evangelical churches, for instance, are not just a place to go to hear the words of the Lord. They are also often true social centers where one can find a job, enter a community after having been imprisoned, or receive help with housing construction or solidarity in the aftermath of traumatic events such as losing a house to a flood …. Evangelical churches are, in other words, often a place where life can actually still be lived in one way or another, even in the merciless conditions of Brazil today. In one of the many contradictions that permeate Brazilian society, those churches are spaces that are necessary for life and that are linked—at least in part—to a life-destroying project.

Therefore, to catalyze a radical organization of people, a good speech is not enough. The right ideas about a given situation are not sufficient, either. The truth—if it is only offered through argument—does not liberate. The first and strongest propaganda of the real takes place in reality itself. It is, for instance, easier to insist that everything must and does have a specific value when reality itself supports that *already* by turning everything into a commodity. To give another example of reality as its own propaganda, often, when we say that education should be free, people point to a present reality as the counterargument: "Come on, look, why do you think education should be free? You have to pay for everything. I have to pay for my car. I have to pay my rent. Why should education be any different?" The real somehow reproduces the conditions necessary to maintain itself. As a result, we cannot oppose the propaganda created by reality with what would merely be another kind of propaganda, but just a more enlightened one, based solely on convincing arguments. We have to *change* reality! In various parts of the world, there are and have been experiences of what are referred to as prefigurative spaces, spaces in which

86   *Small Screws, Big Twists*

there is an attempt to establish relationships that are able to escape, at least in part, the rules imposed by the market and the state. The strengthening of these spaces is an immediate need, since it allows the population better living conditions. There will be no conquest of power without them. These spaces need to be organized in conjunction with one another and collectively transformed into a power that will oppose the state.

This people's power has to be able to meet the needs of the population that the state can no longer or does not want to manage.[9] There cannot be exchanges of commodities—which impose on the exchangers a feverish need to buy at the lowest possible price what they need for a living and sell at the highest possible price what they have to offer, which is often their labor power. Nor can these be spaces guaranteed by right. I do not want to minimize here the importance of the struggle for rights, their expansion, or their maintenance. However, rights, once acquired, tend to make the population passive in the face of them. Often one does not interfere or get involved in the choices of school curriculum that come as a result of the right to education. The right to health does not lead to the creation of patient committees with tasks such as thinking about disease prevention campaigns. Housing programs do not allow the community to participate in the elaboration of the urban design of condos or in their construction, leaving this process in the hands of the real estate market. As a general rule, only the state is responsible for enforcing rights. The aim is to enact the exact opposite: through self-organization, reinforcing the autonomy of a popular movement vis-a-vis the state, performing tasks traditionally incumbent upon the state but doing them better, with the objective of removing part or all of the state's legitimacy. Argentinian social movements seem to have approached this challenge by engaging in mass demonstrations to obtain funds from the state so that they can autonomously manage various spaces that attend to popular needs. The task carries with it not only the danger of charity, but also the possibility of training cadres with sufficient experience in self-organization, people's power, and the creation of a network with great capillarity amid the masses. The question, given what is at stake, does not seem to be whether such spaces should exist or not (in fact, they already exist and are called solidarity networks, community kitchens, mutual aid groups, etc. ...) but how to make them politicizing spaces. In what ways can the sociabilities created in such spaces be truly emancipatory?

Bensaïd, following Lukács, points out a crucial difference between the bourgeois and the proletarian revolution. With the generalization of mercantile exchanges, the capitalist mode of production could develop within feudal society and accumulate forces in it well before reaching political power. The bourgeoisie gained economic power to the point of exercising political responsibilities and had the time to create what were referred to as its "organic intellectuals." The conquest of political power was a crowning achievement of this process.

Whether or not capitalist society today develops the preconditions for socialism—just as it generates its own gravedigger—is unfortunately an open question. What is certain is that, in this society, socialist modes of production do not develop. This, then, is the task for the prefigurative spaces organized through people's power: outlining what this new form of production will look like—even if only tendentially. And just as capitalist modes of production also produce subjectivities that correspond to them, it will be up to the prefigurative spaces to foster and organize subjectivities conscious of the need for revolution.

What is to be done (with art)?

What does the Left think of the arts? What does it think it can do with or for art? Why does the Left think it has to help art?

One argument made in response to the questions above is put forward by people far beyond the Left, including artists themselves and even sectors of the enlightened Right: art is good business.

What Can Art Do in the Anti-Capitalist Struggle? 87

It has a higher return on invested capital than other investments do. From the actors on stage to the popcorn salespeople at cinemas, art can generate thousands of jobs. It also benefits other branches of our economy. What would tourism in Brazil be without Carnival, for example? How many beers are consumed at samba gigs?

I do not deny the economic dimension of the matter. Art and culture are definitely capable of moving considerable sums, which makes demands for increased rights and protections for its professionals more than legitimate. However, this argument—one that frames art as just another economic activity—cannot be sustained for long. Should we eliminate all unprofitable art forms? Should poetry be sacrificed on the altar of profit? Can any use of art that cannot immediately find consumers to pay for it gain any kind of public support? Furthermore, aren't there other, more profitable economic activities? If the argument is solely economic, then art will be in direct competition with all other sectors and will receive incentives only to the extent of its competitiveness. Should we put aside even commercial cinema if the price of oil rises? Should art and culture be subject to market volatility without mediation?

Another argument we often hear is that art allows for the spontaneous, singular, and authentic expression of people or groups who produce and/or consume it. This argument requires more of our focus here given its strength on the Left—a strength that in turn comes from its truthfulness. In art and culture, we can find works that distill historical experiences in unprecedented ways, capturing their density while also somehow helping to unveil them. Dominguinhos' song "Lamento Sertanejo," for example, uniquely helps us better understand the suffering and helplessness of thousands of northeastern workers in the large cities of Southeastern Brazil.

This argument, however, also suffers from certain limitations, especially when it promotes the idea of art and culture as genuine expressions of the genius of individuals or groups. At times it appears to defend a curious circular thinking in which a certain identity would only be legitimate if it produced and consumed a certain type of art and culture. It constructs a kind of flawless parallel between identity and product, but one that more closely resembles a restriction or a fence. Northeasterners would have to listen to and play only the music style *forró* under the penalty of becoming un-northened. This thought that a "foreigner" would always bring with them the risk of a loss of authenticity contains a lack of awareness of the historical processes of identity building, which are always an undoing and a rebuilding at the same time. This way of thinking also leaves another question open: Does a Northeastern worker have nothing to gain from hearing songs of exile from workers who belong to other groups? Can that same worker not listen to anything else, to things that reflect something beyond their own reality as workers from a certain culture? Are Peruvian folk music and Japanese experimental music forever out of reach? Why? I even notice this same argument about art's capacity for authentic, spontaneous expression by the people—which, again, has its share of truth—used, curiously, by militants to legitimize profound depoliticization. If politics is the place of division and conflict, even some militants themselves imagine that art and culture would be, in contrast, the sphere in which differences would never represent power inequalities and where, therefore, everything and everyone could peacefully coexist. In other words, if art is conceived as not political but instead merely "pure" expressions of the people, then we are invited not to judge any artistic contribution. On this plane, the most varied positions and artistic products would be juxtaposed side by side in a regime of general and apolitical equivalence, without antagonisms. The only thing that is not allowed in this addition of artistic products (films, songs, plays) is the confrontation between them. Silvio Santos dances to the sound of Racionais MC, Chico Buarque is welcomed by Chacrinha, and the strangeness that this could generate loses its ground.[10]

If politics is born from the recognition of the inequalities that are at the foundations of our society (between the dispossessed and the owners of everything, between "masters" and those

88 *Small Screws, Big Twists*

who are "supposed" to serve them), politics also unfolds in the struggle that tries to remedy those inequalities and even, who knows, eradicate them. Politics reconfigures diversities, seeing in the vast majority of them the result of processes rooted in history, processes that create power relations marked under the sign of oppression. Put another way, to enact politics is not to acknowledge diversity just *as* diversity, just *as* difference (as in: there are poor, there are rich, there are women, there are men, and these are all separate and innate categories), but to connect them and analyze them together to try to understand how they are linked and even mutually constitutive. In response to the disconnected world of the infinite expression of monadic singularities, emancipatory politics opposes a world architected by social structures that can and must be changed so that equality can prevail. Thus, in opposition to the static world in which anything goes, politics attends to the history that founded oppression, the present as a moment of change, and the future as the prospect of a just society. The engine of this dynamic (the relationship among past, present, and future) is the contradiction and the struggle engendered by it. Struggle is the day-to-day modus operandi of every socialist policy, and socialism's basic practice is the reformulation of singularities into groups, factions, and alliances for that struggle.

If art and culture are understood only as the domain in which all confrontation is excluded for the free coexistence of everything, then, in all logic, it is only up to the politicians who are interested in art and culture to play the role of managers or administrators who will have to do their best to ensure that all artistic expressions are respected and publicized. The fight returns here in clothes that don't suit: the politician becomes the guarantee that the expressions of so-called high culture do not steal the scene (and the resources) at the expense of what we usually call popular culture. Both high culture and popular culture—as suitable expressions of groups or individuals—would have equal right to exist. And that right will be backed up, the left-wing politician will say, by the fact that, as they are authentic and singular expressions, they are necessarily against the current system.

I do not deny that art and culture have logics of their own and that they cannot be reduced merely to minor aspects of the class struggle; still, this conviction that they are *naturally* anticapitalist is strange. Thus, in the field of the Left, it is not so difficult for us to recognize that capitalism is not only a mode of economic reproduction, but also a total system that, through specific mediations, shapes everything in its image and likeness. Many of us tend to have no objections, for example, to thinking that education is at the same time a preparation of the workforce and a concrete possibility of emancipation. From this contradiction, cracks, lines of combat, and struggles emerge. So, too, does a whole range of analyses and actions that are denied *a priori* to the fields of art and culture because both of those fields have, in most cases, been considered anti-capitalist (perhaps because they predate capitalism).

I do not start from this assumption. I believe that art and culture are, in most cases, expressions that do not emerge unscathed from the colonization of our subjectivities by capital. And to get rid of those shackles, the leap into the conceptual or the experimental is not enough. Anyone who regularly watches contemporary dance has certainly witnessed a type of show in which the dancers are not presented as individuals, as singular subjects, but as interchangeable bodies, without any specificity, particular but not singular examples of humanity. And in such shows, these bodies tend to be treated as flesh, subject to almost anatomical examinations. They often endure various tests, or they make movements of agony; from time to time they are even assembled together in images that resemble those of anonymized corpses …. The position offered to the spectator is to see the bodies through a gaze for which the qualitative no longer exists, only the quantitative; everything is measurable. The spectator is encouraged toward an anatomical curiosity about what the body is capable of doing. But this gaze is precisely one of the gazes of dominant subjectivity: that of instrumental reason, which is truly obsessed with

What Can Art Do in the Anti-Capitalist Struggle? 89

exams, evaluations, measuring everything and everyone, because it wants to know the value of everything in order to exchange everything and all. It is actually the kind of reason necessary for capitalism. As abstract as this kind of performance may be, the type of subjectivation it proposes is actually redundant in the context of our dominant subjectivity.

What is true for these experimental productions is true for others, and even more so for those created by the cultural industry. I do not want to say here that subjectivity is only the reflection of material relations, nor that art is only the mechanistic transposition of class relations. How can I not agree with Trotsky, who critiques those who try to interpret Dante's *Divine Comedy* through the "invoices sent by Florentine cloth merchants to their customers"? The reflection of the ways in which people relate to each other, how they find the means to live, what these means are in each different period of history—all of these things can be found in works of art and in culture, but never immediately. Research is required.

Perhaps it is good to pause here to develop a little further what I said above about the first propaganda of reality being made by reality itself. From this statement, another statement arises: time and time again, art and culture operate more as confirmations of conceptions that are produced by our daily experiences than as expansions of our subjectivities. In other words, art and culture certainly are convincing; they help us keep believing in this world as the only possible world. However, the power to convince that is held by art and culture is one that collaborates with the power to convince that is already enacted by reality itself, which has an incomparably greater importance. To change society, it would take much more than having revolutionary Hollywoods for Soviets that arise all over the world. Art and culture are, ultimately, more *shaped by* perceptions arising *from* our routine than they themselves *shape* it.

This hypothesis appears to be confirmed by the recent success of zombie films and series. The success of these products of the cultural industry brings with it an enigma for those who think that art and culture can shape the world. Why does Hollywood—which, just before and after the Second World War, produced films of luminous optimism like those of Frank Capra—today have those box office successes matched by films about the apocalypse and the undead? First of all, what would these films teach us? That something incomprehensible has hit society, something that is beyond our ability to make sense of it. What we can understand from it is extreme violence. Each day and each minute contain deadly perils. To survive, these films suggest, we must confront this violence, and we must ourselves be capable of committing brutal acts in our daily lives. Life can be summed up as an incessant and precarious struggle to find the necessary means for survival. In this fight, we have few friends, and we know that we will lose most of the ones we *do* have, either because they die or because they themselves will turn into monsters. If projecting into the future is an impossibility, the only dimension that time has preserved is that of a constant present where all our strength and intelligence must be summoned to achieve the feat of being able to stay alive a little longer. As readers may have already noticed, these films are actually talking about what life is like for the vast majority of people on this planet. It is not so much that these films inculcate brutality in us; rather, it is the very routine of life in a late capitalist regime that ingrains such brutality. For many people, the pleasure they get from watching such films comes from the confirmation of our impressions of this increasingly aggressive reality that we have to face as soon as we walk out our front doors.

So if art and culture are more conditioned by the sociability of bourgeois society than they are capable of conditioning it, how can they contribute to any emancipatory project?

Before proceeding, it is perhaps important to clarify that the purpose of this text is *not* to set rules about what artists and cultural workers would have to do to help emancipatory struggles.

90 *Small Screws, Big Twists*

In this regard, I believe that the terms of the Trotsky-Breton manifesto (particularly the call for complete freedom for art) remain valid now (in spite of the enormous difference from one historical conjuncture to another), especially for artists who work in art institutions.

However, despite the difference in conjuncture between Trotsky's time and our own, I believe that the demand of "complete freedom for art" for artists who already exist within the institutions of art remains valid. There is no complete freedom in art institutions, and it is precisely when artists demand that freedom to continue their research that they will be able to feel the leashes operated by art institutions, which exist today in forms that are different from those associated with totalitarian regimes. Perhaps, feeling this tutelage exercised by art institutions, they will aspire "to a complete and radical reconstruction of society. This [art] must do, were it only to deliver intellectual creation from the chains which bind it, and to allow all mankind to raise itself to those heights which only isolated geniuses have achieved in the past," as Breton and Trotsky write so lyrically in the manifesto.[11]

It is important that artists who circulate within art institutions can do so freely so that they can try to split these institutions in half, not only inserting and revealing contradictions from within but also trying to bring their audiences moments when they are not hailed by dominant subjectivity. Moments in which other ways of practicing our subjectivities are possible. Moments in which the law of the exchange of equivalents can be partly unveiled or even suspended.[12] Moments in which we come across free experiments that do not obey the valorization of value.[13] Moments when we don't have to fear if our value in the market decreases because we are not producing for it. Moments when we don't have to think of ourselves as small companies that always have to increase our commercial potential. It would not be a little thing if we were able to come across these moments more and more often, possibilities that make an emancipated future present, memories of a world that is larger than its present misery.

In light of these considerations, the question cannot be what artists can do for the Left. Instead, the question must be: How can militants of the radical Left use art to build popular movement organizations?

The most obvious utility that art can offer is its ability to organize people, given that it is a practice that allows for the gathering of countless individuals. In fact, it is evident that art is already being used in precisely this way. In 2019, in Duque de Caxias, a city in the metropolitan region of Rio de Janeiro, the city hall offered a theatre workshop for 30 candidates. More than 1,000 people applied. In a second example, I turn to the Maré favela complex, also in Rio de Janeiro, which is exceptional in many ways. With its official 130,000 inhabitants, it is one of the largest favelas in Latin America. But one of its perhaps lesser known characteristics is the number of theatre groups that operate from within it: over 40. The size of these groups varies: the smaller ones have just under 10 people at their core; the larger ones have more than 40 participants. These theatre groups have, almost by their very nature, a popular rootedness and a territorial capillarity that the political Left does not have. These groups primarily stage their own lived experiences. They embody reflections on the tangible realities these days for residents of these neighborhoods: what it is like to live in a favela itself, to be black, to be northeastern (meaning from the northeast of Brazil specifically), to be a woman, to be LBGTQIA+, to be a worker, etc. The audiences include friends, relatives, and other residents who have a direct connection with what is being expressed. And those artistic expressions are of an absolutely different nature from what can be seen on other stages across the city. The performances relate directly and genuinely to everyday life, and the performers are not unknown actors or, conversely, performers so widely known that their stardom is fetishized. They are each someone's daughter, nephew, or friend, and they talk "about us and to us." Wouldn't it be a tremendous lack of imagination to have no other engagement with these theatre groups besides public calls

What Can Art Do in the Anti-Capitalist Struggle? 91

for funding support? Is there nothing else to be done besides treating these artistic expressions in exactly the same way as we treat those presented in theatres in the richest neighborhoods of the city? (Currently, the only way these groups in poorer and working-class neighborhoods are treated differently from some of those wealthier theatres is that they are often perceived as especially worthy of additional funding resources—and for the specific reason that their flourishing enhances diversity in the arts.) Or let's take yet another example: poetry slams are vibrant spaces with many performers who belong to a group of people who—if the state got what it wanted—would be exterminated: young black people from the periphery. These poetry circles constitute perhaps the most critical spaces that currently exist in Rio—particularly in terms of the perspectives voiced about police and their policies of territorial control through militia groups and genocide. Should we dialogue with the artists who perform in those spaces merely as a means to promote them and help them be funded? And are the problems suffered by these spaces only of a logistical nature? Do we, for example, only have to offer chemical toilets so that these slams can take place in a more pleasant environment? Is there not another possibility here for how artistic practices and political organizations can relate to each other? Could we not instead imagine a possible shift in who carries out which functions in that relationship? In other words, are political organizations limited to interacting with artists only when they are offering them state resources? For example, could militants not try to organize the theatre groups in the favelas or evolve the slam groups into campaigns?

Though I focus here on the function of artists and artistic spaces in political organizing, I do *not* do so to dispute in any way the centrality of workplaces (factories, etc.) themselves as key locations of political learning and organization. With the decline of Fordist capitalism, however, factory floors can no longer function (at least not in quite such a widespread way) as vectors of political organization or as places where the struggles waged can catalyze political learning. Today, submission to exploitation certainly continues (and sometimes it is even more accentuated now), but the ability to build resistance in more "traditional" workplaces, some of which no longer exist, has been partially lost. It is therefore necessary to invest in other spaces—which may eventually also be working spaces, as many art spaces are—and practices in order to be able to create the links and subjectivities necessary to confront capitalism. Here I want to voice the bet that art can be one of these new vectors to support and develop that struggle.

The kind of encounter provided by art potentially takes on distinct forms, enabling the emergence of modes of perceiving the world that could compel those interested in turning the world upside down. Though I have focused a lot here on the arts in a broad sense, theatre specifically will be my core interest for the rest of this essay: theatre more as a spectacle than as a collective construction. Theatre can be a space in which a certain number of individuals come together to build a unique expression of who they are, of their pride, and of their dignity—and a space where they can be visible in a way that interrupts the invisibilization and erasure they often experience at the hands of systems of power. The stage can be the space for the construction of an identity that is defiant in the face of all social impositions, even those of accommodation to the dominant society. The scene can be an instrument both for the transformation of self through the unveiling of oppressions suffered *and* for the study of how we will emancipate ourselves from those oppressions. TO belongs to the family of types of theatre that can offer this kind of space. Brecht's learning plays do, too. They are theatre forms in which the actor is preferably non-professional. In these forms, the seduction of the public, whether to convey a message, is no longer the central objective. Instead, the monopoly of knowledge is broken—even if just as a tendency—by breaking the monopoly of the stage. There are no longer any discourses that are inherently delegitimized right from the start, even before they are articulated, merely as a result of the origins or background of the person formulating them. Every actor has to be the primary

92 *Small Screws, Big Twists*

recipient or audience of their act. Acting becomes a concrete building process, of living knowledge about who we are, who and what we were forced to be, and who we want to become. Acting transforms into a political experimentation—and with the word "politics" I mean to imply an experience of confrontation—with the hope that we will not be limited to what has already been established so that we can freely experience what we want to become.

But *how* that theatre is created is of extreme importance. Countless times political theatre has tried to have its theory guide its practice. For example, if we believe that there should be no bosses in the economy, there would also be no place for directors in theatre. The critique of the hierarchy centered around the figure of the leader logically unfolds into a critique of the social division of labor. The work belongs to everyone; the specialization of tasks has to give way to the participation of the collective as a whole in all aspects of the work. This kind of comprehensively collective approach, however, has rarely been fully enacted. In any group, there are differences in availability and in acquired knowledge. Fatigue and exhaustion are factors, too. However, the idea of this approach—this criticism of the dominant way of doing things theatrically—is based on never accepting the social construction of production as natural or a given. As the reader may have understood by now, I believe that our daily practices are loaded with meanings and create ideas and ways of thinking. The capitalist mode of production is then, of course, itself an ideological and political practice of great importance for the legitimization of society as we know it. Therefore, resistance to fundamental aspects of the traditional mode of theatrical production must not only be linked to the critique of hierarchy but also go beyond it. What will be needed to guide our forms of theatrical production will be radically different from the elements that guide capitalist production. Theatrical development cannot be subject to the requirements of increasing productivity or saving work time. There should be neither mechanization nor the incessant intensification of the labor needed to take care of the artistic tasks involved. Thus, this mode of theatre production will not be subject to the law of value: a value that can never be determined by the amount of abstract work needed in order for the art to be created. This mode of theatrical production for which I am arguing has to be guided by the perspective of offering the possibility of a free praxis where there is neither loss of self nor a calcification of capacities.[14] This way of making theatre will instead hold the possibility of experimentally accounting for the "free development of each one" as a "condition of the free development of all"—in other words, the destiny for everyone as described in the Communist Manifesto.

Though, as a general rule, all the various genres (from Shakespeare to vaudeville to even musicals) can be interesting when produced by artists working in this specific mode of production that I am describing, there are some texts, exercises, and materials that might be more useful than others. The kind of theatre that I am proposing can serve as a practical scenic exercise to brush off the dominant aesthetics and discover conservative ideologies in them. Though—as I previously suggested—representations do not play a predominant role in the creation of reality, they can certainly serve to preserve or combat it. And these representations are present in the dramaturgical/formal construction of countless scenes from films, soap operas, and other series that we absorb, sometimes on a daily basis. The presence of conservative ideologies in these scenes does not stem from a conservative conspiracy by writers, directors, and producers. Such ideologies of scene structure spring, as if spontaneously, from the assemblage of the world, from everyday relationships. In most cases, they are, at the moment of their emergence, a *symptom* of capitalist society. But as soon as they exist, they become *agents for the maintenance* of that same society. We must therefore pay the greatest attention to the dramaturgical structures and formal tropes that incessantly return. We must examine them onstage—dislocating them, moving their parts around, playing with them to better interrogate their meanings. And if, in a Hollywood scene in which two super or heroic beings fight, we introduce the point of view of a city

What Can Art Do in the Anti-Capitalist Struggle? 93

resident living where the fight takes place, would the scene be as beautiful if the destruction of the "ordinary" resident's home was in the foreground? What would the story of the ball where Cinderella meets her Prince Charming be like if it were told by the prince's servants? How would we portray a story in which we watch a rich villain forced to do evil simply to remain rich? To paraphrase Brecht, what would it be like to stage a story in such a way that we would not focus on the unfair use of power but *on power itself* as the source of injustice?

The theatre practice I am advocating here should be an exercise of ideological detoxification, of deconditioning, of breaking with the representations that we construct—consciously or not—of the societies in which we live. Such theatre is an invitation to permanently question our views of the world, given that they help to sustain the world as it is in all its horror.

This constant work—to denaturalize our unstudied, seemingly spontaneous and instinctual views of everything and everyone—takes, at its essence, a critical disposition. In this sense, it is a negative theatre that I propose. What happens onstage is shown in all its artificiality, all its historicity, and all the possibility of its mutability. And this critique must not have any inherent barriers, neither in its objectives nor in its strength. But for the transformation to this kind of theatre to be effective, we must combine the stage with other forces, so that theatre becomes a moment inserted in a larger process of political work. The stage is certainly not the best place to chant slogans or to show infallible certainties, and that is precisely why—just as the spectator must become a spect-actor—the actor must become a militant within a movement. Only by entangling art in other dynamics beyond the arts will the actor-militant be able to extract their full political potential. We have to create a political movement by merging a critical, negative analysis onstage with the optimism of popular theatre groups already organized in their territories!

Lenin's formula for literature is well known, and I am inclined to extend it to all art forms: "Literature must become 'a cog and a screw' of one single great Social-Democratic mechanism."[15] At the time of his statement, social democracy was the future of the Bolshevik party—the vehicle for the revolution and nothing like the parties of today that claim to be its inheritors. As to be expected from Lenin, this definition, however short in length, is still dialectical. A screw is common hardware. It could even be tempting to consider one screw insignificant in the context of a larger machine. The fact that a screw is small would seemingly diminish its importance even further. However, in a machine, every part is important. Only with all of its parts can full functioning be expected. The absence of even a little screw can cause an entire machine to break down. We need to know where to fit this screw—and by that I mean art—now. The issue is complex. We no longer know if we still have the machine. There does not seem to be a strategy to match what is at stake today. What party or organization today has the practical and theoretical perspective on how to take over state power in 5, 10, or 15 years? And yet, the urgency today is perhaps greater than ever before. The world's midnight is fast approaching. According to Bensaïd, beginnings always take place in the middle. This text aims to reflect on some of the means for beginnings. And here, at the end of this essay, I also want to reflect on a few certainties. The state has to be overcome so that capitalism can also be overcome. In post-Fordist times, people's power has gained even greater importance as a way of organizing the masses and preparing them to assume the tasks that are currently confiscated by the state (and to do those tasks better). Within the mechanism of people's power, art (and theatre in particular) takes on the role of both critical analysis and the aggregation of peoples. Art becomes a space for the development of human capabilities. This conception of art bestows on it a great importance. These certainties that I am posing need opposition and revision. It is my most sincere wish that they serve as a basis for discussions that can either deepen or deny some of their assumptions. But what I most passionately hope for is that any refutation or further development of these ideas arises from practice. May the hands return to work!

94 *Small Screws, Big Twists*

Notes

1 When I am invoking the idea of society as a totality, I am referring to the notion that there are no relationships in a society—however minor those relationships might seem—that are not somehow connected to the other relationships that also structure the society. For example, racism, as a system of relations, is linked to capitalism and so on and so on ....

2 Here I refer to statutes in the sense of a political-legal-professional group. In the Middle Ages, each of these had specific rules that distinguished one from another.

3 Karl Marx, *Crítica da filosofia do direito de Hegel* (São Paulo: Boitempo, 2010), 137.

4 See https://www.marxists.org/archive/marx/works/1843/critique-hpr/ch03.htm. Accessed 22 August 2022.

5 Antoine Artous, *Marx, l'État et la Politique* (Paris: Syllepse, 1999).

6 Ibid., 132.

7 In New York City, fines for infractions such as jaywalking or running in school halls are the city's second source of income. See Keeanga-Yamahtta Taylor, "Révolte noire aux Etats-Unis," *A l'encontre – La Brèche*, http://alencontre.org/laune/revolte-noire-aux-etats-unis.html. Accessed 1 June 2022.

8 See Walter Benjamin, *On the Concept of History*, trans. Dennis Redmond (2005). Available via Creative Commons license at: https://www.marxists.org/reference/archive/benjamin/1940/history.htm. Accessed 10 August 2022.

9 I mean people's power in the sense of a power created through self-organization by the people who recognize the need for the abolition of the bourgeois state.

10 I refer here to well-known Brazilian figures. Silvio Santos is a television station owner and an anchor for entertainment television shows. Chacrinha was an anchor for similar entertainment programs. Both of these individuals are right-wing. Chico Buarque is a very famous samba singer, and Racionais MC is an also very famous rap group; both of them are extremely politicized and critical.

11 Andre Breton and Leon Trotsky, *Manifesto: Towards a Free Revolutionary Art* (1938). Available at: https://www.generation-online.org/c/fcsurrealism1.htm. Accessed 29 August 2022.

12 Here, when I mention the law of the exchange of equivalents, I refer to a law that rules us most of the time: When you pay for something, you expect to have something in return that is the equivalent of what you spent. But when art is at stake, how can you make this law work? Art, at its best, is invaluable and therefore suspends the reign of this law.

13 The valorization of value is another basic aspect of capitalism, one according to which we need to create more value all the time: for the companies for which we work, for the national economies in which we live, and even for ourselves. Within this law's logic, we need to increase our value at every turn.

14 Here I refer to a calcification in the sense of one's capabilities beginning to become permanently limited by the division of theatrical labor.

15 Vladimir Lenin, "Party Organisation and Literature," *Lenin Collected Works*, trans. R. Cymbala (Moscow: Progress Publishers, 1965), 44–49. Available via *Marxists Internet Archive* at: https://www.marxists.org/archive/lenin/works/1905/nov/13.htm. Accessed 29 August 2022.

Part III

Are There No Alternatives?

9 Examples but Not Models

Against Well-Made TO and for Well-Adapted TO

"It is when the theatre ends that our work begins": The example of Jana Sanskriti in India

Jana Sanskriti, "People's Culture," is a political movement that is very likely unique in the true sense of that word. Maybe for the first time—or at least that I know of—in histories of links between art and politics, the link in Jana Sanskriti's case is not about a political organization that built a cultural front with the purpose of attracting new militants or instructing them. Jana Sanskriti, by contrast, started as a theatre group and went on to become one of the great political forces in the state of West Bengal, India. This strength manifested itself, among other occasions, on October 22, 2006, when more than 12,000 peasant members of Jana Sanskriti went to Kolkata, many of them traveling a journey estimated to take tens of hours, to participate in a demonstration in favor of the creation of the Indian Federation of Theatre of the Oppressed.

The history of Jana Sanskriti begins in 1985, when a group of young townspeople decided to leave the PCIM (Indian Marxist Communist Party), whose functioning they criticized for being undemocratic and incapable of realizing the political program it proclaimed. The decision was not made out of a disgust with politics, but out of a desire to create a movement that actually represented the aspirations of the popular masses, a movement where militants would actively contribute to the elaboration of the politics of their organization.

In this sense, Jana Sanskriti's path is representative of the creation of what are now referred to as Indian Grassroots Movements. In the 1980s, many urban activists across India decided to create political organizations (meaning ones that were outside the bounds of parties and unions) in rural areas. These organizations all share the common traits of representing a specific audience (peasants of that local geographic area, populations affected by dams, Adivasis[1]), rejecting party structures considered to be anti-democratic, refusing money from foreign institutional financiers (considered participants of neocolonialism), and always dealing with problems particular to their local context. The Narmada Bachao Andolan, in which Medha Patkar and Arundhati Roy are militants, is the best known example of a Grassroots Movement: the movement is made up of thousands of peasants who militate against the construction of dams that would flood the valleys where they live.

Jana Sanskriti's decision to settle in the countryside was certainly influenced by Maoism. In 1985, the Naxalite movement[2] as well as Gandhism (and its desire to create "an India of villages") were still reference points present for most people. The choice to live and organize in rural space was also driven by two absolutely concrete facts: first, the PCMI's fierce repression of dissidents in urban areas, which could even go as far as murder, and, second, the very social structure of what are referred to in India as slums. When there are no tasks to be carried out in the countryside, peasants come and go, moving temporarily to the city in search of short-term jobs; as a result, the slums are intermittently packed with inhabitants.

DOI: 10.4324/9781003325048-13

98 *Are There No Alternatives?*

Settling in the countryside was, as is common in such cases, very arduous at first. Living conditions were extremely difficult for this little group—these dozen townspeople—who had decided to quit their jobs to live in the villages. Apart from material problems (lack of money, lack of sewage systems, among others), this group had to face another difficulty: the peasants were more than suspicious of the young militants. The newcomers had no specific social role in the villages, no reason to be there. The reason for their presence was open to different interpretations: they were by turns bandits coming to rob the villages, guerrilla fighters trying to enlist peasants in the armed struggle by force, or—since some of them were bearded—Catholic priests who were going to convert them to Christianity.

It is the absence of a defined role within the villages that led these young militants to become artists. Sanjoy Ganguly, one of the only founding members to still be part of Jana Sanskriti, says that it was only when they started performing that the village doors opened. The idea of doing theatre came to him after having understood how rich the cultural life of the villages was, particularly in terms of performances of traditional theatrical forms.

The peasants came regularly to attend the performances organized by the first members of Jana Sanskriti. These spectators began to offer their hospitality, and some even joined the group. Years later, according to Ganguly, the group has a sense that, though the spectators attended the performances, in those days no real dialogue was established between the audience members and the actors afterward. The people who attended the performances considered the actors as holders of a talent and a discourse that were completely foreign to them, and as such they saw no way to appropriate and use them. The possibility of theatre truly democratizing the exercise of politics seemed compromised. And it was then—while sharing Jana Sanskriti's concerns about this issue with one of his friends—that Sanjoy Ganguly got a hold of photocopied pages of the English translation of *Theatre of the Oppressed* and that Jana Sanskriti decided to draw inspiration for their work from the experiences and theories of Augusto Boal.

Jana Sanskriti currently has more than 30 groups, who perform pieces from a common repertoire that the group has developed and, in most cases, readapt those pieces or create new ones. As someone who has observed work by Jana Sanskriti but whose observation has been only partial in nature, it is difficult to define a common denominator that represents the diversity of themes and artistic languages/vocabulary of the movement. There is, however, a Jana Sanskriti play that I had the opportunity to watch several times, performed by different teams on different occasions, across a period of about ten years. The name of the play is *Shonar Meye*, which translates to *Golden Girl*. It has been performed over 3000 times in India by Jana Sanskriti. It focuses on the living conditions of women in rural areas. *Shonar Meye* does not have a straightforward narrative plot, per se. The play is articulated in three different moments: life in the family home, marriage, life at the home of the in-laws. These moments, though they are performed in chronological order, could, however, be presented separately. In other words, each fragment of the play has an internal logic, and each of them could, strictly speaking, be performed on their own or in a different order without the play suffering. This fragmented form may be due to the place where the performances occur: the squares of small villages of West Bengal. The performances do not necessarily begin with large audiences (which is part of why the play is often preceded by songs and dances that have no relation to its plot: they give the public time to gather), and it is likely that many spectators will leave before the end. In fact, this fragmentation is what allows for the "de-individualization" of the story presented: it is not a question of presenting the story of a singular woman, but the different stages of women's lives in rural areas. Most of the women present in the audience are at one or another of those stages. As for the overall performance composition and acting, they tend to favor a certain distance. The transitions between the scenes consist of singing, dancing, and human statues underlining various themes or arguments.

The actors will sometimes address the audience directly. The father-in-law expresses himself only through a Grammelot-esque gibberish, but his gestures are so "typical" that the audiences laugh at each appearance. The protagonist, after having cried profusely, dances with the other actors, who abandon their character-specific roles as immediately as she does ....

Though the play denounces the dowry system[3] as a primary issue and the greatest symbol of patriarchy, it shows with the same clarity that all stages of a woman's life are situations of oppression. In the system depicted, there is no oasis of peace for the woman in either the biological family or the husband's family. The family is headed by the eldest man and consists of his wife, daughters who have not yet married or are not going to marry for some reason, sons, daughters-in-law, and eventual grandchildren. The family is a company in which women's chores—though they are daily and extremely painful—are considered worthless, since only men's activities are geared toward the market (mainly rice production as a commodity) and therefore generate direct income. The education of women is regarded as a useless investment because their working strength will eventually go to someone else's family. The dowry marks that alleged uselessness of women, with the logic that the burden of "importing" a woman into another family has to be compensated with what are often astronomical sums of money. Women's autonomy is unthinkable in a context where they are always under the yoke of a patriarch who is at the same time the owner of the fields where the family works, of the house where they live, and, in a way, of the family itself. Though the play shows that men as a group benefit from this system (especially in terms of their education or their opportunities to occupy public spaces or have a minimum of autonomy), it also shows that only the patriarch has the power to decide for the entire family. The other male characters are presented as powerless to show any concrete solidarity or as servile and unintelligent puppets.

Shonar Meye is always the first piece presented by Jana Sanskriti when they initially arrive at a village. That is the case for two reasons. First, Jana Sanskriti is strongly convinced that only when women can freely discuss their living conditions can the village as a whole be able to engage in a broader process of political struggle. Put another way, only once one of the central contradictions within the village is addressed can other alliances be built. Second, the critique of patriarchy is not identified as a threat to the interests of local leaders, so those leaders do not prevent the play from being performed.

Jana Sanskriti always follows the same steps when it deploys members to a particular village. First, a group who has already formed inside the village (an association, militants from other grassroots movements, etc.) invites Jana Sanskriti to come. Three separate performances of *Shonar Meye* follow, with an interval of approximately one month between each performance. The possibility of taking the stage in Forum Theatre is a novelty for the audience, and they need the time to become accustomed to it. At the first performance, some spectators will feel brave enough to step onto the stage, but, after a few performances, the number of interventions will increase. And, above all, those interventions will become even more thoughtful, with audience members having had the time to consider their future interventions between performances. That is why Jana Sanskriti offers the same play several times to the same audience.

Here is a brief description of a typical village in which Jana Sanskriti operates: when you are born in a village in West Bengal, it is more than likely that you will die there or within a radius of about 30 kilometers (if you are a woman and the marriage takes place in another village). All the members of a village—the largest of which has a population of approximately 2,000 people—know each other. Many of them are in fact of the same family, or they are neighbors with each other, or they are business relations. Or a villager may be several of those things at once to the same person, since one of those types of relationships does not preclude another. It is therefore extremely courageous to step up onto the stage to fight fictional oppressors because

100 *Are There No Alternatives?*

their very real counterparts are in the audience. For example, when women "improvise" struggles against patriarchy during a Jana Sanskriti forum, they are doing so in front of their family, their in-laws, their husbands.[4]

During the three different presentations of the play, members of the Jana Sanskriti team transcribe all the interventions of the spectators. As a result, Jana Sanskriti knows who spoke and what was said. After the group reviews and analyzes the records of the interventions, the people who came onstage to say or do things that resonated with the political analysis of the situation by Jana Sanskriti will be approached and asked if they are interested in creating a Jana Sanskriti satellite group in their village. If there are enough interested people, Jana Sanskriti offers that group two week-long sessions at its center so that prospective members can get away from both their day-to-day concerns and their oppressors (in-laws, PCMI activists, drug traffickers, situations caused by illegal drinking …). The first week combines theatrical training (expression exercises, singing, and games), creation of human sculptures in which participants must try to reflect their realities and the oppressions they face, and a political training. The second week focuses on the construction of a play for the new group, on a theme decided by them. After having performed the play a few times under the supervision of members of Jana Sanskriti, the group is able to perform alone. The group regularly returns to Jana Sanskriti's center to follow up on their training, learning pieces from the Jana Sanskriti repertoire, performing plays, and watching plays by other groups. The new group only officially becomes a satellite group of Jana Sanskriti after two years.

That recently formed group will then work in their village as well as in the surrounding villages (each group works in approximately ten villages), facilitating TO workshops, participating in Jana Sanskriti's political actions, etc. Being part of Jana Sanskriti also requires respecting certain rules. For example, accepting a dowry is grounds for a man to be excluded or removed from Jana Sanskriti.

Each group within Jana Sanskriti is also a form of soviet or local council that elects two representatives for the general council of the movement. The representatives from any one group are required to be a man and a woman, respectively, who can be immediately removed if those they represent regard them as having failed. The broader council meets once every two years, more if necessary to respond to an extraordinary event. The council will decide on the campaigns to be carried out, their themes, their strategies, the alliances to be formed, the sums that will have to be spent.[5] Once the general political orientation is defined by the council, it will be implemented by the central group of Jana Sanskriti based in Badu, a group whose members practically never change. The core group is made up of about 15 members where we find the only 2 founding people from the city who remain part of Jana Sanskriti: Sanjoy and Sima Ganguly. The members of the core group are the only ones to receive a salary from Jana Sanskriti, when money allows. Their tasks are enormous and extremely varied, ranging between performing shows, organizing demonstrations, running workshops, accounting, forwarding food to a flooded area, etc. The fact of having to respond to emergencies led the core group to have great autonomy. (As just one example of the kind of emergency they have had to address, we could look to the struggle that took place in Singur and Nandigram from 2006 to 2008 against the forced eviction of more than 40,000 peasants, which led to the Nandigram massacre on March 14, 2007, an event that constituted for David Harvey "the most shocking case" of violence against peasant populations to pave the way for big capital.[6])

Due to democratic demand, Jana Sanskriti gave rise to the creation of another type of organization: spect-actors' committees. The committees exist because not everyone can or wants to become actors; these groups are primarily designed to preserve an independent space where the peasants can gather without the presence of Jana Sanskriti in order to formulate the demands coming from the villages in the most autonomous way possible. It is, ultimately, the spect-actors' committees who decide on the themes for the next campaigns and what activities should accompany them, who judge the quality of the plays and their suitability for addressing the problems at hand, etc. Though Jana Sanskriti itself counts around 600 members only, the members of the spect-actors' committees total more than 20,000.

Jana Sanskriti's campaigns are diverse in their themes, forms, and breadth. Before the elections, members of Jana Sanskriti dress up as clown-candidates and enact parades to—as they put it—treat politicians the same way that they treat the population. During a campaign in favor of the creation of a law that would guarantee the state pay for a minimum of activities inside the villages (so that its inhabitants do not have to emigrate seasonally to cities where their working conditions will be even worse), 50 members of Jana Sanskriti traveled—by bicycle— the 1,307 kilometers that separate Kolkata from Delhi.[7] At each stop, an allied grassroots movement organized a presentation or performance by Jana Sanskriti. The performance in Delhi took place in front of thousands of people.

A longer campaign was carried out against the sale of illegal liquor. The consumption of these drinks is a serious problem in rural Bengal. These liquors are extremely harmful to one's health, and the places where they are consumed are also gambling spaces, causing some peasants to lose even their homes in one night. The performances denouncing such liquor and the relevant discussions in the committees set the stage for such fury on the part of the peasants that they immediately decided to destroy the places where alcohol was sold or stored. Jana Sanskriti, not agreeing with this solution, followed the peasants in their actions, if only because the owners of these warehouses comprise a violent mafia. Another tactic was eventually found: blocking the road near the warehouses. As a result of this tactic, police officers showed up to clear the road. The crowd then asked the police to seize the illegal drinks, a task the police did not do before because they were receiving bribes to prevent them from doing so. In front of around 400 people, however, the police are obliged to obey the crowd's demands.

The most recent campaign that I witnessed perhaps allows for a better understanding of how Jana Sanskriti works: here I refer to a campaign related to education of children under six years of age. Across four years, Jana Sanskriti had built schools for around 2,000 children. In those settings, the children had a higher quality education than the one provided by the state. In addition, because it was generally women who had been taking care of the children at home, Jana Sanskriti's creation of the schools gave them more free time, which allowed women to become more involved in the movement. In a second phase, Jana Sanskriti started closing these schools and putting on performances about education. A population of approximately 150,000 people had the opportunity to attend, on average, four of these shows each—and to participate in various debates on the same topic. All interventions were noted, and the record of them was returned to the spectators' committee in each village, which then could decide on the next steps: they could take on the task of maintaining the schools that Jana Sanskriti closed, or they could demand that government schools of the same quality be opened in the villages.

Jana Sanskriti takes banal facts of life and problematizes them so that a large population of approximately 300 villages can collectively debate them. Not only can peasants publicly present their discontent; their analyses occur within a framework where they have to take into account what others have said and, with those others, build a collective response to the problem being discussed. Jana Sanskriti organizes the population by asking them what they can do to transform their daily lives, whether that transformation will happen through building alternatives, such as schools, or by confronting powerful locals. The common thread uniting all Jana Sanskriti campaigns is that they are designed in such a way that the peasants can have full decision-making power in relation to everything that goes on in the villages.

102 *Are There No Alternatives?*

TO, as practiced by Jana Sanskriti, caught the attention of several grassroots movements across India. Jana Sanskriti has organized countless workshops with these movements and built alliances with them. Thus, in October 2006, the Indian Federation of Theatre of the Oppressed was created. The federation has more than 30 member movements. These movements sometimes come from very different regions; the languages spoken are not the same from one state to another. As these movements are viscerally linked to the specific problems of their localities and of the populations with whom they work, the problems that they address are not necessarily the same from one movement to another. And the lenses of political analyses from one movement to the next are even less similar; they range across disparate currents of Marxism and Gandhism, often in original syntheses and certainly not shared by all. The challenge for this federation is precisely to try to build a platform where these organizations can overcome their differences and work out a common political perspective together. More than 15 years after its creation, the federation continues to struggle to overcome those gigantic challenges. In those conditions, the very permanence of the federation is a victory in itself.

Jana Sanskriti has become a major player in politics in West Bengal and India at large, while creating a very horizontal structure. The march held on October 22, 2006, to celebrate the creation of the Indian Federation of Theatre of the Oppressed seems to demonstrate the significance of Jana Sanskriti. The central group had organized a march with an expected participation of about 3,000 people. Ultimately, 12,000 peasants traveled from their villages to Kolkata under particularly difficult conditions, which required mobilizing important logistics (transportation, food, and water for trips that often exceeded 12 hours, constitution of nuclei so that peasants did not get lost, etc.) without the central group being informed of anything. Therefore, the total numbers for the march were determined not only by Jana Sanskriti themselves but also through a combined process of taking into account numbers provided by the police and numbers provided by local Jana Sanskriti organizers. The fact that Jana Sanskriti did not know what the numbers would be ahead of time demonstrates both how decentralized their processes are and how they were able to promote autonomous decision-making in the villages.

Though Jana Sanskriti's action and impact on the Indian political scene appear to be extremely positive,[8] their impact in the immeasurably smaller world that concerns me here—the one created by TO practitioners across the planet—is more ambiguous. Jana Sanskriti is probably the most recognized TO group today. Every two years, a festival called Muktadhara (a Bengali word meaning "free-flowing stream") attracts dozens of participants from all over the world to West Bengal, where they have the opportunity to present their plays, attend a workshop with members of Jana Sanskriti's central coordination, and visit the villages, among other things. These spaces are, however, not very formative. Jana Sanskriti seems not to want to get into any debate that might offend anyone, whether out of a sense of respect for the guests or, more prosaically, because they need the foreign participants for many reasons, including the strengthening of an international support network, which is important given both the ruthlessness of Bengal's political system and the very limited resources that Jana Sanskriti possesses. In my experience, at least, even the most discordant TO interpretations are accepted at the festival, without any real spaces for debates so that these differences can actually be discussed and—who knows?—even be overcome. Jana Sanskriti's own vocabulary—which takes a lot of inspiration from Indian mystics like Vivekananda and in which we find expressions about the need for "an inner revolution," a "new spirituality," or "a journey within ourselves to a discovery of ourselves"[9]—encourages the tendencies of some of the participants, mostly young Westerners, to rejoice in an alleged encounter with a New Age mysticism that seems to be more of an occidental creation than a deep understanding of Indian spirituality. Foreign performances contrary to Jana Sanskriti's political views are presented in public squares in front of peasants, whose reactions range from boredom in front of plays that are incomprehensible to them to a fascination with white people.

This lack of a more marked positioning of Jana Sanskriti perhaps helps account for why—although probably hundreds of non-Indian participants have passed through Jana Sanskriti—it has not developed a specific line of thought or action, and therefore it does not exert a great international influence on the world of TO as such. Another reason for this relative lack of influence may simply be explained by the fact that the material, concrete conditions of Indian peasant life are nothing like those of a mixed group of practitioners from all over the world. In a way, though the Indian families with whom Jana Sanskriti works are undeniably humble, they are also less dependent on wages, with many of their needs being met through means other than the exchange of commodities. Their houses belong to them; their lands produce much of the food they eat. In both of those cases, the mediation of the market and money do not exist. Therefore, it is possible that a family will decide to "release" one of its members so that they can fully participate in Jana Sanskriti, while other members of the family are hard at work to make up for their absence. That was, for example, the case with Satya Ranjan Pal, one of the most important members of Jana Sanskriti. The iron law of wages has not yet fully disciplined those populations, who have not suffered a complete separation from their means of production. For this and other reasons, Jana Sanskriti is simultaneously both an example of the utmost interest for those wanting to learn about a productive use of TO *and* an impossible model for most urban practitioners who are trying to survive in one way or another, through the sale of their working strength to the state or to outsourced institutions like NGOs.

Óprima! Criticism as a Concrete Practice, or: "We don't give a shit!"

In the summer of 2011, Portugal had just experienced its largest demonstration since April 25, 1974. A few months earlier, on March 12, around half a million people had taken to the streets to fight against precarity, convened by four unorganized precarious youth groups. The manifestation—which was called "Geração à Rasca" (Generation in Peril) and influenced by the new winds of the Arab Spring—indicated the beginning of a new cycle of social struggles in Portugal, animated by what were called "inorganic" movements, given that they did not belong to any previously created organization. This wave of protest culminated in (between the end of that year and the end of 2014) five general strikes and some of the most massive demonstrations in the country since the return to democracy, with those convened by the platform "Que se lixe a Troika!" ("To hell with Troika!"—a slogan that emerged in 2012) being perhaps especially notable. It is in this context that the first preparatory contacts and links were formed for what would become "Óprima! An Encounter of Theatre of the Oppressed and Activism." The first edition of this gathering took place in Lisbon in February 2012.

Óprima!'s goal was to bring together individuals who had TO experience with activists of these emerging mobilizations. The context seemed favorable for this type of meeting.

On the one hand, this period was marked by the search for a new repertoire of collective action and forms of organization that tended to be more horizontal and fluid, capable of including those who were not part of the existing organizations, whether those organizations were partisan, unionized, or smaller associations with a specific topic (a collective wanting to discuss feminism through artistic actions, a group of precarious workers wanting to talk about their working conditions, etc.). Given TO's critique of the specialization of theatre and politics—and the fact that it is fundamentally based on a logic of participation that breaks with the separation between actor and spectator and proposes that each person speak and represent their own reality—TO seemed like a form of engagement that would resonate with the spirit of the manifestations.

104 *Are There No Alternatives?*

On the other hand, the arrival of a new generation—and its awakening to these struggles—urgently guided the creation of spaces for gathering and sharing in order to construct common reflections and means of action that could be both interesting and critical at the same time.

The first Óprima! formed around an initial nucleus of a dozen people who belonged to five different groups of militants: the March 12 movement (M12M), with the organizers of the "Geração à Rasca" demonstration; the World March of Women—Portugal (MMM), including Portuguese representation of a worldwide feminist network formed within the alter-globalization movement and the Social Forums of the 2000s; UMAR—Azores, a feminist association from the Portuguese islands in the Atlantic—a group that, at the time, had developed a theatrical project with fisherwomen for the recognition of their work; activists from the Khapaz Association, including the Prison Intervention Group and the "Ghetto Platform" (Plataforma Ghetto), who had carried out an action on the outskirts of Lisbon with a radical program against racism and police violence (and whose activists had participated in a project that included TO); a small TO collective from Pombal, a city in central Portugal, formed shortly after a workshop; and finally the "Estudantes por Empréstimo" (Students For Loan), a collective that had presented Forum Theatre in dozens of schools the previous year on the issue of democratic access to higher education and the group's opposition to both the reduction of scholarships and the corresponding expansion of the presence of banks making loans within universities.

Óprima! began with a number of political experiences that established a relationship between art and theatre. The gathering convened people who first met as members of activist groups, not originally conceived as theatre groups. As a result, most people at the first Óprima! meeting had never had experience with TO. Then there were those who, having had contact with TO, intended to use it in concrete political struggles. At the same time, and thanks to those struggles, there were also groups present who had a critical view of the increasing commodification and neutralization of TO. Their critique extended to TO's consequent transformation into a good for consumption and exchange *or* a technique of social intervention in the hands of professionals for projects that—even with the best of intentions—always end up being dependent on the funders' agenda, leading to ambiguous relationships with the state and the various powers that compose it. "Students for Loan," for example, is a group of militants from the student movement who were involved in a project associated with a parliamentary mandate from the Bloco de Esquerda (Left Bloc) party, clearly committed to the struggles against austerity policies. The group Khapazes de Semear Konsciencia (KSK—Capable of Sowing Consciousness)—composed solely of children of immigrants from Cape Verde and Mozambique—has been running a highly politicized campaign against racism for years, but at that time, it was looking for other points of reference in the world of TO, since it had a critical view of the project in which it had just participated.

From the beginning, the gathering of these collectives was self-funded by choice but also out of lack of time and a concern for autonomy. All the necessary preparation work was done on an unpaid basis, fueled instead by personal will. The meeting consisted primarily of a workshop and the presentation of Forum Theatre plays. It ran for five days in a Lisbon space that belonged to several associations with whom the organizers thought it was important to establish a relationship. This first gathering was the beginning of a process between groups who barely knew each other. It confirmed—at least for the groups who continued on to the following editions of Óprima!—that there was a desire to work together.

Óprima!'s second edition was organized in a more participatory way by the four groups who stayed on after the first edition: "Students for Loan," the KSK group, the World March of Women—Portugal, and the Theatre of the Oppressed Nucleus—Braga (NTO-Braga), an association created in 2011. The latter group—which joined Óprima! after a workshop led by a

Examples but Not Models 105

member of "Students for Loan"—is a collective whose identity and type of interventions were very close in nature to those of the groups in the first Óprima!, with participation in street demonstrations, an organic link to the social struggles against austerity, and the fact that none of them were TO professionals or made it a paid activity.

The second Óprima! took place in Braga, which is located in northern Portugal. The central activity of this edition—meaning the activity in which all those present participated for three of the five days of meetings—was a workshop that I facilitated. The workshop focused on Forum Theatre dramaturgy. The main objective was not merely to tell personal stories of oppression. We also aimed to question our very ways of representing reality. We wanted to avoid repeating individualistic models centered on simplistic contradictions between oppressor and oppressed, models that fail to account for the structural foundations of oppression, its systemic nature, the collective aspects of conflict, and the multiple dynamics that oppressions bring into play. We instead sought models that could portray oppression as something routine, something both central to social relations and concrete, composed of material dimensions that cannot be reduced to its most visible aspects or the subjective capacities of choice on the part of the oppressed or the oppressor.

This second edition of Óprima! strengthened the relationships of trust between the groups as well as their political-theatrical sharing. In addition to the workshop, the gathering included discussions on the Portuguese political situation that were able to generate common analyses, and—from that point forward—joint struggles were built. There was also an important space allotted for criticism about the world of TO—and about the method itself. From the Braga workshop came the embryo of a scene that was presented a dozen times, allowing the groups from Porto and Braga to work together in an ongoing way on the intertwined topics of precarity, youth unemployment, and the problem of micro-entrepreneurship. This collaboration was perhaps the first concrete result of a continuity that the organizers of Óprima! had hoped to accomplish, one that moved beyond the moments of the gathering itself. In other words, the energy and commitment underneath Óprima! was not exhausted by the ecstasy of a good event. Instead, Óprima! offered the space to form a constellation of bonds and connections that extended beyond it, structuring an intervention that—over 18 months later—resulted in the presentation of Forum Theatre in various contexts (schools, unions, associations, meetings of movement militants), in partnership with the collective "Precário Inflexíveis" (Inflexibly Precarious).

The Braga edition of Óprima! was probably the one that brought together the most diverse group of activists. That fact can partially be explained by the Portuguese conjuncture at that time. In 2013, Portugal was in the midst of a turbulent period of contestation. Less than a month after Óprima!, a gigantic demonstration brought together approximately one million people—10% of the Portuguese population—in dozens of cities across the country. With the slogan "O povo é quem mais ordena" ("The people are the ones who organize")—a verse from the Portuguese song "Grândola, Vila Morena" by José Afonso, which signaled the start of the 1974 revolution—the march arose out of a call from an informal collective that included some members of Óprima!.

The third edition of Oprima! took place in Arrentela, south of Lisbon.[10] There, thanks to the relationships of trust established between the organizers, Óprima! reached a new stage, one that made it a relatively rare kind of space on the TO landscape: a space of genuine critical generosity. This peculiar form of generosity came about through the following method: each group presented their piece so that, the next day, within the context of the workshop, it would be criticized by the other members of Óprima!, who identified the challenges that seemed to be arising with the scene that was presented. Then, in small groups, the workshop participants recreated scenes from the play in question, proposing dramaturgical alternatives to respond to the

106 *Are There No Alternatives?*

problems that had been noticed. In this way, the criticism of TO is no longer simply a discourse aimed externally, meaning at groups who do not belong to Óprima!. It becomes, rather, a learning experience for internal use, an exercise in political-theatrical questioning of the dramaturgy used by the groups *and* a collective search for concrete alternatives to respond to the issues that the groups have encountered. However, at the Arrentela gathering, a certain hopelessness was also palpable. That feeling arose at least in part from the ebb of the recent large mobilizations and the search for ways of rooting the struggle so that its continuity went beyond large protests.

Arrentela was also where Óprima! established contact with a French TO group, "Féminisme Enjeux" (Feminism Onstage), a connection that allowed for the organization of a workshop following Óprima!. Out of that workshop arose a piece that was later presented at a feminist festival in a marginalized French neighborhood, in November 2014. Much of the group who created this play still performs a reworked version of it in various contexts in Portugal, trying to fuel organizing and other action against sexual harassment.

The next Óprima!—held in Porto in 2015—was the one that had the most people who had traveled to the gathering from outside Portugal. Groups from other countries came to present their plays—Theatre of the Oppressed Group-Montevideo (GTO-Montevideo) and Féminisme Enjeux—and researchers and practitioners from several countries attended. The Óprima! planning group carefully conceived the geographical expansion of the universe of practitioners present so that it would not be in contradiction with the fundamental concerns of the gathering. A certain political identity and a critical, non-fetishizing perspective on TO formed the common ground on which the meeting could take place. This complicity with one another—this shared analysis in relation to TO and political struggles—meant that the same critical generosity could be exercised at this gathering as before, and to the extent that a Brazilian participant declared in the final evaluation round that she was left with the impression of having witnessed one of the famous Arena Theatre Dramaturgy sessions that began in 1966. (The exaltation with which those original Arena Theatre session participants criticized each other was precisely one of the reasons that the sessions became so well known.[11]) The character of this event, the most internationalist Óprima!, echoed in the concerns of the participants, who looked beyond Portugal to Greece—which had brought to life the hope, soon to be betrayed, of a transformation that did not obey the dictates of European institutions—but also to several other European countries whose elections demonstrated a clear progression toward the extreme Right. And in Portugal—which had lost around 400,000 people across the four years of the crisis, with young people constituting a massive portion of those who had to leave—Óprima! was also a moment of reunion, due to the presence of former members who had been forced to join the contingent of economic exiles.

The essentially descriptive account above, however, does not render visible the main reasons that Óprima! is an unusual encounter in the TO universe—or the tensions, contradictions, and debates that cross Óprima! as an initiative. Next I will try to take on some of these topics.

With its democratic planning processes, its horizontal way of sharing perspectives, the meals organized collectively, the shared cleaning, the housing accommodations provided in solidarity, and its sliding-scale cost of participation, Oprima! tries to anticipate in its practice the type of relationships that the participants would like to see established in the world. It tries to cultivate the types of relationships that function, as much as possible, independently from mercantile logic and the principle of competition. For these reasons, Óprima! is an event of its own kind in the world of TO—in which, as a general rule, meetings are financed primarily by selling workshop seats, a dynamic that creates a sense of always needing to satisfy "customers" to ensure short-term or long-term sustainability. Ulício Cardoso, KSK member and organizer of Óprima!'s 2014 edition in Arrentela, publicly declared, "We hold these meetings for ourselves, and we open the doors for other people to attend. If they like it, we're happy. If they don't, we don't give a shit!"

Examples but Not Models 107

And with that sentiment, the radical difference of being at a gathering not guided by any commercial concern becomes clear. In this sense, Óprima! is a prefigurative experience, inhabited by contradictions inherent to these processes and guided by the desire—using Rancière's terms here—to take equality as a presupposition and not as an objective. The differences between the members of the Óprima! community are obvious. Their origins, routines, and expectations in life seemingly do not have any particular common denominator. The son of an immigrant from Cape Verde has little in common with a member of parliament from the Left Bloc. The context of Óprima!, however, rejects the divisions imposed by society and maintains equality of access across people who—outside its space—are subject to hierarchies according to their professions and/or origins. Those factors—alongside the freedom to be critical and the reality that all members of Óprima! have organized meetings in their own cities at least once—smooth out the differences between members of the group until they are barely noticeable.

Many theatre meetings—and in particular ones that are focused on TO—group people around a common interest in a specific technique. Though it's good to debate with those who use the same weapons, Óprima! operates from a different logic. It is an attempt to build a group around those fighting the same enemy. The origins of Óprima! are certainly based more in militant practices than in an exclusive interest in technique. That distinction also gives Óprima! a profile that is very unusual in the TO universe. The complicity between its members, however, far from constitutes consensus. The fact that some members belong to the Left Bloc, for example, is always regarded by other members of the group who are critical of the party as carrying the possibility that Óprima! could be co-opted by partisan interests. In other words, in this case, people and groups with different political and aesthetic sensitivities coexist. Until now, a sense of kinship, the sharing of common values, and the always-open possibility of criticism have made the conflict and confrontation of experiences, views, and struggles collectively productive.

One of the points that unites all Óprima! participants is the attempt to carry out a radical critique of the existing world of TO. The participants' relationships to TO can be reduced neither to an acceptance of reproducing its technical and theoretical corpus nor to a unilateral rejection. The members of Óprima! sought and managed to establish a relationship of a different nature with TO, an unorthodox and critical fidelity to its principles, one that does not even dispense with questioning the usefulness of the method in the current conjuncture. Put another way, it is the very respect for the legacy and history of TO that imposes the demand for a radical critique of its practices and its appropriations by work in service of already-dominant power structures. This stance implies the rejection of the assumption that TO would always be a useful tool. It also admits that there could be truth in a hypothesis of TO's potential obsolescence or inadequacy now, with the possibility that it does not carry the same emancipatory scope that it had in the historical context that saw its birth. As I will explore below, the discussion around this issue was particularly incendiary at the 2015 meeting.

The question of TO's connection (or lack thereof) to the present conjuncture is a constant concern for the participants of Óprima!. The crisis in Portugal could not in any way be left out of the analysis when people experience precarity month after month. Óprima! does not give in to the wonder produced by moments of encounter, sociability, and sharing. Without denial of the importance of its moments of joy and companionship, organizers and participants of Óprima! think of it first and foremost as a place for the elaboration of strategies and future actions. Just like a Forum Theatre session, the encounter wants to be incomplete, since it must have the potential to trigger action outside and beyond Óprima!. It is what happens *outside* the encounter that gives meaning to what happens *inside* it.

The plays have to meet the reality outside Óprima!, just as this same reality has to be represented in the most concrete way possible onstage. Though, in the first editions of the gathering,

108   *Are There No Alternatives?*

the plays that were presented veered heavily toward depicting examples of oppression in ways that partially divorced them from their concrete contexts, the plays presented more recently tend to focus more on the materiality of how oppression works. Increasingly, the dramaturgy—or at least the criticism of the plays presented—steers away from a conception of TO as a presentation of values or ideas that we would have to distance ourselves from in order to be free. Óprima!'s principal investment is not in TO's potential to unveil false discourses or an "exhortative tendency" of which A. Boal himself was a great supporter.[12] In other words, the disposition of the event is not about fighting a form of alienation, understood as a bunch of erroneous ideas that prevent us from action, nor is it about training to make our will even more inflexible and intransigent in the face of such ideas. Ultimately, the objective is less to combat mentalities than to try to show onstage how these mentalities are materially formed.

The 2015 edition of Óprima! took place in a context in Portugal where austerity policies seem to have installed a lasting hopelessness in the population. At the same time, emigration and crisis literally emptied movements and struggles. Here lies the biggest challenge facing Óprima! today: knowing how to overcome the situation that saw its birth. How do they avoid the calcification that would transform what was born from a living practice into a bureaucratic ritual? The vast majority of people who participate in Óprima! are very happy to do so and this form of joy can also be considered a form of resistance, a way of meeting within the limits of society to imagine plots against it. At the same time, many already know that these reasons for the gathering cannot be the only ones. Thus, in the final evaluation round of the 2015 gathering, José Soeiro, member of parliament from the Left Bloc and one of the founders of Óprima!, raised the question of whether it was really necessary to plan a next edition.

In fact, there was a deep ambiguity in that meeting held in Porto in 2015. There was certainly an important audience for the workshops and the plays (it is pivotal that, for the dimensions of Óprima!, its total never exceeds 80 people). In addition, the quality of the workshops was praised, and the atmosphere was palpably enthusiastic and jovial across the five days. There was, however, despite all of these aspects, also an anguish that felt more pressing by the day. The collective concern had as its object TO itself and its ability (or possible lack thereof) to oppose a reality that seems to have revoked the possibility of alternatives to the low quality of life imposed by austerity.

To explore this concern further, let's turn to the thesis completed by researcher Inês Barbosa on TO as a militant tool. She analyzes the example of NTO-Braga, of which she is a founding member, explaining how the Portuguese audience for their Forum Theatre play (presented in Braga itself) felt very discouraged and desperate. The themes of the Forum Theatre play she discusses were youth unemployment, precarity, the hyper-exploitation that those who still had a job had to endure in order to keep it, and the discourse of entrepreneurship, which frames the crisis as an opportunity of which only the most courageous can take advantage. Barbosa shows us the dismay of the audience's reactions, which, in their most combative moments, sent "everything to hell!" by not accepting what the workplace dictated and going back home, in what seemed more like an act of self-destruction (in the sense of a choice that would lead to losing one's employment) to keep dignity intact than a concrete construction of viable struggles.[13] The participants appeared to be saving face, so to speak, by essentially saying "fuck off" to their boss, but such a stance, of course, doesn't ultimately lead anywhere—except, again, perhaps to losing one's job.

> Even though we were in an aesthetic space and, as such, in a space framed as fictional and protected, the difficulty of organizing work colleagues to initiate a collective action was evident in the Forum Theatre sessions that we held with *OMET2* (the title of the play presented). This difficulty was due, first of all, to the absence of lasting relationships between colleagues and of spaces and times for shared conviviality.[14]

Examples but Not Models 109

Thus, for those audiences Barbosa describes, precarity seemed to have become a form of unfailing domination, a constant blackmail that prevented the elaboration of any opportunity for resistance. In this respect, Portugal in 2015 would confirm the somber analysis offered by Pierre Bourdieu in 1997:

> Precarity profoundly affects any man or woman exposed to its effects; making the future uncertain, it prevents any rational anticipation and, especially, that minimum of belief and hope in the future that is necessary to revolt, especially collectively, against the present, even the most intolerable. [...] The unemployed and workers deprived of stability are not subject to mobilization, because they have been affected in their ability to project themselves into the future, the indispensable condition of all so-called rational conduct, starting with economic calculation, or, in a completely different order, by political organization.[15]

Barbosa, who is familiar with and widely cites Bourdieu's text, is not, however, unaware of the reality in which precarious struggles often emerge in Portugal. The question or concern here is not so much about the idea that the horizon for struggle has been eclipsed altogether; instead, it is about how such struggles can or cannot be enhanced by TO. It was a question that, in a way, was present for most of those who took part in the 2015 meeting. All the plays presented seemed to fall short of an adequate presentation of the oppression that each chose to address. There was a demotion to the drama of problems that could not fit into this form without giving the content a fake frame, one that was limited to the intersubjective. This approach staged conflicts in which conscious dialogue was the great vehicle of action. In a logical response to that structure, the interventions tried to convince the oppressor or at least to ridicule him, oscillating between a rhetorical contest and a joke competition. Those present for the scenes debated and criticized the aesthetic contradictions, the simplistic presentation of the oppressors as either perverse individuals to be battled straight-on or fools to be (re)educated, and an almost-photographic reproduction of reality in some moments, a dramaturgical device that, at least in that case, gave no other possibility for action besides the demonstration of individual courage. Related to the last concern on that list, a scene about harassment in the subway was particularly criticized for implying that the solution to the problem would be that the women experiencing that oppression in the scene should simply be braver. Somehow no Forum Theatre session, however, was ultimately able to move beyond these errors; participants widely recognized and accepted that there were problems with the scenes, but without that criticism leading to any proposed alternatives. TO itself seemed unable to surpass these limits.

Curiously, what gave hope to the collective of groups and individuals who gathered at that version of Óprima! was the Forum Theatre play that was least hopeful.

KSK, a group of young descendants of Cape Verdean immigrants, created a play based on testimonies collected in literacy classes organized with women of their mothers' generation. In the play, the protagonist Maria finds herself inside a contradiction: she cannot continue to work as a maid, given health problems that are precisely a consequence of her work. Neither can she stop working, however, since her labor rights are denied because, as an immigrant, she has worked her whole life without her employer legally declaring her activities. The employer offers Maria—because she is "almost part of the family"—an unacceptable solution: for Maria's daughter, a nursing student, to take Maria's place working at the boss's house. Despite the real affection Maria felt for her employer's family, this offer was an insult, a degradation. When Maria talks about it with her daughter, she tells her that she hasn't worked her whole life so that her daughter would end up cleaning "white people's shit." The dialogue between these generations mirrors contradictions that stretch far beyond the individuals onstage—contradictions

110   *Are There No Alternatives?*

that permeate even the language used. Maria expresses herself in Creole, the language of Cape Verde, to her daughter, who answers her in Portuguese only.[16] But the contradictions extend even further: to life expectations themselves. Though, for Maria, precarity was the price her generation had to pay for integration into life in a foreign land—a sacrifice so that her children could have a better life—her daughter replies that she cannot escape racism and job uncertainty, either. With this intergenerational scope, the oppressions they experience can no longer be regarded as a stage or moment that time would take care of overcoming, but an endless horizon with no mirage of integration. According to Maria's daughter, there is no guarantee that she will be able to practice as a nurse, a profession for which she studied. And, in any case, she says nursing does not pay much better. For this reason, and because the daughter does not accept the prospect of her mother sacrificing her own health to pay for her education, the daughter is willing to accept the employer's offer. The social contradictions that cross the characters' lives become the motor of the play. The concreteness of these contradictions shifted the focus away from a conflict of individual wills that we find in the vast majority of other Forum Theatre plays.

There were several interventions from Maria's perspective, and those interventions could only try to find a breach in the system as it exists. Such a breach was not found. In other words, the participants were not able to think of ways to organize resistance to the system, to extort any possibilities inside the system that had been previously unnoticed, or to create ways of living that would make the problems irrelevant. The implicit position was that of an individual who, with existing resources, tried to solve the problems she faced. We were, in a way, asked to assume the position of ultra-effective social workers, not movement militants. However—despite the fact that there was no scope for the construction of lines of combat or desertion—this was the play that most favorably impressed the audience at that year's gathering. The inability to find an alternative to that situation did not create more despair; on the contrary, it seemed to redouble the strength of those present. I cannot go beyond hypotheses here to explain how this demonstration of impossibilities became a beacon of hope. Perhaps it was due to the impeccable dramaturgical construction, which was capable of giving an account of Maria's story in the form of a concrete reality "which is the universal character of the case," stripped of any false particularity that we often find in TO plays.[17] Sometimes we fill those plays with so many specific (and even true) anecdotes that we diffuse and distract from the stark and fundamental reality of the oppressions at the heart of them. Maria's story had none of that adornment; the rigorous and brutal mechanisms of social relegation that she experienced were underscored by an equally austere scene. This time, the exercise of taking the stage and trying out alternatives did not trigger the finding of solutions that were as easy as they were false, a phenomenon that unfortunately occurs in so many Forum Theatre sessions. The interventions were instead, in this case, part of an ongoing effort to analyze reality. The investigation proceeded with the help of the audience members, who were called upon to test the strength and hardness of the cage in which Maria was struggling. In this situation, there was not that strange combination of arrogance and a certain infantilization that I have found countless times in the world of Forum Theatre. When I say arrogance here, I refer to a presumption that intervening spectators should rise to the "level" of the actors and demonstrate onstage the qualities that the actors themselves supposedly already possess. And I use "infantilization" in this instance to speak to what I perceive as a desire to convince spectators that their interventions could easily be carried out. These approaches give the curious impression that, for most Forum Theatre groups, emancipation is regarded as just around the corner. The fact that the play paid us the respect of avoiding this double condescension also probably made room for the feeling of hope to be born, not from a magical solution provided by a spectator, but from having been able to reflect intensely on stories that today seem—at least when taken individually—hopeless.

Examples but Not Models 111

This dialectical construction also allowed the performance to be built on bases that were not prosaic. The daughter seemed to manifest a kind of hatred when the mother refused to let the daughter replace her at work, but it was clear that such a strong feeling could only be driven by the daughter's deep love, which viscerally rejected the mother's impulse to sacrifice herself for her daughter. The actress playing the daughter always seemed to take the mother's refusal of the employer's offer as an affront: "Who do you think you have raised if you think I would be so selfish as to accept that my education would be paid for with the sacrifice of your health?" The intense beauty of this scene—and the others in the play—can perhaps also be glimpsed in the fact that the militants at the gathering left the Forum Theatre sessions without the anguish of the previous nights. That night, the last one for Óprima! 2015, we saw the emergence of the possibility of a kind of Forum Theatre whose function was precisely to stimulate a certain despair, but with the paradoxical effect of sharpening our intolerances for the world as it is.

In his essay "On the Fetish-Character in Music and the Regression of Listening," Adorno writes that music produced by the cultural industry enacts in its listeners a paradoxical "denial and rejection of pleasure in pleasure itself."[18] He argues that entertainment music audiences—while they may be seduced by commercially successful songs—feel that these same songs do not allow them to fully develop their senses. "While they feel pleasure, deep down people perceive themselves as traitors in relation to a better possibility, and simultaneously they perceive themselves to be betrayed by the prevailing situation."[19]

Just as this "denial of pleasure in pleasure" is possible, perhaps there is also a denial of despair in despair that would occur *precisely when* a Forum can demonstrate—without frills—both the impossibility of the immediate realization of a "better possibility" *and* the uncompromising refusal to betray oneself by becoming content with the prevailing situation or by posing solutions that are demeaning in their failure to rise to the burning stakes and complexity of the situation at hand.

A brief history of the Popular Theatre School (La Escola de Teatro Popular—ETP), or: political-theatrical learning in times of collapse

In June 2016, I was given the opportunity to organize an international meeting on Theatre of the Oppressed (TO) at the Florestan Fernandes National School, the most important training space run by the Brazilian Landless Movement. Artists and activists from several countries participated, including activists from the popular movement known as La Dignidad (Movimiento Popular La Dignidad—MPLD), who had been part of the creation of the School of Political Theatre (La Escuela de Teatro Político) in Buenos Aires, Argentina. At the meeting, these activists from La Dignidad explained how both their movement and their school worked. La Dignidad is a movement that tries to organize the working class through the construction of spaces and services that meet the concrete needs of the population. For example, the movement created popular cafeterias, schools, day care centers, health centers, a fire department, a network of ambulances, a distributor of bottled gas, and other elements of popular infrastructure.[20] Each of these structures generates jobs for the militants of the movement and tries to create a sociability of practice that distances itself from the relations imposed by the market and the state.[21] The School of Political Theatre itself participated in such efforts as it responded to some demands of the movement: training firefighters, creating plays on domestic violence for the feminist collective within the movement, etc. The school also, however, formed their own student base, recruiting mainly from beyond the movement and creating ways of building a kind of theatre that was explicitly political and did not obey the forms inflicted upon them by the capitalist regime.

112 *Are There No Alternatives?*

It was the example of this school that spurred the creation of the Popular Theatre School (La Escola de Teatro Popular—ETP) in Rio de Janeiro. Its founders Geo Britto and I knew that our school could not be a replica of the one in Buenos Aires because the two cities have very distinct political scenes. We assessed that there was no such movement precisely like La Dignidad in Rio; therefore, the school could not belong to a single movement or be open to anyone interested in political theatre in general. Instead, the school would have to belong to movements plural and be open to militants only. In April 2017, the first group to comprise the Rio school took shape. It was made up of militants from MST (Movimento Sem Terra, or the Landless Movement), MTST (Movimento dos Trabalhadores Sem-Teto, or The Roofless Workers' Movement), RUA (Rua—Juventude Anticapitalista, or Street—Anticapitalist Youth), and the Levante Popular da Juventude (Popular Youth Rise). All these movements had representation within the Political-Pedagogical Coordination of ETP, where the school's management occurs. The primary objective of the school was (and still is) to train militants so that they can return to their movements to strengthen the construction of the cultural collectives within those organizations.

Another important difference between the contexts of Buenos Aires and Rio de Janeiro was that the approach of each ETP militant was already imbued with the cultural practices of their own movements, at least in the cases when those movements had such practices. As a result, many of the students from Rio de Janeiro had preconceptions about what constituted political theatre. Often the theatrical practices in their movements tend toward artistic representations that idealize reality. In other words, they represent powerful and perverse subjects who decide of their own free will (and often thirsty greed) to oppress heroic and pure subjects. What's more, the victory of those heroic subjects is guaranteed by their own unbreakable will, or it is instead imagined through an altruistic sacrifice that will pave the way, ensuring the victory of future generations. These representations are—often unconsciously—inherited from the style known as socialist realism. They dominate social movements in Brazil today. And ultimately—according to the evaluation of the ETP pedagogical team—such representations contribute little to a concrete analysis of reality and possible ways to overcome it. In that sense, the school positioned itself as being constructed with movements and for movements, but also—to a certain extent—against movements.

We devoted the first part of Year One of the school to the study of plays from the repertoire of the most fertile period of Brazilian political dramaturgy, which spanned from the mid-1950s to the early 1970s. In this period, Brazilian theatre moved away from models of bourgeois drama—where subjects endowed with free will make choices based on their personal ethics, without ever confronting any social contradictions or other social dynamics—to Epic Theatre, where characters are dialectically subjects and objects of social forces that condition them and that they, in turn, construct. This same historical period also witnessed the transformation of theatre from an object of consumption intended for leisure into an instrument for cultivating political forces driven to oppose the dictatorship. Based on ETP's study of this dramaturgy, we performed a show called *Theatrical Guerilla* (*Guerrilha Teatral*), an expression used by A. Boal in his autobiography to describe the performance event known as *São Paulo Fair of Opinion*. In *Theatrical Guerilla*, we told a story that traveled across excerpts of distinct plays and styles. It started with *Eles não usam Black-tie (They Don't Wear Black Tie)*, continuing on to *Revolução da América do Sul* (*Revolution in South America*) and *Mais-valia Vai Acabar, Seu Edgar* (*Surplus Value Will End, Mr. Edgar*), then the musicals of Arena Theatre in São Paulo—and ending with a Newspaper Theatre scene[22] whose culmination was a theatricalization of a news item from that same day: the 1st of May speech by then-Brazilian President Michel Temer. The intense repression of the general strike that had taken place in Brazil a few days before the performance of *Theatrical Guerilla* made the room particularly receptive to the show, which was also intended to be—at the same time—a process of teaching the audience about the varied forms that political theatre has taken in Brazil.

Examples but Not Models 113

Soon after, ETP's study of Brecht began. We aimed to learn models of scene construction from the teachings of the German playwright. In particular, we focused on what we could glean from him about how to build scenes in which the dominant ideology is fought through the use of dialectics. The study of reality as constituted by dynamic contradictions became the central point of this phase of the work. In fact, we had a particular criterion for the choice of texts that we would explore in-depth: we looked for those in which the work of militants appeared as a theme. As a result, we studied plays that do not normally receive so much attention—plays like, for example, Brecht's *The Mother*. At the end of this stage, we concluded that rehearsing Brecht texts required a degree of skill and knowledge that we had not yet collectively reached. We therefore preferred to organize a large, one-day workshop, open to social movement activists, during which ETP students conducted exercises based on the use of dialectics in theatre.

The next phase of ETP was catalyzed by a political event, the execution of councilwoman Marielle Franco. On April 14, 2018, one month after the assassination, the school opened its doors for more than 30 people, regardless of whether they had already been participants in ETP—for a several-hour session focused on building scenes that were then presented during the rally and protest that had formed in reaction to Franco's assassination. The school presented these scenes wherever people gathered (bars, squares, etc.); we wanted to dialogue with the population in a way that went beyond what the march itself already made possible. Though, at some presentations, we encountered negative reactions ("Why don't they talk about the police officers killed?", "They only talk about the killing of Marielle, but her driver, Anderson, was killed, too, and nobody talks about him"), in most cases we were received with attention and sympathy.[23] But in some ways what was even more impactful for us in the long term was the emotion felt by those who created and performed the scenes:

From that moment on, the school felt the need to open up, to act in a way that turned outward more. A Forum Theatre scene we developed—"Questions of Occupation," about domestic violence in the occupations—was performed in several spaces, including the very occupation where the participants who helped the most to conceive the scene lived.[24] During the 2018 electoral campaign, following the model we had used to mark one month since Franco's execution (scenes assembled quickly to be presented as part of acts in the streets), we opened our doors several times to welcome people who wanted to express themselves through theatre against the advance of authoritarianism. We called that process of rehearsal and street action "Theatre Against Fascism." We also created the Rio de Janeiro Fair of Opinion, an event designed to pay tribute to the 50th anniversary of the São Paulo Fair of Opinion. But our version of that event aimed to do something else, too. We wanted to bring together theatre collectives who were uncomfortable with the present Brazilian political situation in a process that focused on creating an alliance between those groups. In total, we counted 12 theatre collectives across the two days of the fair, with an estimated audience exceeding 150 people. But in another sense, we were also part of a larger effort in which 100,000 Brazilians participated: the fight against Bolsonaro's election. It was a moment teeming with the insistence that we could not leave politics on the side nor hand it over to professional politicians. This moment, which combined an intense beauty with a certain ingenuity, was ultimately defeated by the victory of Bolsonaro. Once again, ETP had to reformulate its tactics.

For the third year of ETP, we did not let the creation of ongoing workshops in favelas and other places simply unfold as "spontaneous" creations of the activists. Instead, we ourselves took on the task of creating those workshops. We began to think of ourselves not only as a school for activists and not only as an activist school, but as a school in partnership with social movements so that they could grow by having theatre groups created for them. The first class—on March 16, 2019—was attended by members of the following collectives: RUA, Levante Popular da Juventude, MTST, MNLM (Movimento Nacional de Luta pela Moradia, or National

114 *Are There No Alternatives?*

Housing Struggle Movement), UNMP (União Nacional por Moradia Popular, or National Alliance for People's Housing), Coletivo de Cultura da Zona Oeste (Cultural Collective of the West Zone), as well as some individuals (generally with particular knowledge of theatre) who were not already inside movements but who had, in many cases, already participated in the "Theatre Against Fascism" experience. At that moment, we felt that it was good to open the school to non-militants (people not already acting from within movements) for two reasons. The first reason is that we believe that good anger is organized anger, a feeling that finds a space to be productive, to organize itself into concrete actions. In that case, we were specifically organizing actions against the new regime that was being designed in Brazil. Many of the actors we met were not already organized in spaces of movement militancy, and therefore their yearnings for struggle might not have extended beyond the 2018 election if we had not opened the school for them. The second reason for opening the school to non-militants was that we understood that our training was quite rudimentary and needed to be complemented with practice. For the practice of creating theatre workshops, we believed that it was beneficial for the movement activists to be accompanied by people with more theatrical experience in their backgrounds.

Perhaps it is important to emphasize here that ETP's use of TO began after the use of TO by other social movements, especially the Landless Movement. Therefore, our experiences and learning benefited from the knowledge that had already been accumulated by those movements, particularly in terms of the limitations of TO that they had previously identified. Those insights come into play especially as we try to make Forum Theatre go beyond a merely intersubjective drama so that it can more accurately encompass the social contradictions that permeate the themes addressed. A "typical" presentation of Forum Theatre places an oppressor against an oppressed person in a binary confrontation where motivations are found in the subjectivity of the characters. For example, in such a confrontation, the heavy bureaucracy of universities—which makes it difficult for students from poorer backgrounds to be accepted—would be reduced to the ill will of an individual university official who is motivated by overt racism. Or the complex problem of domestic violence and its social roots and context are boiled down to a harmful relationship between one man and one woman, without trying to tackle any systemic elements. In such dramaturgical frameworks, the criticism that is intended as corrosive actually emerges as quite mild: for institutional problems to disappear, it would be enough to have or hire a more understanding individual university employee. For domestic violence to cease, it would be enough to have a resolute individual woman leaving her house. ETP's use of TO—and more specifically of Forum Theatre—tries to reconcile spectators' specific interventions with a play structure and composition that do not evade the reality that each oppression only exists thanks to a broader social framework that partially overdetermines its agents and victims.

Soon after, ETP began to open a new front for its older participants or those with more theatrical background. This phase corresponded to a strategic turn by the school, which no longer considered sufficient the training provided in its own spaces; that training process had to be completed by monitoring its participants who are ready to become facilitators. With eight ETP members divided into four pairs, we formed four groups in different units of *+Nós* (+Us) in the cities of Caxias and São Gonçalo, the favela complex of Alemão, and The Institute of Philosophy and Social Sciences.[25] The objectives of this new phase were threefold:

1 To create spaces where young people from poorer or working-class neighborhoods could exercise their critical thinking skills in the construction of scenes about their own reality.
2 To promote more relationships between young people and social movements: young people often attend spaces created by social movements—such as courses where students prepare to take the test that allows entrance into universities—without identifying

Examples but Not Models 115

much with the movements that run those spaces. With these classes we were hosting in movement pre-test schools, we aimed for the plays that resulted from them to circulate within militant spaces (camps, meetings, etc.). We hoped that these plays could present the worldviews of the young people who created them and help participants consider the question of what constitutes these social movements *beyond* the pre-test schools that those movements run. We knew that the project could bring more militants into the social movement, in this case RUA. As we first began offering these classes as part of this project, the intention was to develop at least four theatre groups over the next four years. Our aim was for those theatre groups to be able to build policy collectively with RUA (through both theatre and debates on aesthetics) and with people who can be won over by the movements. We wanted to make it possible to have theatre groups performing more frequently and creating interventions against governments, against capitalism, sexism, and racism, on the streets and in different territories, giving capillarity to the political interventions of RUA and involving people in a way that extends beyond what the university preparation courses can offer.

3 To reclassify culture as a powerful instrument for the political struggle of the masses. Far from being just a fun adornment for political parties, culture can be a training tool for popular organizing. This potential has been proven by past movements such as the Popular Culture Movement, the Centers of Popular Culture, the Basic Ecclesiastical Communities and—to a lesser but equally interesting extent—by A. Boal's mandate as a *vereador* (city councilperson) in Rio de Janeiro. It is a potential that needs to be urgently reclaimed. ETP bet on this project as a pilot plan capable of demonstrating through practice the potential of critical art as an instrument for struggle. We had already witnessed that many militants trained by ETP have nowhere to "return," given the inexistence of cultural collectives in their movements. Therefore, we felt the need to take a step forward to demonstrate through practice.

Our challenges in building this project were many. The participants came, in most cases, from especially precarious sectors of the working class: residents of occupations who sometimes take six hours of transportation to attend a five-hour class, students who combine their studies with work and movement organizing, inhabitants of working-class or popular neighborhoods who were sometimes prevented from attending our classes because of situations caused by violent (and often deadly) police interference in the areas where they live, alongside other factors. ETP's very limited resources were barely able to contribute to the transportation of some participants, and even those resources had their days numbered as they were attached to a project that was over at the end of 2019. Our pedagogy had the task of taking into account both those who came regularly and those who could not attend the course as often. The participants' theatrical experience and knowledge varied widely, a reflection of the disparity that exists within the working class itself. Each participant learns in different ways, and we strive to consider the learning needs of everyone without really knowing how much we have achieved. Another difficulty is that various distinct sensibilities and political practices coexist within ETP. Militants of youth movements who oppose each other in their university elections rehearse scenes together during classes. The array of movements that compose the school do not all share the same analysis of the current political conjuncture, nor do they build the same alliances. ETP is also a space where militants/organizers from distinct organizations can build unity from the grassroots and through practice (of theatre, but we hope that the dynamics established in the theatre are not limited to the stage). We continue to ask: How do we maintain a balance between (1) avoiding the dilution of important debates and (2) not letting the conflict

116 *Are There No Alternatives?*

inherent to politics reach the point that it makes ETP as it exists today unfeasible? We knew that, in this scenario, we were about to see an accentuation of authoritarian tendencies, while the current economic policies would show their potential to destroy Brazil's remaining common goods, as misery and discontent would increase.

Little was said in the preceding pages as to why ETP uses theatre for its goals. The reasons are many. In and around Rio, there is a real interest in theatre on the social periphery or margins—an interest that is not met, thus opening up spaces for movements who want to tap into this genuine desire as a way to engage in dialogue with the rest of the population. Theatre is a form in which a critique of the social division of labor can be exercised quickly through practice. The artisanal nature of its creation allows for the possibility of an especially collective process in which each person takes on several roles and therefore participates in something potentially richer than what happens in situations where the commodity regime pigeonholes us into one role exclusively. This collective creation—when its themes are the lives of the people who participate in the workshop in question—contains the possibility for a high degree of reflection. As a result, it helps generate a better understanding of the reality that surrounds us. There are still, however, other and varied reasons to do theatre. One of them—and perhaps not the least of them—is its ability to show in the field of art that, as the slogan goes in Brazil, "[i]f the working class produces everything, everything belongs to them." That idea means that art belongs to us, too. To say that something belongs to us in this sense is not to say that we are legitimate owners of it or that we can sell it at retail. Instead, I mean that, if art belongs to us, we can make it better. If production really belonged to the working class, it wouldn't be as chaotic and destructive as it is today, to the point that we don't know if there will be a tomorrow. It would be harmonious, able to bring more sense to the world and to each person in it. If culture were really ours, all the problems and all the narrow-mindedness that we see on petit-bourgeois stages (politically petit-bourgeois, if not socially petit-bourgeois) would disappear. We are the ones who can make culture—and art specifically—better. All our difficulties, our lack of time, our lack of accumulated knowledge and experience—all of these, in our best moments, mirror the difficulties of the working class in the task of taking over the world. We are the weak and magnificent bearers of tomorrow. And that's why, despite all of our problems, all of our difficulties, ETP has such a strong meaning for those who belong to it. And, if we do our work beautifully, we will be proof that it is possible to overcome these difficulties, that it is possible—to use Walter Benjamin's terms—to make something new and beautiful emerge "with the sobriety of dawn."[26]

Notes

1 Adivasis is a term used to designate Indian aboriginal populations.
2 The Naxalite movement was born out of a split in the Indian Marxist Communist Party. In 1967, riots led by former members of the PCMI broke out in the village of Naxalbari. The Naxalites claim to be Maoists, try to rouse the masses, and advocate an immoderate use of violence. The Naxalite leader, Charu Majumdar, even declared that "he who does not dip his hands in the blood of an enemy of the people cannot be called a revolutionary." cf. Prakash Sing, *Histoire du Naxalisme* (Paris: Les Nuits Rouges, 2004).
3 The dowry goes from the woman's family to that of the husband. The sums can be very high. The father of the bride often has to sell his land or his house or borrow money. In this sense, in order to fully experience the privileges of Indian rural patriarchy, it is not enough to be a man; one must be the father of boys. The play shows how the dowry is framed as a "compensation" (a beyond-fictitious construction, and not only because the woman will work tirelessly in the new home) for the supposed

Examples but Not Models   117

"inferiority" of the woman. If the dowry is not paid after marriage, which is often the case, that non-payment becomes the justification for mistreatment.

4   The beautiful film by Jeanne Dosse—*Jana Sanskriti: A Theater on the Field* (Paris: Mémoire Magnétique, 2005)—captures admirably the atmosphere of a Jana Sanskriti performance in a village that is new to them, as well as what is at stake for actors and spectators.

5   The local teams, however, have enough autonomy to be able to carry out campaigns on topics that are uniquely relevant to their areas, whether or not they form alliances with other teams.

6   David Harvey, (2011), 47.

7   A total of 1,307 kilometers is the equivalent of 812 miles.

8   An important warning to be made here: I don't speak Bengali or any other Indian language and what little I know about Indian politics came to me largely through conversations with members of Jana Sanskriti, especially Sanjoy Ganguly.

9   All of these expressions were drawn from the Jana Sanskriti website (http://www.janasanskriti.org/index.html) on 12 Jan. 2016.

10   To my knowledge, this was the only TO meeting to have been held in a neighborhood on the social margins. Arrentela is a neighborhood built in the 1970s to house workers from Portuguese colonies in Africa. Today, Arrentela suffers from the common ills of similar neighborhoods across several European countries: a lack of public services with the exception of the omnipresent police, degradation of buildings, populations with unemployment rates even higher than the national average, racism .... Without fetishizing suffering or life on the social periphery in general, I still believe that the fact that Óprima! was the only gathering—that I know of—to have happened in such a context says a great deal about Óprima! itself—and about the currently existing world of TO.

11   Though the legend of the dramaturgy seminar gives this exaltation a very destructive rage—a legend put forward in the book by Paula Autran, *Theory and practice of the dramaturgy seminar at Teatro de Arena* (São Paulo: Portal Editora, 2015)—the evaluation rounds that are part of Óprima! are marked by a camaraderie that judges the plays of others from an equal position. There is no didactic arrogance here on the part of anyone, but in everyone a sincere concern to find the forms that are best adapted for the reproduction of reality.

12   Augusto Boal, "Depoimentos sobre o teatro brasileiro hoje: Augusto Boal," TUSP, SP. *Revista aParte* (March–April, 1968), 4.

13   Inês Barbosa, *Crise, Austeridade e ação coletiva: experiências de aprendizagem crítica com Teatro do Oprimido* (Braga: Doutorado na Universidade do Minho, 2016), 280.

14   Ibid., 283.

15   Pierre Bourdieu, *Contrafogos* (Rio de Janeiro: Jorge Zahar Editor, 1998), 73 and 75.

16   The particular use of language by KSK was an extremely astute way to represent the life of Maria (as well as thousands of other Marias). To her boss and to her doctor, she would have to speak Portuguese, a language with which she was not at ease. In her house, she would speak in Creole to her kids, who would answer back in Portuguese. The only place where she could find some linguistic intimacy was on public transportation, where she could speak and hear Creole with all the other women her age, who would, like her, go to and from their homes on the periphery of Lisbon to clean the houses and workplaces of the capital of a country that had colonized hers.

17   Herbert Marcuse, *One-Dimensional Man* (London and New York: Routledge & Kegan Paul, 1964), 113.

18   Theodor W. Adorno, "On the Fetish-Character in Music and the Regression of Listening" (1999), 71.

19   Ibid., 102.

20   Here, again, I do not mean popular in the sense of "well-liked" but instead in the sense of being by and for the people.

21   In the movement's schools, the children's parents are invited not only to help repair and clean the spaces and to prepare food, but also to participate in monthly assemblies in which the school's pedagogical project is debated and built. The spaces created by the MPLD try to break with the immobility imposed by both the rights "given" to citizens and the logic of merchandise being presented to the consumer in its already finished form. MPLD spaces tend to be open processes; they do not provide a finished product but instead propose a way of doing, a type of action, in a manner that requires the participation of the supposed "receiver" of a particular social service. Therefore, the "receiver" becomes hardly that at all, instead genuinely participating in the realization of the process and in its conception,

22 hence making it open to change, modification .... Schools constitute just one example of a setting where MPLD enacts such processes.
22 The reader who already knows the very important book by Iná Camargo Costa, *A hora do Teatro Épico no Brasil,* can already guess how useful it was for us to read it. It served as a script, and in it we found several of the analyses of dramatic form that were provided to the audience between the scenes.
23 Anderson Gomes was the driver of the car in which Marielle Franco was traveling when she was assassinated on March 14, 2018. He, too, was fatally shot that day.
24 In Brazil, an occupation is an unproductive or unused piece of land or an empty building that is—in accordance with the law that stipulates that every piece of land or building needs to have a social purpose—requisitioned by movements in order to make it possible for families to live there.
25 +Nós (+Us) is a network of what are known in Brazil as pre-test schools. The network was created by the social movement Rua—Juventude Anticapitalista (Street—Anticapitalist Youth). In Brazil, due to the destruction of public education enacted by so many governments, the public schools are often not very good. Therefore, in various working-class neighborhoods, many social movements organize schools that teach all that is necessary to pass the test in order to be accepted into college.
26 Walter Benjamin, *Passagens* (Belo Horizonte: UFMG, 2006), 518.

10 The Search for a Subjunctive Theatre

The limitations of the bourgeois dramatic form

As I discuss elsewhere in this book, it is an apparent contradiction that Augusto Boal—the founder of the Arena Theatre Dramaturgy Seminar, a student of John Gassner, a professor at Escola de Arte Dramática (School of Dramatic Art, a major theatre school in São Paulo), and the author of such a critical essay on Aristotelian dramaturgy—has written so little about the need for a specific dramaturgy for Forum Theatre. This contradiction appears to be resolved if we consider the centrality of his bet on the emancipatory virtues of the spectator's onstage interventions. From that perspective, we might begin to understand how such a wager may have come to eclipse all other considerations (things like dramaturgy or acting style), rendering them minor or even conservative issues for him in comparison to the revolution of having spectators enter the space of the stage.

> Thus, in the first place, it is a question of seeking the opposite effect to that of Aristotelian catharsis—it seeks to dynamize the spectator: instead of eliminating *harmatia* (that is, the subversive, transforming, revolutionary character) that exists in every oppressed person, we try to increase it, stimulate it, make it grow. Brecht tried the same, but in my view he was halfway there. What is insufficient in Brecht is the lack of spectator action. His theatre is also cathartic, because it is not enough for the spectator to think: it is also necessary for him to act, activate, perform, do. Brecht's mistake was not realizing the indissoluble character of ethos and dianoia, action and thought. He proposes to dissociate and even oppose the spectator's and the character's thinking, but the dramatic action continues to be independent from the spectator, who remains in the spectator's condition.[1]

Here A. Boal identifies the source of theatre's coercive power not so much in a dramaturgy whose call to identification purges any anti-system impetus. Instead, he focuses on the theatrical coercion enforced by a division of the world that establishes the stage as a place where one can speak and act in contrast to an audience of undisturbed passivity, a division parallel to the one that operates in society as a whole. The question of theatrical writing—of dramaturgy itself—then becomes logically obsolete for anyone who wants to make true political theatre. Though several concrete examples are given, the indications about dramaturgy itself are almost non-existent in his writings. In the book *Theatre of the Oppressed*, on theatre-debate, the first way of referring to Forum Theatre, he states only that "a ten- or fifteen-minute skit portraying that problem and the solution intended for

120   *Are There No Alternatives?*

discussion is improvised or rehearsed, and subsequently presented."[2] In the book *Stop, C'est Magique!*, a long passage insists on the difference between psychodrama and Forum Theatre, a difference attributed to the fact that Forum Theatre would be "the theatre of the plural first-person."[3] Though individual accounts constitute the basis for the construction of a Forum Theatre play, "in the process of its elaboration, however, the individual story must grow, multiply, and must contain in its final fabulation the majority's problem and not only that of an individual who originated the model for the story." He gives no indication as to how this dramaturgical transposition operates. Even more surprising given the later success of Forum Theatre specifically, it is Forum Theatre that is not even mentioned in the 1982 edition of *Games for Actors and Non-Actors*.

Only in the book *Legislative Theatre*, published in 1996, does A. Boal feel the need to establish "a well-structured, reliable scheme" for Forum Theatre dramaturgy. This need arose from the proposal of Legislative Theatre itself. In 1992, he was elected as a vereador (city council member) for the city of Rio de Janeiro; he had been put forward as a candidate by the Workers' Party (Partido dos Trabalhadores, or PT). Swimming against the PT's current (from 1994 onward, the PT no longer bet on the creation of popular nuclei and witnessed a decline in its internal democracy[4]), A. Boal collaborated with advisors, social movements, and favelas to create 19 Theatre of the Oppressed (TO) groups. Those groups had the task of creating presentations that demanded input from the population about the kinds of laws necessary to solve the problems posed by the plays. The responses from the population then passed through a "metabolising cell" that transformed some of the proposals into bills. Thus, 13 laws were enacted, one of them being the first witness protection law to exist in Brazil.

This intense work of multiplication of groups in popular (poorer or working-class) neighborhoods explains the need for a "formula," a more defined dramaturgical structure that can make the transmission of ideas easier—and can simultaneously transmit *too much* ease in the sense of making the proposals that arise out of that structure more facile. Other moments that called for schematization—a kind of container for the dramaturgy to make it more portable—continued to emerge over time. There were major projects that A. Boal and his collaborators brought to fruition, like the one carried out in various prisons across the country, thanks to funding from an English agency. Then support from the Lula presidential administrations allowed the Center for Theatre of the Oppressed—Rio de Janeiro (known as CTO-Rio)—to carry out several additional projects and the important work of TO dissemination "inside Brazil and around the world," to quote an expression often used by the group.[5] Thus, CTO-Rio held Joker training workshops all over Brazil, especially in the north-northeast of the country, as well as in Guinea-Bissau, Angola, Senegal, and Mozambique. Those latter trainings were always carried out with African partner groups who continued to multiply the techniques (GTO-Mozambique, for example, currently has several dozen theatre teams). We must also take into account the numerous workshops carried out independently by members of CTO-Rio as well as workshops by A. Boal himself (workshops that I followed as an assistant for eight years), in which the structure below was invariably used to explain Forum Theatre Dramaturgy (Figure 10.1).

We can find several points in common in the dramaturgical frames or formulas communicated across many of these kinds of projects and trainings. The first is a rehabilitation of Aristotle, whose "three unities are useful, not as laws, but as general rules, guidelines, suggestions."[7] What actually made those Aristotelian unities [those of time, place, and action] useful for TO in this case is that they helped oppose the tendencies of groups to "relate sagas that stretch in time and space," "to want to include everything in their plays," and to dissolve the action into a patchwork "to be avoided."[8] More importantly, A. Boal framed Forum Theatre as having as its essence—as he suggested all theatre did—"the conflict of free wills, conscious of the means

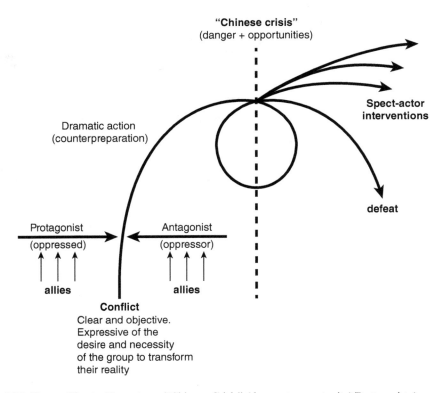

Figure 10.1 [Forum Theatre Dramaturgy/"Chinese Crisis" (danger + opportunity)/Protagonist (oppressed)—dramatic action—allies/Antagonist (oppressor) counterpreparation—allies/Conflict—Clear and objective. Expressive of the desires and needs of the group to be transformed into reality./Outcome/Alternatives from the spectators.][6]

they employ to attain their goals, which must be simultaneously subjective and objective."[9] Though these wills must express forces that are social in nature, this transposition from the social reality to the stage is carried out by reducing oppression to actions consciously performed by the character of the oppressor.

> The dramatist must pit the Protagonist against the representatives of these abstract powers. Sure, society is the oppressor, but who are its agents? One cannot present a character called "Society" or "Education" or "State Repression": we need to personify, to concretise in a person, a character, the means by which society, the education system, or the repressive power of the state, oppresses the Protagonist.[10]

What is left out here is precisely the impersonal rule of capital or other systems of oppression. In other words, this conception does not attend to the mechanisms by which oppression is exercised without the mediation of conscious subjects, though it could easily be argued that these mechanisms are precisely the most important in society. Thus, to say that in a play "on racial prejudice the nucleus of the conflict must treat precisely that: a victim of prejudice struggling against the prejudiced discriminator" leaves unanswered a series of questions that could

122　*Are There No Alternatives?*

legitimately be asked: Why does the discriminator discriminate?[11] Why do they have the power to do so? Why does society accept this kind of attitude? Are there forms of racial discrimination that do not require the mediation of a conscious agent? ... By avoiding those questions, we would, to rephrase Brecht, deal only with the abuse of power by an individual and not with power itself, constituted at a given moment, in a certain society. This theatrical form that reduces everything to the relationship between individuals has a name—drama—and there is already a long history of criticism of its limits.

According to Peter Szondi, the dramatic theatre reproduced on stage the emancipation from a god-centered cosmology that Renaissance society was experiencing as a whole. Therefore, what was most important on stage were the relations between individuals (and no longer their relations with angels or demons). The most important act was the one of deciding; the decision was the proof of freedom. Dialogue had a supremacy in order to mirror the fact that the arena of life was exclusively that of the relationship between equals. In this sense, drama was absolute and autonomous. Nothing beyond the stage existed, nor was there anything underneath the character's dialogue.[12]

It can be debated how much Forum Theatre—and drama itself as a form—would in fact be absolute and autonomous. After all, typically, in introductions to Forum Theatre plays, jokers explain the origin of the group performing, the need for the play, and the rules of a forum process. All of those could be interpreted as prologues devoid of drama, bringing into the play the externality that is banished by the form of the drama itself. In addition, Forum Theatre scenes are rarely performed on a proscenium stage, which is, according to Szondi, the only stage configuration appropriate for the drama. The illusion of full reality is difficult to maintain, for example, in favelas or public squares.

I maintain, however, that Forum Theatre comes close to drama in essential ways. If—in causal, narrative-based drama—"each moment contains the germ of the future, each scene must imply the next, hence imposing the unity of time and space,"[13] Forum Theatre works with "1. assembling the framework of the conflict; 2. unleashing the climax, the explosion; 3. producing the outcome; and so on, in succession, with greater intensity each time."[14] This sequence of time, which accumulates energy toward an explosion, was precisely a characteristic of dramatic theatre criticized by Brecht, in which, according to him, everything carried out onstage prepares the catastrophe to come, making the whole a sort of introduction to the catastrophe.

But the profound kinship between narrative drama and Forum Theatre happens in the construction of plays that pose intersubjective relationships as an insurmountable horizon for the themes presented and find dialogue to be their most powerful tool. Today there are some Forum Theatre plays that proceed without words, without voiced dialogue. At the same time, that does not necessarily avoid the characters in a scene being portrayed as conscious and free subjects. By that I mean that often, even in these scenes without spoken text, characters who are absolutely transparent to themselves—unaffected by unconscious divisions or social constraints— face each other, thus approaching the "pure drama [which] seems to attribute to the human person a privileged position, of almost absolute autonomy"[15]—and where the relations of power take place without mediations, between individuals.

It is by no means my intention to deny that this dramaturgical schema has been able to spark several extremely interesting processes. Even Brecht, a staunch critic of drama, recognized that, on certain occasions, what he called Dramatic Theatre could be more productive than Epic Theatre. According to the German author, the Dramatic Theatre could be, in extremely tense social situations, the spark that ignites the fire, politically speaking, while a non-dramatic theatre would face more difficulties in promoting an immediate action.

The Search for a Subjunctive Theatre 123

I am interested in probing the limitations (any formula or schematic has them) that this dramatic schema may have, limitations that have already been observed on many of the occasions previously described. These limitations appear to be of two distinct kinds.

First, we have the interesting paradox that Forum Theatre—which aims to make us realize that the lived reality is one of many possible realities, where the virtual is summoned with all its weight to explode the assumption that reality is inevitable, and whose creator affirms that it is not just that another world is possible but that *many* other worlds are possible—would have only one dramaturgical schema to fit all the oppressions that exist. Are there alternatives to everything but Forum Theatre dramaturgy? Would this one dramaturgical schema be the only exception to the universal contingency of the world? Wouldn't that be a fetishism of a supposedly universal dramaturgy? It is impossible for me not to think here about the story of Brecht's Mr. Keuner, where the latter, tasked by a gardener to carve a tree in the shape of a ball—failing to achieve the desired shape, cutting too much on one side, then too much on the other—ends up reaching the sphere but only after having cut almost all of the branches off. The gardener, upon returning, admits that it is a ball but asks, disappointed, where is the tree? Aren't we, TO practitioners, doing just that? Of course, we have Forum Theatre plays that follow the model, but how does that model fully account for the reality of oppressions that we intend to fight? Though, for A. Boal, "techniques were created to help people; people were not created to serve the techniques," this advice seems not to have been followed in the actually existing world of TO, much of which seems to believe that a single dramaturgical model can tackle, for example, both homophobia in a family and the consequences of the 2008 crisis in the labor market.

The second category of limitations that I want to address relates to the constraints of this specific model. As I explored above, portraying the real as only constituted by intersubjective relationships necessarily leads to individualizing problems that simply cannot be understood on such a scale. In this sense, A. Boal's proposal to surpass the reach of previous political theatre falls, both feet together, right back at the contradictory place where it was born in Brazil. Let's return to the problems exposed by Iná Camargo Costa regarding the play *They Don't Use Black Tie*.

> As scholars of Brecht's work know, work strikes are not a matter of a dramatic nature, as the resources offered by dramatic dialogue—the drama's instrument par excellence—hardly reach their breadth. Drawing on the repertoire of the old formal logic, we could say that the extent (the size) of this subject is greater than the vehicle (the dramatic dialogue).[16]

In the best case scenario, we fall into an aesthetic opposition between form and content, wanting to solve problems that constitute society as a whole, but in the more circumscribed sphere of the family. In the worst case scenario, we resolve this opposition by creating representations that are perfectly attuned to the dominant discourse so effectively summarized by Margaret Thatcher when she said that there is no society—only individuals. We have already witnessed the issues linked to this kind of representation: the moralization of political problems, the invisibility of the very structures that promote impersonal domination, the need to designate the oppressors as perverse individuals, the supposed accountability of the oppressed people who, as individuals, would always be imagined as having the possibility of "turning around" their role as victims of oppression. If Forum Theatre is, in fact, as A. Boal said, a question asked of its audience, then the way in which this question is formulated through drama limits the interventions made by the spect-actors to certain types of answers. I would like to focus next on offering a typology of these interventions, one based not on static evidence but on observation

124   *Are There No Alternatives?*

of countless Forum presentations. I believe that this typology encompasses almost all types of interventions that I have witnessed.

The first—and most common—category of interventions could be referred to as abstract heroism. In a scene about domestic violence already described in this book, one abstractly heroic alternative proposed by a spect-actor intervention had a woman facing abuse simply packing her bags and leaving, slamming shut the door of her marital home, without further difficulty or details to figure out. Where will she go (knowing that, in most cities in the world, securing a spot in a refuge for victims of domestic violence can be an arduous task, and that, if she goes to a friend's house, her husband might go after her there)? How will she support herself? What will the husband do the next day? Does she have children, and how might that reality shape the situation? In other words, with a proposed alternative that is based on abstract heroism, concrete questions or problems tend to be relegated to the distant background. The important thing in such interventions appears to be the demonstration of one's ability to choose. Pondering the concreteness—or not—of the possibilities proposed does not seem to be a relevant concern. Such an approach frames solving the problem as being all about willpower alone. The motto of French Maoism "Drive the cops out of your heads!" today becomes Nike's slogan: "Just do it!"

A variation of this first type of intervention is one in which the spect-actor calls into the scene a representative of the law as a way of solving the problem. In most situations, the cast and the audience tend to respond favorably to this alternative. I myself witnessed a play in which Justice—an integral part of the same state that, in the first scene, had appeared as the perpetrator of the genocide of black people through its military police—intervened favorably as soon as requested to resolve a case of labor discrimination in which the victim's Afro hair style didn't fit her employer's beauty standards.[17] Faith in the ability of a Brazilian justice system to provide for all who need it is obviously not a result of the life experiences of those people who were gathered together that night. The source of this belief is probably to be found paradoxically in a complete inability to imagine a solution that is not illusory. The obstructed horizon of the struggles against oppression—or the very inexistence of that horizon for many of that generation who were present there—opened up space to a phantom presence of state power as a manifestation of a desire for reparation.

The second type of intervention is that of accommodated oppression. In this type of intervention, the spect-actor does not confront power but accepts it so as not to suffer its most fearsome manifestations. In the United States, for example, one group showed how to react when you are a person of color and your car is pulled over by the police. Interventions followed, and, one after another, we saw spect-actors push themselves to increase their ingenuity on stage: keeping their hands on the steering wheel, turning on the car light, lowering the window carefully, making only the slightest possible movements when reaching for the papers in the glove compartment, etc. The only question that hadn't been asked was why a black person, a Latino/a/é person, or anyone else should fear for their lives in front of a police officer? The world presented was immutable; the task that remained for Forum Theatre was to teach us how to adapt to it.

The third and last category inside this little typology that I am constructing here speaks to a type of intervention that comes up more rarely. In it, the spect-actor tries to represent on stage how much they are being dehumanized by the oppressor. The latter, faced with that spectacle, becomes aware that, by submitting the oppressed to such treatment, they also dehumanize themselves. The oppressor, therefore (at least as it is presented), stops oppressing. In Austria, for example, an Iranian group presented a version of *Antigone*.[18] The recent popular demonstrations in Iran at that time had been harshly repressed; bodies in the streets were guarded by soldiers, who prevented family members from burying their dead. The intervention in the forum version of *Antigone* that was hailed as the most successful was performed by a spect-actor who remained

The Search for a Subjunctive Theatre   125

motionless at first, letting tears run down their face. After a while, with a slow dignity, their watery eyes fixed on the soldier, who remained petrified. The spect-actor, as Antigone, approached her brother's body to hold him in her arms and carry him, stepping back, always keeping her tearful gaze on her oppressor, who was unable to carry on with their oppressive stance.

Many are the Forum Theatre examples in which the lack of mediations between these dualist (individual oppressor versus individual oppressed) contradictions limits the space of the scene to clichés and abstractions. The characters then become a mere transposition of the figure of the small producer, a foundation of capitalist subjectivity: this small producer is individualistic, reduced to a scale of one, and self-focused—a small entrepreneur full of will to win in a society that they perceive as—and that objectively is—hostile to them. These characters are just the flip side of the commodities that we need to buy and sell to have a life in our societies.

Can dialectics break bricks (and help Forum Theatre)?

I am not trying to propose *a* "solution," a dramaturgy 2.0 capable of overcoming all of the problems I have explored here so far. This section's hypothesis is not that these problems have as their only origin a kind of idealist deviationism from Epic orthodoxy on the part of A. Boal, and that, once Epic dramaturgical self-criticism is carried out here, Forum Theatre can be the finally found instrument of theatrical emancipation. My goal here is much more modest.

I want to try to build a more dialectical scheme (the oxymoron in this expression is not lost on me) for two main reasons. The first is that I believe that, when faced with another dramaturgical possibility for the construction of Forum Theatre, practitioners can think of these schemes as propositions, and it is up to them to know which is the most suited to the material they wish to treat—or to invent other schemes so that those dramaturgical structures can correspond in the mostly finely honed ways to the problems that they want to address. The invention of a new dramaturgical schema is a step, I believe, for such structures to be revealed as tools and not dogmas.

The second reason for proposing this more dialectical scheme is that I believe that it is possible to find a dramaturgical structure that, while maintaining interventions by the audience, is more capable of dealing with the mediations through which oppression manifests without falling into the opposite of Guevarist voluntarism, a kind of fetishism of an absolute irrelevance of human activity that was denounced by Erwin Piscator in 1962.

> [...] a historical drama would no longer be possible as a drama of decision, under the pretext that decisions would no longer be possible for the man taken by anonymity, under the mask of devices and socio-political constraints, in the absurd construction of an existence where everything would be decided in advance.[19]

I seek a model that would be created from the assumption that the possibility of praxis still exists, that we act within a world which is in part *already given* and partly *yet to be built*. This model would try to remain equidistant between these two poles, and it would have a protagonist with a certain sense of awareness of the problem inflicted upon them. After all, if the only problem in the situation is the protagonist's lack of consciousness about their oppression, that issue would be quickly solved by interventions in which spect-actors just add their own consciousness to the supposedly more deficient understanding held by the play's protagonist. A spect-actor in the place of a protagonist like Brecht's Mother Courage would, for example, then discover in a second that "[w]hen a war gives you all you earn/One day it may claim something in return."[20] In this model, the fact that the protagonist has a consciousness of their situation, even if a partial

126   *Are There No Alternatives?*

one, would also serve precisely to mark the limits of its importance, since to have a consciousness of what is happening to them would only underscore that the protagonist is incapable—at least all by themselves—of changing the concrete situation that they are suffering.

This consciousness of the protagonist could never be total, but instead should be fragmentary, intermittent, perhaps like the characters in Brecht's play *The Days of the Commune*, who sometimes understand the need to invade Versailles and sometimes fall in love with themselves and the event that they created, to borrow Slavoj Žižek's expression about Occupy Wall Street protesters. This partial consciousness would be affected by the need to face an unavoidable difficulty. One example could be the need to find support so that a friend who has suffered domestic violence can feel safe to at least talk about what happens to them, as in the play *Claire's Party* by the French group Féminisme Enjeux. Or another example could be the need for employees to organize themselves in a cafeteria so that they are entitled to lunch, as in the piece *In the same boat?* by the group GTO-Lavapiés in Spain. But the idea is that being confronted with the difficulty in question would be just the motivation necessary for the protagonist to go looking for other oppressed people with whom they can possibly form alliances.

Therefore, it would not be a matter of putting on stage decisive confrontations between monolithic characters, and instead a matter of attempting to show the present moment not as "homogeneous and empty," but full of contradictions, of dynamics to navigate.

I am talking here about an attempt to represent oppression not as an impenetrable and smooth system, but as a system composed by flaws, edges, and hollow spots that could possibly—when taken together—sketch the outline of the narrow door through which our hopes could pass. The scenes between the "great oppressor" and the primary oppressed character would then lose meaning as representations—reduced to a narrow individual dimension—of fables about a "Grand Soir," a unique and redemptive revolutionary event.[21] "[T]he course of events cannot be changed at its peaks, not by heroic virtue and resolution, but only through strictly ordinary habitual actions, through reason and practice," as Benjamin wrote about Epic Theatre.[22] The goal of this new dramaturgical schema would be to create a structure that avoids the specter of an ecstatic final struggle, instead grounding itself in the search for alliances and the contradictions that follow.

These possible allies should be "subjugated subversives," following here a fruitful definition of the oppressed posed by A. Boal.[23] This split—between the potential for subversion and the reality of submission—could follow some of the theses on Mao Tse-Tung's dialectic summarized by Alain Badiou.

In a process (that is, in a system of contradictions) there is always a contradiction that is primary.

Every contradiction is asymmetrical: in other words, one of the terms of the contradiction is always dominant over the general movement of the contradiction itself. It is the theory of the primary aspect of contradiction.

There are contradictions of different types whose resolutions come from different processes. The main distinction to be made in the matter is [the one] between antagonistic and non-antagonistic contradictions.[24]

Here the possible allies would be figures crossed by such contradictions that—even if they somehow help maintain the antagonistic contradictions—they are not antagonistic in and of themselves. One pole of a contradiction—which would hold them in submission—would

The Search for a Subjunctive Theatre 127

always be dominant. This pole shouldn't be an absolutely material constraint. (An example of an absolute constraint given frequently by A. Boal in workshops was a character with his hands tied, blindfolded, in front of a platoon about to execute him; that character has no alternative.) Yet neither should the dominant pole of the contradiction be strictly ideological in nature. The overestimation of the ideological factor tends to create characters who appear unintelligent, who are somehow brainless zombies lazily reproducing television discourses—people who in fact only exist for those who deny the vigor of commodity fetishism. This overestimation of ideological factors goes hand in hand with another overestimation, that of the role of activists, teachers, artists, and others whose task is, in many cases, precisely to work on representations. The overestimation of those roles is linked with the underestimation of the "common people" who would need the help of the artists to emancipate themselves from the chains that television, social media, and other forms would put on their minds, as if the spectators were completely helpless in front of those representations. The other pole of the contradiction, the potentially subversive one, should also be material in some way. By that I mean that a character could not be materially dependent on war for their survival and, at the other end, only have pacifist opinions. The character of *Mother Courage* loses her children—whom she loves, but who are also productive forces in her work—to war.

The protagonist's task would then be to try to influence these contradictions so that they are resolved in the sense of combating oppression. These contradictions, embodied in characters, should tentatively represent the specific contradictions that cross the terrain inhabited by oppressed people in a concrete situation of oppression. To give some tangible examples, let's turn first to a workshop where a scene featuring a driver of a motorcycle taxi was created. That driver lived in a favela, and the gentrification of the favela simultaneously placed him in a situation of advantage and disadvantage all at once. Gentrification was favorable for the driver because he could charge triple for his rides on weekends—when people from outside the favelas would go there to visit or drink in hip bars that were cropping up in some of those favelas at the time—but it was unfavorable because it entailed a significant increase in rent prices and in the general cost of living. In another example, a play by the group Féminisme Enjeux, it was somehow precisely because a teenager knew what sexism was all about that she did nothing to prevent her friend from being victimized by it. The fear of reprisal immobilized her in the face of what she knew was oppression. How can we build an alliance with that taxi driver? How can we respond to that teenager's concrete fear so that she can help her friend? These would be the questions that the audiences would have to face in a version of Forum Theatre intended to represent the difficulties in building alliances in these asymmetrical struggles against oppression.

A concern expressed by A. Boal—in an essay on the dialectical interpretation of the actor—could be useful here. A dialectical interpretation is not just the addition of different aspects to a character, but an articulation that combines those characteristics, showing how they are mutually constitutive for a character: it is precisely because there is the one aspect of that character that the other aspect exists. We can find an example in the character of Vidinha in the play *O Patrão Cordial (The Cordial Boss)* by Companhia do Latão (based in São Paulo). As the boss's daughter, Vidinha does not exploit, nor is she exploited, allowing her to truly believe in the oneness of humanity to the point of being able to fall in love with her father's driver. However, by pursuing this passion, she would put herself at risk of also becoming an exploited person, a risk from which she ultimately runs away. It is because of her class position that she simultaneously can and cannot love whomever she wants. The need for this sequence of events is in turn linked to the need to show the instability of these processes, or, in Brecht's wording, to show that "it is because things are what they are that things will not remain what they are."[25]

128 *Are There No Alternatives?*

These characters in turn should be divided into different groups. These split characters, who are at the same time oppressed and pillars of oppression, are located in different spheres whose effects conjugate each other, voluntarily or not, and reinforce the system of oppression. To engage the above example again, the fight against sexism in a school takes place both at the level of the students (where we find the teenager who is reluctant to help her friend precisely because she knows that she would be exposing herself to the same mistreatment) and at the levels of the teachers and the parents' association. A play must show these different spheres so that oppression does not appear to be caused by a single agent. By multiplying the foci, we can represent oppression as a system that necessarily exists through a variety of mediations. The graphic representation of the dramatic structure could then shift from the confrontation between two forces without internal flaws or cracks (individuals who are imagined as pure oppressors or pure oppressed) to something closer to Alexander Calder's mobiles: unstable structures always liable to be unbalanced if one of their parts suffers interference—an obtrusion that would lead to a rebalancing but not necessarily cause the collapse of the structure. This schema would have the task of helping outline a dramaturgy capable of dealing with oppression as a central category of our society. In it, the oppressive and oppressed groups, categories that would refuse any moralistic definition, would oppose each other within a conflict with countless mediations, whose initial conditions would determine a landscape of possibilities without mechanically determining who would win. A contingent element, open to the intentional action of a collective subject, would constitute this terrain. The spect-actor, upon entering this field, would have to intervene in it to extract all the possibilities at the same time present in it and constrained by it. This exercise would allow the spect-actor to consolidate a "practical sense of the possible," to quote Daniel Bensaïd's beautiful expression.[26]

Notes

1 Augusto Boal, *Stop: C'est magique!* (Rio de Janeiro: Editora Civilização Brasileira, 1980), 83–84.
2 Augusto Boal, *Theatre of the Oppressed*, trans. Charles A. and Maria-Odilia Leal McBride (New York: TCG, 1985), 139. Translation copyright 1979.
3 Augusto Boal, *Stop: C'est magique!* (Rio de Janeiro: Editora Civilização Brasileira, 1980).
4 In this sense, see the enlightening testimony (in Portuguese) by Luiz Mario Benkhein, A. Boal's advisor in his mandate as city councilor, in the catalogue for the exhibition on Augusto Boal at Centro Cultural Banco do Brasil. Available at: http://culturabancodobrasil.com.br/portal/wp-content/uploads/2015/01/boal_catalogo_COMPLETO.pdf. Accessed on 17 November 2016.
5 Luiz Inácio Lula da Silva—usually known simply as Lula—was president of Brazil from 2003 to 2010.
6 This drawing was made by my father for use as part of CTO-Rio's pedagogical work.
7 Augusto Boal, *Legislative Theatre: Using Theatre to Make Politics*, trans. Adrian Jackson (Abingdon and New York: Routledge, 1998), 55.
8 Augusto Boal, *Legislative Theatre: Using Theatre to Make Politics*, trans. Adrian Jackson (Abingdon and New York: Routledge, 1998), 54–55. Here we have to take into account the fact that A. Boal always thought realistically about the possibilities of these groups of non-professionals—often with very precarious lives—to be able to find enough time to produce theatre. His recommendations always took into account the concrete situations of the people with whom he worked, people who typically had no previous theatre experience and who did not live in the sort of conditions that were most conducive to staging a performance.
9 Ibid., 58.
10 Augusto Boal, *Legislative Theatre: Using Theatre to Make Politics*, trans. Adrian Jackson (Abingdon and New York: Routledge, 1998), 62.
11 Ibid., 63.
12 Peter Szondi, *Teoria do Drama Moderno* (São Paulo: Cosac Naify, 2011), 24.
13 Anatol Rosenfeld in Szondi Ibid. 196.

The Search for a Subjunctive Theatre 129

14 Augusto Boal, *Legislative Theatre: Using Theatre to Make Politics*, trans. Adrian Jackson (Abingdon and New York: Routledge, 1998), 64.
15 Anatol Rosenfeld, *O Teatro Épico* (São Paulo: Editora Perspectiva, 2008), 44.
16 Iná Camargo Costa, *A hora do teatro épico no Brasil* (Rio de Janeiro: Paz e Terra, 1996), 24.
17 This performance occurred at the Third International Conference on Theatre of the Oppressed and Universities on August 5, 2016.
18 This performance occurred at the World Forum Theatre Festival, held in October 2009.
19 Erwin Piscator in Olivier Neveux, *Politiques du Spectateur* (Paris: Éditions la Découverte, 2013), 41.
20 Bertolt Brecht, *Mother Courage and Her Children*, trans. Eric Bentley (New York: Grove Press, 1955), 33.
21 "Grand Soir" is a French expression. I use it here to gesture toward the portrayal of a revolution as an event that could be carried out in a single night.
22 Walter Benjamin, "The Author as Producer," trans. Jon Heckman, *New Left Review* 1/62 (1970). Available at: https://www.marxists.org/reference/archive/benjamin/1970/author-producer.htm. Accessed 21 September 2022.
23 Augusto Boal, *The Rainbow of Desire,* trans. Adrian Jackson (Abingdon and New York: Routledge, 1995), 42.
24 Alain Badiou, *Théorie de la contradiction* (Paris: François Maspero, coll. Yenan «synthèses», 1976), 48.
25 This phrasing is a popular aphoristic translation of a notion expressed by Galileo to Andrea in Brecht's *Life of Galileo.*
26 Daniel Bensaïd, *Penser/Agir* (Paris: Lignes, 2008), 44.

11 Exercises Toward a More Dialectical Practice of Forum Theatre

Here you will find the games and exercises that I use the most in the work we do at the Popular Theatre School (Escola de Teatro Popular—ETP) or in workshops that I facilitate beyond ETP. These are exercises that I find useful and that are not included in the book *Games for Actors and Non-Actors*. The purposes of the exercises vary. Some serve to break the ice between participants, others to talk collectively about oppression. The ones that I consider the most important here try to develop a more dialectical performance.

If a new dramaturgy for Forum Theatre demands split characters—who are at the same time oppressed and pillars of oppression—then it also requires a different performance in which the actor learns to perform two feelings at the same time. The goal is not to act happy *or* serious, introverted *or* explosive, but to try to embody the dialectic: a performance in which the actor somehow shows the audience that they are hiding their feelings from another character, a performance in which the audience can understand what is happening to the character precisely while seeing the character *not* fully comprehending what is happening to them, a performance through which a spect-actor can think of alternatives as they see that the action onstage is only one among many possibilities.

In fact, this way of approaching performance is nothing new; in this case, it is just an attempt to bring to Forum Theatre ways of acting that were already present in the work developed by Augusto Boal at the Arena Theatre in São Paulo. It is impressive how—almost without fail—A. Boal places contradictions at the core when talking about the actors' work in Arena, whether in his more developed essays, like "Structure of the Actor's Interpretation,"[1] or in his evoked "invented memories": "Vianninha was playing a character who was supposed to be feeling the anxiety of a person who is climbing up a gorge to save someone and is torn between solidarity and fear."[2]

Almost all the exercises that will be described here aim to help actors develop a contradictory performance that follows Brechtian precepts, according to which, for example, the good actor whose character is supposed to be inebriated must not interpret the drunkenness, but the effort to try to appear sober. These exercises have multiple origins, although many of them have been taught to me by Sergio de Carvalho and Helena Albergaria when I have had the privilege to work with them at the theatre company *Companhia do Latão* in São Paulo.

None of the exercises that will be described in this chapter are universal recipes. Some of them work better in certain environments than others. The facilitator can obviously adapt a given exercise to the places where they decide to use it and allow the participants themselves to adapt how they do it, given a range of factors, including disabilities, pain, and questions of degrees of comfort with physical touch. There will of course also be differences from one cultural context to another or from one person to another about what themes might be considered

DOI: 10.4324/9781003325048-15

Exercises Toward a More Dialectical Practice of Forum Theatre   131

"too serious" for a brief exercise or about who should be able to play whom in such exercises. In ETP's practice, however, we tend to take the approach that the realities that many of the school's participants live right here in Brazil are already concretely serious enough that we don't need to avoid engaging those realities even in short exercises, and we also have collectively allowed the inhabiting of identities very different from our own in terms of the roles played in exercises or even onstage. As A. Boal always maintained, the exercises exist for the people doing them, so each group or facilitator can handle these questions in whatever way they deem best.

Games and Exercises

Chen's good morning

Some games work differently depending on the number of participants. I believe that this one works best when you have ten or more people. Participants should walk at a fast pace around the room. Then the facilitator indicates when it's time to shake hands, and the participants will have one second to find another participant with whom they shake hands and introduce themselves to each other. After that, everyone resumes walking. This time, the facilitator will say "2 people in 2 seconds," then "3 people, 3 seconds," and "5 and 5," until the total number of participants is reached. This is a good game for warming up a group quickly.

Capoeira-chi

I learned this game in a capoeira class; however, I always thought of the game as ultimately functioning in a Theatre of the Oppressed (TO) workshop more like a Tai chi exercise, hence the hybrid name. Two people face each other, arms touching. The initial position of the arms does not matter, but the two must be able to reach the other's face, as this will be precisely the objective of the game. There are, however, certain rules. The arms must be constantly touching. The point of contact between the arms can always be changing, but they must always remain in contact. The movements must be slow and continuous; you cannot make quick, sudden moves to surprise your partner. Feet are not allowed to move. With feet always glued to the same spot, participants will have to contort themselves to reach their partner's face or dodge not to be touched, sometimes mimicking *Matrix* effects! The objective is to touch the other's face, not hit them! Most importantly, it is necessary that no force is used, that the arms remain absolutely relaxed. This is something that should look more like Tai chi than sumo wrestling or arm wrestling! Once the face is touched, the game continues. The game is not about winning or losing, but trying to touch without ever blocking, with movements as fluid as possible. After some time, the facilitator can ask the pairs to break up to find new partners with whom they play the game again. The facilitator can also ask each one to pay attention to their new partner: What do they do differently? How does your height, whether you are taller or shorter than your previous partner, affect your movements? What new strategies can you develop to counter each other without ever blocking your new partner's movements?

Pascal's eyes

Participants are asked to walk around the room. No one is allowed to walk in a circle; each person needs to change directions every three steps. Collectively, participants should always use up the whole space. The speed changes from 0, which would be a complete standstill, to 10, which would be running, but these poles (standstill and running) are never spoken overtly. After a while, the facilitator stops the exercise and introduces the following variant: the participants

132 *Are There No Alternatives?*

form pairs and look straight into each other's eyes. Then the exercise starts again exactly as before; only now each pair will have to move in the space without either member of the pair looking away from their partner's eyes. The facilitator will indicate that it is not a question of following each other's movements, of making parallel moves; each one should move autonomously, the distance between the partners always changing, increasing and decreasing.

Samurai march

Participants are walking around a space until the facilitator asks them to pair up. All pairs will have to play characters with contradictions. The first contradiction, inspired by the duel scene from the movie *Rashomon*, is the one that gives the game its name. Each participant has to imagine themselves as temporarily inhabiting the situation of a samurai in a duel. There is no need, however, to interpret this samurai as many people often imagine them: theatrical and full of unique skills. On the contrary, each participant has to be on the verge of collapse due to the fear of dying, imagining the other participant/samurai to be the most fearsome opponent ever encountered, the best samurai there ever was! Anyway, they must fight, yes, but on the edge of panic. The movements, expressions, and even breathing have to translate how much one inspires terror in the other. This exercise needs to be performed with the utmost realism and with the maximum seriousness!

The facilitator can go on to propose other situations of contradiction to explore. One example is a scenario that is inspired by the beach scene in the film *Moonlight*. Two teenagers of the same gender meet in the most romantic place imaginable. The two are attracted to each other, but ... they are teenagers, and they live in an extremely anti-queer environment. They absolutely want to kiss, touch, but, on the other hand, they almost panic with the thought of being discovered. What if the signs they think they're perceiving from the other are just illusions? What if, when trying to kiss, they are rejected? What if the other tells everyone they're not heterosexual? Desire and panic must go hand in hand in the improvisation inspired by this scene. It is the most excruciating flirtation imaginable, in which you want the other to know but also fear it at the same time. In this improvisation, the fundamental scenario is to explore the contradiction of desire in a situation where the expression of it is strictly forbidden.

Another possibility is to propose a scenario of a duo that belongs to a common group (chess club, social movement, theatre group ...). The two characters have to convince the audience to join them. However, the two members of the group hate each other. One is convinced that the other is going to make an inappropriate comment, or some other concern arises that makes it such that the task for each is to stop the other from speaking. Each one has to try to steal the focus but cannot do it openly. In the most "Freirean" way possible, the most "dialogic" way, one has to get the other person to be quiet ....

Line of power

All participants stand in a circle, and on their backs are taped pieces of paper on which various social roles or functions are written. These roles can be as different as possible: banker, street sweeper, teacher, Uber driver ... but also why not include familial characters such as "father" or "mother" and a few famous people? Everyone will then be able to see the "title" for each other's characters, but they will not be able to see their own name or title. At first, everyone will enter the circle at the same time, mingling. The idea is for each person ultimately to be able to guess what "role" they have on their own back. But be careful! The idea with the mingling is not to represent each other's character! The task is to act as if you were in front of the character you

Exercises Toward a More Dialectical Practice of Forum Theatre   133

are facing! We have to act as we think society would act *in general* toward someone asking for money on the street, a sex worker, a police officer … What would I do *if I ran into* Messi? Do not *act like* Messi! All of this happens without speaking. As participants begin to understand who they are, they must act as the characters they think they are, just as these characters would act in front of others. After everyone has an idea about who their respective characters are (or might be), then a line must be formed that goes from the most important character in society to the least important character. Only once the line is made will the participants have the right to remove the papers they had fixed to their backs to see who they really were. There are no mistakes here, or, rather, even errors can have meaning. I remember, for example, playing this game in the Czech Republic. As the country had been part of the so-called socialist bloc, I put "communist" on the back of one of the participants. The poor guy got scornful looks, people pretending to spit on his shoes. When he was finally able to see who he was, he smiled in relief: "I thought I was a pedocriminal!" After this step, with the participants still lined up, the facilitator can launch a debate: "For whom was it easy to identify one's character? For whom was it not so easy? Why?" The most important question to ask in this debate, however, is whether the participants believe that they have composed the order of the line "correctly," accurately representing the distribution of power in society. Every time I have facilitated this sequence, the answer has been "no," and the debates have begun on what power is and what category or role should be placed where in the line. After this time for debate, a third step can begin: participants are asked to construct an ideal image of society. Generally, the participants cannot reach the objective, but the process is enriched by the possible discussions. Is a line the ideal form to represent a society? If not, what should its form be? Should all the roles given exist in an ideal society? In this case, as in many others, the debates are much more interesting than reaching a consensus.

Zé's The Sun Shines

This game, as the name implies, is a variation on the game The Sun Shines, which I learned from my good friend José Soeiro. At the beginning, we play the game The Sun Shines as it already exists: one person stands in the middle; the others are in a circle, sitting in chairs or standing. The person in the middle then says, "The sun shines for those who …" And that person always looks to say something that could be common for the largest number of people possible: "The sun shines for those who …" like chocolate, ate breakfast today, etc. Then, for those who believe that what has been said is true for them, the task is to get up and, as quickly as possible, move and stand somewhere else. Up until now, everything in my description here corresponds to the traditional version of the game known as The Sun Shines. After a while, a variant is introduced: people in the center of the circle are invited to name oppressions that they have experienced, always with the same intention of trying to formulate their versions of "The Sun Shines for …" in such a way that most people there have experienced something similar. This game seems to me to be very useful in trying to approach the issue of oppression without doing so through the exposition, often painful, of an individual account. What we attempt here is, on the contrary, to build a feeling of commonality or unity by facilitating opportunities to notice that other people have also lived experiences that are similar in some way.

Yes, But

The "Yes, But" game is one already in the TO arsenal, yet it has never really been given the same importance as Colombian Hypnosis, for example, even though it is just as excellent. Two actors will start an improvisation. One of the actors determines which character the

134 *Are There No Alternatives?*

other one is playing and accuses them of something. The second actor has to immediately accept the character, the situation, and the accusation. "Yes, but ...." Then the second actor has to use all their imagination and intelligence to argue against the objection that lies at the heart of the accusation, stating that it is completely normal to have done what they did. What the second actor did, they must somehow argue, constitutes behavior that is in no way reprehensible, quite the contrary. There was no other option .... It has always been done that way .... What would others say if they hadn't done it? The first actor cannot be easily satisfied and must follow up with new accusations, for which the second actor will have to find justifications once again, always starting by saying, "Yes, But ...." The second actor has to find all the possible ways to defend their character. After a certain time, the pair can reverse roles.

This exercise can serve at least two functions. It can be a form of Forum Theatre rehearsal, a situation in which we can rehearse how we will avoid quashing the intervention of our spect-actors with a categorical "no" and instead encourage them to find other arguments to oppose ours. This scenario can also be used in the process of developing scenes, since it can show that possible allies may want to fight against oppression ("Yes ...") but there also might be concrete reasons that make joining the fight difficult ("but ...").

To avoid the participants limiting themselves only to the realm of verbalization, after a while we can ask for some variations. In a variation, the actor-accuser will always have to manipulate objects (real or not), creating spaces as the improvisation takes place. The "Yes, But" actor will not be able to respond verbally before expressing in the most realistic way, with facial expression and body movements, the feeling that the accusation provoked in them (indignation, desire to laugh, pity, etc.).

Yes/no/no/yes

In this exercise, one of the actors asks another for an object or to perform an action, and the other refuses to do so. The action is not intended to be particularly serious in nature, e.g., "Lend me your coat. I'm cold." "No, I don't want to." The first then has to intensify their frustration, becoming more and more annoyed and trying different tactics until the second agrees and decides to hand over the object or perform the demanded action. At that moment, the first person then has to find a reason not to accept the object anymore. The second, appalled by the refusal, then also has to convince the first to accept it again, to do what they said they would do: take the object. Then the first has to refuse again. And the merry-go-round goes round and round until the actors' imaginations have exhausted their possibilities of reasons to refuse.

In this exercise, the balance is the back and forth, the movement. The characters' quarrel not only takes place as an instrumental means to obtain a certain thing, but it also becomes an end in itself (as is true in so many quarrels).

The two poles and the rubber band

This exercise is done with three people. Each in turn has to stand in the center between the other two. When in the middle, the person has to imagine that each of the other participants is a specific character within a contradictory relationship. Each time you approach a pole, it becomes more and more difficult to move forward; the attraction to the other pole gets stronger and stronger until the moment you give in to the tension and move toward the opposing pole. But the tension rises again with each step toward the other pole. There is no resting point. The participant in the middle is like a stone in a slingshot that, by extending further and further, causes the

Exercises Toward a More Dialectical Practice of Forum Theatre   135

force pushing in the opposite direction to increase. The following are two examples of situations that have been performed by participants in response to this prompt: a spouse and lover (with each step toward the lover, the guilt for not being with the beloved spouse and child increases; with each step toward the spouse, the attraction to another life and to the possibilities of a new passion increase); someone suffering from domestic violence and a social worker (with each step toward the spouse, the pressure increases to go to the social worker for a possibility of life without violence; with each step toward the social worker, the fear of being caught increases, the doubts about what will happen to the children, the lack of support from the family—all of these things become heavier).

Helena's circle, or: "I must but I don't want to"

The participants form a circle. A participant starts off paired with the person standing next to them. The improvisation consists of playing a scenario in which you have to touch (or pretend to touch, according to whatever agreement the group in the room or a pair makes) the other person when you don't want to do so. For the purposes of the exercise, all characters and situations are valid, even the ones in which we portray oppressor characters. (Once again, it is fundamentally up to the participants and the facilitator to decide what is acceptable in the workshop room.) As one example, one participant here in Brazil was inspired by this prompt to perform a situation that had happened to her personally, stepping into the role of a racist doctor who had not wanted to attend to her because she was a person of color. Other possible situations that could arise in response to this prompt include a security guard who doesn't want to expel a friend who is stealing food from the supermarket where he works or, as my father proposed to Vianninha, a person who is in the position of having to save someone about to fall from a cliff but, at the same time, is scared of losing their life …. The important thing is to explore through these improvisations some of the contradictions that often arise between individuals and their social functions. Once one of the participants touches (or pretends to touch) the other, the latter launches a new improvisation with the next person in the circle. The exercise ends once everyone in the circle has done their improvisation.

The neutral

Two participants stand face to face, acting in front of the rest of the group. One of them will act with great internal contradiction. The "neutral" person is there primarily to be helpful. The facilitator provides different types of situations as prompts. The one I like to give first is one that so many of us have been through: a couple who have recently separated meet in a bar. The meeting has a purpose: one of them has to return the house keys, or Ophelia has to return Hamlet's love letters to him …. In this scenario, the one who wanted to separate is more or less fine: it's a painful process, but it has to be done, and they don't want to hurt the other person at all. In this scenario, they are the "neutral." The other person is in bad shape: not sleeping or eating properly, thinking solely about their love …. This character is naturally looking forward to the meeting. Yet there is more complexity than that: in front of the former partner, the person will not admit to being down. On the contrary! The character who didn't want the relationship to end at all will say how they "never felt so good," how they've lost weight, not due to sadness but because now there is "finally enough time to hit the gym!" Here we see that performing contradictions does not lead to artifice; rather, it just means that we are having a more attentive eye to what people already do in life. Once this improvisation is over, the person who acted the most contradictions leaves, and another comes into the scene. Whoever was already in the scene

136 *Are There No Alternatives?*

is going to perform the next contradictions offered by the facilitator. Here are some examples of scenarios of contradiction that we use in ETP:

- The burial: In a chapel, while one character mourns the death of a dear family member, the other character, who works for the cemetery, both feels sorry for the grieving relative *and* has to clear the chapel for the next funeral, which is about to start! The employee's job depends on getting the family member out of the chapel as soon as possible, yet they simultaneously have complete empathy for the despair of the person in mourning. I always ask that this situation be acted out in the style of an Italian comedy: very exaggerated!
- The awkward militant: In an occupation, a middle-class militant organizer has to get an occupier to perform a task, attend the assembly, etc. .... The squatter is delighted to finally have a home of their own and is unaware of their precarity. For the militant, this precarity is something that they have never experienced, something they have never known. The militant can't help but be disturbed by the glass of cloudy water they are offered, the meat served in a way that includes parts of the animal that they would never eat, and the only available bathroom being a hole in the ground. But, at the same time, the militant absolutely doesn't want to let the fact that they are disturbed show. This scene is inspired by a person I met when I went to Nepal. This person was organizing against the caste system, even though he was of a very high caste. To demonstrate his politics, he, among other things, ate food made by the untouchables, which is a great taboo. He did that to demonstrate the absurdity of the system. However, he couldn't keep this food in his body; he felt sick every time and ended up throwing up. But the next day, he again ate what was considered "unclean" food. He could neither extract himself from the society that had created him nor be content with it.
- The cell: This situation is inspired by my father's imprisonment. When Heleny Guariba received him in prison, she gave him advice on how to "act" there and, specifically, during the torture session that he was likely to suffer.[3] This advice was useful and useless at the same time. On the one hand, it was more than necessary to welcome my father, to try to calm him down. But it would not have done much good if the torture had been even more brutal; we all have a breaking point. It is in this contradiction that improvisation initiated by this prompt must develop. Everything must be done to try to appease someone with words that we know do not actually have the power to eliminate the threat that surrounds the two characters.

Greetings

Four people are gathered together, and a fifth person arrives and has to greet the group. Each time the motivation is different. The person might want to hide their shyness or that there is someone in the group they hate or love; the person greeting might have a sense of mild superiority or is interested in seducing everyone .... With each new participant, a new motivation will be tried out. This exercise aims to develop an actor's performance based on their ability to show the audience that something is being hidden from the other characters.

Applause game

This game is inspired by the French film *The Taste of Others*. The participant has to pretend to be an actor bowing to their audience, being saluted after a premiere. Among the different actions in front of the public, the actor first has to look for the loved one in the audience, be sad as a result of not finding them, and finally smile when the loved one is spotted. Of course, other versions can be introduced. The participant may find something or someone in the audience

Exercises Toward a More Dialectical Practice of Forum Theatre   137

that causes repulsion, or a panic that will need to be controlled …. The important thing is that we are able to identify—within an action as simple as greeting the audience—all the variations introduced by the participant.

Models for Theatre of the Oppressed

ETP, almost from its onset, used models to construct our scenes. What are models? It has been said countless times, here in this book and elsewhere, that there is no strict compartmentalization between form and content and that critical content cannot be expressed through conservative forms. Worse than that, in fact, the content will become conservative if the chosen form is such. This concern is not new in dramaturgy. Models are scenes that already exist and that were able to find formal solutions to adequately express their contents. Furthermore, these scenes are constructed in such a way that formal structuring principles for other scenes can be extracted from them. Just as, for generations, painters learned to paint by copying those considered masters of their art form, we believe that we have a lot to learn from reinventing scenes from the dramaturgy that came before us. The model scene is *a starting point* for our imagination and not a space for its captivity. It is not a contradiction that the rules we give often serve to set us free. In a way, humans are almost always using models when writing, only unconsciously. These unconscious models are those of the cultural industry to which we are exposed on a daily basis and that we end up reproducing without even realizing it. The decision to use models allows us to, on the contrary, free ourselves from this conditioning by consciously choosing which rules should guide our dramaturgical constructions.

Here I will give examples of three types of models. The first type of model serves for making exercises that try to better understand reality. This model carries dynamics whose objective is not necessarily the construction of a scene but instead a fuller comprehension of a situation. Brecht's didactic pieces are similar, in the sense that he considered them—as I have explained elsewhere in this text—dialectical warm-up exercises for dialectic athletes who are communist militants.

The second type of model serves for the creation of Forum Theatre scenes. I am more and more convinced that a good Forum Theatre play cannot contain only scenes in which there are interventions. The fact that there are interventions into the scene necessarily leads to a representation of the real in which the individual decision has a predominant weight. I am not saying that the individual cannot do anything. I am only saying that the individual cannot do everything. Therefore, it seems to me a satisfactory solution to put these scenes where there are interventions aside and focus on scenes of another type that perhaps point more to how oppression works as a structure of society and therefore cannot be modified on an individual scale only.

The third type of model is composed of scenes whose structure may be interesting to develop in a forum. Usually Forum Theatre sessions, in the dramaturgy conceived by my father or in the one that I proposed earlier, are arenas where a character will try to convince or oppose another. These spaces always host relations between two individuals in which one tries, through argument, to influence the other. It is precisely to break this pattern that I propose the following models.

Model exercises

The subaltern's point of view

There are countless scenes that are constituted precisely by what they exclude: characters who are absolutely necessary in a scene and who might not have their point of view represented. These invisibles often belong to the world of work, but not only. Take the final scene of the film *Breakfast at Tiffany's*, for example: Holly Golightly has just left the police station with Paul Varjak.

138   *Are There No Alternatives?*

She has decided to leave the United States, even if the case against her could get much worse if she flees and even if her Brazilian millionaire has already told her he doesn't want to marry her anymore. She will leave! Paul, on the other hand, is convinced of the need to make her stay. Why keep running away from everything and especially from herself? After all, they love each other and should give this love a chance! All the tension in this scene comes from where they are when it takes place: a taxi. There's a whole game about where she should go: to the airport or the hotel. The taxi will be stopped three times. The third time, Holly gets out, leaving all her luggage behind, looking for Paul, who himself is looking for the cat that Holly left out minutes before. But what would the scene become if it were not staged from the protagonists' point of view, but from the taxi driver's? How did he feel about having to watch a couple fight in his workplace? What were his feelings each time he was asked to change destinations or stop the car? What did he think when he was abandoned along with the suitcases?

The purpose of this model is to include in famous scenes the invisible presence of so many characters who are in fact essential for the scenes to exist in the first place. What do the servants of the Prince who is in love with Cinderella think? Do they think it's funny that they have to work until after midnight? What do the residents of a house destroyed by the quarrels between Batman and Superman think?

Bringing these points of view to light puts a perspective on who the protagonists of the dominant narratives really are, expanding the picture to the point where it fits a little more of society.

Success and failure of the same tactic

Ensuring that a social movement is not defeated requires an astuteness always capable of foreseeing what will be new in the political conjuncture. It is essential to be sensitive to each change that is happening in order to be able to extract from it a lever that can open new paths. The exercise proposed here starts from the assumption that we do precisely the opposite most of the time, that our tendency is to transform tactics that once worked into magic formulas that are always capable of guaranteeing victory. This exercise is based on scenes from a didactic play by Brecht, *The Horatians and the Curiatians*. In it, we encounter an archer who was able to injure his opponent thanks to his position. Although his bow was not that good, he placed himself against the sunlight, blinding his opponent at sunrise. The sun, however, continued rising, and the archer's position was no longer an advantage. The archer ends up dead for not being able to see how the situation was changing and for not accepting that he would need to continue the fight in other ways besides shooting arrows.

With this model, the participants must create a scene in which a certain tactic proves to be very successful at one moment but then later causes the defeat of the group that uses it in another moment. When I think about this model, I can't help but think about the manifestations of June 2013 in Brazil.[4] At the beginning of the June Journeys, the Black Bloc did a most important job; they faced the police, expressing the desire of the masses present to be able to demonstrate without repression. I will never forget the extent of the violence used to repress the teachers or the sarcastic social media post of the police officer showing his broken baton with the phrase "sorry, professor." I remember popular indignation as the next demonstration was being prepared. I remember 100,000 people marching, wanting the police to understand as clearly as possible that their right to go out into the streets could not be impeded. I also remember the satisfaction we felt when, the next day, a photo of an overturned police car with an anarchist on top of it, bearing a huge black flag, was captioned with the words "Sorry, police!" and went viral as a social media post. We had our revenge! But I also can't forget that, when the movement began to die down, the violence of the Black Bloc remained the same, only under different conditions, and it

Exercises Toward a More Dialectical Practice of Forum Theatre   139

became another element leading to the emptying of the streets. At the beginning, the police force let the Black Bloc approach the City Council in Rio, threatening to invade it, setting fire to trash cans. When the television stations had enough recordings of the degradation, however, then the police advanced, beating up both Black Bloc members and protesters. In other words, the same tactic was used in two different moments, with two very different results.

Models to enrich Forum Theatre by contextualizing the scenes that invite spect-actor intervention

Gestus

Many are the debates about the notion of gestus articulated through Brecht's body of work. ETP's understanding of this tool-concept is that it is an image that expresses something typical of society, but precisely in terms of the contradictions that society holds. In other words, gestus is not a question of representing what would be a characteristic gesture of a capitalist, for example, by making him smoke a cigar, but of noticing through images how much our societies force us to act or behave in contradictory ways. Perhaps it is better to delve into the plays of Brecht, who was first and foremost a playwright, not a theorist. The character of Mother Courage carries a contradiction in her name. On the one hand, she is a mother and wants to protect her three children as much as possible. On the other hand, she has the courage to follow an army into the middle of a war to try to sell goods to soldiers. Notice how this contradiction is not just a juxtaposition. In order to feed her children, she needs to be a saleswoman. However, her children are not merely an expense for her. In the first scene, the children pull Mother Courage's cart. They are a production force for her, not just family. In this contradiction evidenced even in her name alone, one side needs the other. In this first scene, we also have a beautiful example of gestus. The recruiting soldiers need to return to headquarters with a new soldier; otherwise, they will be punished. Seeing Mother Courage's children, they get excited and try to seduce them into enlisting. One of the children even seems to want to join them. Mother Courage realizes the danger, calls her children, and asks them to pull the cart again. She's already standing on the cart when one of the soldiers tells another: "Buy something!" "What?" To which the answer is: "It doesn't matter! Fast!" The second soldier takes a coin with one hand and, with the other, takes his belt and shouts that he needs a buckle. Mother Courage, still standing on the top of the cart, twists her body to be able to see him. She gets off the wagon, bites the coin to see if it's good silver, and starts haggling over the buckle. Meanwhile, the first soldier escapes with her child. In this twist of her body, we can see her contradiction. On one side she's a mother, on the other a trader.

In this case, the use of the model proposed is simple. It is only a matter of building a scene in which there is an image that is capable of expressing a contradiction that refers to something greater than the scene, greater than the relationship between those individuals, one that refers to society more broadly. The gestus allows us to go beyond inter-individual relationships without having to bring allegorizing abstractions to the stage. It allows us to witness how society partially sculpts individuals and how the most banal gestures can demonstrate how the structures of oppression are present in the most commonplace relationships.

I have worked a few times with a movement for which I have great esteem, the Roofless Movement of Bahia (Movimento Sem Teto da Bahia, or MSTB). In the first workshop I gave with that movement, I introduced an exercise for gestus creation. All the scenes came alive and were interesting, but one caught everyone's attention. A woman was setting a breakfast table at disproportionate speed. Her two children arrived with a ball, wanting to play. The woman interrupted what she was doing to yell at them, furious that she was now late for work. Once the

140   *Are There No Alternatives?*

table was set, she barely said goodbye to the two of them before running to catch a bus that took her to another stop, where she had to catch a second bus, only to then have to catch a third. Finally, she arrived at her work, where she was greeted by her bosses. She was so good with children; what patience she had! And then with her bosses' two children she would play in a range of ways, including singing songs and playing ball. After work, she would run back to her house again. But as much as she ran, she could never get home in time to catch her children still awake. They were already asleep. She saw a drawing made for her: "Mom, we love you!" She tried to wake them up a little by singing the same songs she sang to the boys at work. But her two sleeping children gestured for her to stop. Precisely because she was a mother, she couldn't be a mother. The *gestus* allowed the emergence of this contradiction so common in Brazil, where domestic work is, at least until recently, the number one job inhabited by women in the state of Rio de Janeiro—and, I imagine, in many other parts of Brazil.

On another occasion, I was working with the Landless Movement, and I asked them to do the same exercise. In the first scene that the participants from the movement constructed, a father tried to play with his son to distract him from his hunger. After a while, the child began to cry. Distraction failed in front of an empty stomach. The father then heard that an enslaved woman who was pregnant had escaped where she was being held and that a good reward was going to be given to anyone who found her. In the next scene, we saw the father with the woman who had been enslaved, telling her that he knew a quick way to get to what is known as a *quilombo* (a community of formerly enslaved persons who are running from slavers). Immediately afterward, the father appeared, caressing the enslaved woman's belly with one hand only to receive with the other hand the reward money from the plantation owner. In the last scene, he fed his son but with a dead man's expression. The whole scene was contradictory. The fun and play exhibited as the father tried to distract his son were both ultimately motivated by hunger. The father, who was asking the woman seeking refuge to trust him, was in fact tricking her. The father had empathy for the woman even as he turned her in. And at the end, the father could no longer relate to the son for whom he had committed such a horror.

"The evilness of the poor"

"The evilness of the poor" is a model designed to show the weight of social dynamics on the individual decisions of the oppressed. We often fall into the ease of portraying oppressed people as being necessarily good, generous, morally superior .... Left-wing films are crammed full of these images. However, most daily empirical evidence shows us that this moral and ethical homogeneity projected onto oppressed peoples does not reflect reality. This model, therefore, does not discuss whether the oppressed are good or bad, but instead how society is structured in such a way that certain actions become almost mandatory for certain categories of people.

I will describe a model here that is, again, inspired by Brecht. In his play *Saint Joan of the Stockyards*, the main character, Joan, goes to the stock exchange along with unemployed workers. Her intention is to show the large-scale capitalists the misery of the unemployed people so that they—taken by pity at the sight of such poverty—decide to lift the lockdown that had been imposed and start employing again. The tactic obviously fails. However, the senior boss, the mighty Mauler, is touched by Joan's candor. He suggests that she visit the factories. She only pities the poor, he suggests, because she doesn't know them, because she doesn't know how bad they are. Joan accepts the challenge and will visit the factories together with Slift, Mauler's assistant.

Joan's first encounter in the factories is with a foreman and an unemployed person. The foreman offers the unemployed individual a job if he will get rid of the jacket of a worker who'd had

Exercises Toward a More Dialectical Practice of Forum Theatre 141

an accident, fallen into the boiler, and will now be scattered across the United States in hundreds of crates of canned beef. The jacket's presence makes a bad impression on the workers .... The unemployed young man accepts the job, but, once alone, looks with real sadness at the jacket—what a sad fate for its owner!—until he realizes the obvious: the dead person doesn't need to keep warm anymore, but he does! So he keeps the coat!

Later, Joan meets the widow of that worker who was killed in the machines, Mrs. Luckerniddle. It has been four days since Luckerniddle's husband left for work, and he, of course, has not returned. She is desperate. Her husband would not have disappeared like that. They loved each other! He was the home's breadwinner; he wouldn't have left her in misery. At the factory gates, Mrs. Luckerniddle demands to be told the truth about her husband. Slift gives her a choice: either she files a lawsuit against the Mauler factories, or she eats for free in the factory cafeteria for three weeks!

The next day, despite Joan pleading with her not to renounce her husband, Mrs. Luckerniddle will be in the factory cafeteria eating peas while the stored meats are in danger of rotting because of the lockdown. To all of Joan's arguments, she will always reply: "I haven't eaten in two days." The formerly unemployed young man turns up with the stolen jacket. Slift asks him to sit opposite Luckerniddle, who recognizes the jacket. Slift asks him: Where did that jacket come from? Slift demands the truth—otherwise he will sack the young man! The young man ends up confessing that the jacket belonged to a man who fell into a boiler. Mrs. Luckerniddle, who can no longer eat or stop looking at the jacket, gets up, feeling sick. She leaves the scene, saying she will be back—so nobody should touch her plate—and that she'll come for lunch every day for three weeks. When Slift asks Joan if she has now seen how bad people are, Joan says no. She did not see the evilness of the poor. She saw on their faces the suffering imposed by their social conditions: "Your tales of their debasement you will see/Refuted by the face of poverty."[5]

In the model inspired by these scenes, participants have to create a scene where a narrator utters a sentence that is only partially true. The scene has to show a broader reality that comes to deny what that sentence affirmed. The difficulty of the model lies in the choice of phrase. It cannot be merely a false, unreal, nonsense sentence. It has to refer to something true but at the same time should only be a narrow explanation of the reality.

In the city of Porto, Portugal, together with Sergio de Carvalho, I once held a workshop where members of Tortuga, a TO group from Madrid, were present. They were creating a play about the situation of The Kellys (Las Quelis, named as such to denote "las *que li*mpian," or those who clean), who are hotel cleaners. Their scene began with a narration: "You will see now that there is no solidarity among cleaners!" A woman, alone, made quick gestures to show that she was cleaning a hotel room. Another worker arrived, her arm bandaged. "Are you ready to return to work?" asked the first woman, who seemed both surprised and doubtful. "I have to," answered the woman coming back. "That's what the doctor said." The two then resumed work. The one with only one arm available for work bravely struggled in every way but couldn't manage to change the bedding or carry the vacuum cleaner around. The other helped her, albeit annoyed. At the end of the day, the manager arrived. They hadn't finished all the rooms, so they weren't going to get full payment. The manager dismissed the woman with the injured arm. He had a new recruit. The eyes of the remaining worker sparkled upon seeing the new recruit: "You'll get used to it soon. I'll teach you!" Solidarity was simply too expensive for this woman.

I also used this model with the Roofless Movement of Bahia—MSTB. This time, the phrase used was: "You will see that poor mothers in Bahia exploit their children." I remember the astonishment that such a statement caused in the audience watching: the silence grew thicker. On stage, children played with paper airplanes. One of the kids sniffed the air, the smell of food obviously wafting across the space, and asked the mother, who we saw cooking, "Is it ready?"

142   *Are There No Alternatives?*

When she said yes, the kids immediately lined up, turning the paper planes into little cones that their mother stuffed with peanuts. As soon as they had closed their cones, they walked toward the audience: "Peanuts, peanuts!" "One for three, two for five! Who wants peanuts?" "Please, buy it, young man, it's to help me!" As soon as they had sold all the peanuts, they turned their cones into banknotes. A line then formed for the children to hand the little money that they had earned to their mother. Realizing that, with that sum, she would not be able to buy enough food for her children, the mother felt anguished and started screaming at them. The scene ended with the mother looking at the audience, crying. Yes, mothers from Bahia—and from many other places in the world—put their children to work. But if being hungry is not enough to guarantee one's food, how are people supposed to earn the money they need so that they can eat?

Powerful people belong to power

This model is, in a way, the inverse of the preceding one. It focuses on investigating how the powerful are subjected to the power that they hold. We tend to believe that having power means doing what we want. Here we start from the opposite assumption. We don't have power, it's the power that has us. Being powerful means being forced to act in certain ways in order to ensure that we continue to occupy our place of power. In other words, people who have power have to act and think according to what benefits power.

In a scene from *Life of Galileo*, the new Pope is talking to the inquisitor. This new Pope is a friend of science; he himself is a mathematician. He defends Galileo against the inquisitor. Galileo is, after all, "the greatest physicist of [his] time, the light of Italy."[6] The inquisitor argues against Galileo's theses. By questioning the celestial organization, Galileo also puts in doubt the organization of men. The debate between the two continues, but what really convinces the Pope is not an argument of any kind. Incessant murmuring is heard coming from behind the door: influential members of the Church want to know what the decision will be. But while the Pope had been talking to the Inquisitor, the Pope was *also* being dressed up in the official garments that accompany his role. At the end of the scene, fully dressed, he looks in the mirror, glimpsing the official version of himself. He decides to have Galileo silenced.

Participants who use this model have to build a scene where a protagonist has an internal split between their personal will and their social role. This internal split must be rendered visually in the form of a disagreement with another character, who asks the protagonist for something that would require them to make a choice that corresponds to only *one* of the sides into which they are divided internally. The protagonist must act in such a way that—through the use of objects (the pope's clothes) or how they relate to other elements of the scene (the incessant noise behind his door)—it is understood that the character will side with their social function.

In a very privileged school in Switzerland where I facilitated workshops, the students had extreme difficulty in embodying the models I proposed to them until I proposed this one, perhaps because it was a model that correlated more to the social positions to which they were already accustomed. In the scene they made, a student was feeling low. After class, the teacher approached him and asked if he was okay. The very anguished boy replied that no, once again, there were problems at home. The teacher seemed to know what those problems were, so she got even closer to the student and hugged him to try to comfort the boy. The student burst into tears. Because of whatever was occurring in his home, he had not been able to take the exam properly. And he was afraid of what his parents' reactions would be in case the results of his exam were bad. Maybe he would repeat that year. What would happen then? He asked—and then begged—the teacher for a chance to retake the exam. The teacher, seemingly stunned by the situation, then broke contact with the student, standing up and walking back toward

Exercises Toward a More Dialectical Practice of Forum Theatre   143

the chalkboard. Sitting behind her desk, she told the student that she couldn't allow what he was asking for, that it would be against school rules. As much as she was individually well-intentioned, being a teacher was not only about listening to students and their individual needs; being a teacher was, in this case, also about obeying certain protocols that she could not oppose.

Diffusion of oppression

This model goes against the preconceived idea that there must be a visible oppressor for there to be oppression. The oppressor is often not found where oppression takes place. For example, I remember a Forum Theatre play about a price increase for public transportation tickets in Rio de Janeiro. The group, driven by the need to present an oppressive character, wrote the story in such a way that, by a giant coincidence, on the day of the protest against the increases, the owner of the transport company had decided to go and inspect his fleet. I understand that art does not need to be a realistic reproduction of our daily lives, but I had the feeling that the group could not imagine a Forum Theatre dramaturgy in which there was no dualistic confrontation. In the situations in which we live, however, it is much more common to have mediations of various kinds, factors that functionally mean that often oppressors and oppressed are not in direct contact like that. As a result, a dualistic confrontation between oppressor and oppressed is often not only implausible, but absolutely unreal.

In John Cassavetes' film *Opening Night*, we have a beautifully rendered example of diffused oppression. The protagonist is a well-known actress. Her newest theatrical role is very problematic for her, as she finds her character too similar to herself in many ways. The character is a woman who is getting older, who has not had children, and who is not in a relationship that gives her pleasure. All this is a source of suffering for the character in the play, but even more so for the protagonist of the film (as we can easily understand in a society such as ours). She starts to miss rehearsals and have anxiety attacks and even hallucinations. On opening night, she arrives at the theatre completely inebriated. The other actors, the director, the author of the play, everyone involved in the show—they all look at her with compassion as she lies on the couch. But it is a full house, and some audience members are already complaining about the delay, calling out the actress's name. What to do? All those theatre workers have empathy for the actress, but, if she doesn't take the stage and act, it would be bad for the production of the play, and maybe even worse for her reputation. They try to get her on her feet, give her very strong coffee, holding the cup so she doesn't get burned. One of the actors holds her up, waiting for the moment she must enter the stage, until finally she does so and begins, as best as she can, to play this role that made her suffer so much but that she could no longer refuse.

This was the first model that I learned thanks to Sergio de Carvalho, and I am very grateful to him for that. Here, with this model, a member of a group must collapse, no longer able to follow a routine that is oppressive to them. The other members of the group are not oppressors; they are oppressed. They must not know very well what to do in a particular instance—and then they must lead the collapsing character back to the same activity that caused the collapse. For her to stop would be bad for the group, but it would be even worse for her.

In the first weekend of workshops for ETP, I proposed this model to the participants, many of them coming from rural or urban occupation movements. The scene that was developed took place, logically, in an occupation. In it, a woman was the most important point of reference for the other members of the movement. She was willing to do all the tasks; she was already a long-time member of the movement and knew well how to coordinate the space. All the fellow occupiers saluted her work and respected her. But when, in the scene, police came with an eviction order, this militant organizer froze, even as everyone went to her to find out what they had to do.

144 *Are There No Alternatives?*

She asked for the name of the commander who led the battalion. When she heard his name, her anxiety intensified. She almost fainted. Those who made the scene had been smart enough not to have the scene reveal whether she had a personal history with this commander or if she had been in another occupation that was evicted by him. Either way, the occupants insisted: Who else could talk to the police? They couldn't risk losing the space they were occupying! She had to go! And, little by little, the militant recovered and went to talk to the captain who frightened her so much. The group had made her do what she didn't want to do, yet the other members of the occupation couldn't be called oppressors.

Contradiction between action and locale

This model, like all the others described here, is not only for building Forum Theatre scenes. This one, perhaps even more so than the others, does not deal directly with the issue of oppression. However, it is very useful so that the space in which an action takes place has a meaning that shapes the action itself, rather than the space merely providing decoration. In fact, the space of the scene always does more than merely decorating it. As I talked about many pages above, the fact that the play *They Don't Wear Black Tie* is developed solely within a house makes the intended topic of the play become somewhat secondary in comparison to family relationships. Thus, the strike and developing actions (the general assembly, distribution of pamphlets, pickets, and repression) are only narrated. What actually happens onstage is an engagement and a breakup, a fight between father and son, etc. The play wanted to talk about the dynamics of class struggle but, among other things, because it takes place only inside a house, it ends up being a bourgeois drama.

In A. Boal's *Revolution in South America*, the contradiction between space and action is no longer an obstacle; on the contrary, it is a resource that the author uses to create another dimension of meaning. The revolutionaries meet inside a nightclub. The play's themes are both the seizure of power through armed struggle and the characters' new love affairs. Here, the space partially determines the action so that the scene can, based on its own dynamics, serve as a criticism of the tavern revolutionaries, who prefer parties and fun to the rigor of clandestine organizing.

The model here demands that participants be able to create a scene in which action and location are in significant contradiction. This is what we have in Brecht's *The Mother* when the protagonist, Pelagea Vlassova, asks herself what she can do to keep cooking decent food now that her son is earning less. She is inside a very small house on a huge stage, with the scenery painted with dozens of other houses as small as hers. And on top of these houses, there is a huge factory. The music invited by the script underlines what we are already told by the scenario: the problem she has within the four walls of her house cannot be resolved within those four walls.

In Barcelona, I tried this model. Participants used it in a very funny way. We were made to imagine that we were spectators coming to see a performance of *Revolution in South America* in a very fancy theatre. An actress came to the front of the stage before the performance to thank both the public authorities and the generous sponsors who had allowed such a genuine Latin American voice to be heard in a national theatre in Spain. She also informed us that to follow was a cocktail hour where we would have the opportunity to greet the so-talented director. Soon the performers began to act out precisely the nightclub scene from the play, but with absolutely random acting intensities and vocal pitches, their eyes always staring away, never looking at their stage partners, in a clear parody of the mannerisms of a certain contemporary theatre. They saluted the public so that soon afterward the much-acclaimed director would come to give an account as emotional as it was insipid about the conditions of Brazilian sex workers. The scene

Exercises Toward a More Dialectical Practice of Forum Theatre   145

was hilarious because the participants had found a thousand ways to always return to the main contradiction between place and action. In this case, the contradiction was one that resulted from the specific ways that the particular space and the text combined.

Models for forum scenes that involve spect-actor intervention

Divide the unity

It is undoubtedly one of the most urgent political tasks to be able to divide those who have diverging material interests but who are united by a certain ideological discourse. In many countries, women end up voting for politicians who are against women's rights because they believe in the other values proposed by those politicians. Around the world, we often witness workers who were born in the country where they reside joining their employers against the interests of workers who immigrated to that country, and precisely to defend an abstraction such as the nation .... Unfortunately, there are too many examples of ideological alliances that unite people who have no concrete common interest.

We find—again in Brecht's body of work—a model about this division that must be forged—a rift we must drive between oppressors and the oppressed people who identify with them—in order to struggle effectively against oppression itself. In *The Mother*, a scene begins with the protagonist lying down. Her son, a Bolshevik militant, has just been executed at the Tsar's behest. Two neighbors, worried by the sound of her crying, come over to her house. One, the poorest, brings soup. The other, her landlord, brings a bible. The two try to comfort her, asking to see a picture of her son. The Mother, Pelagea Vlassova, shows them the only photo of her son that she has: a "Wanted" poster circulated by the police. For her, someone who moves inside the clandestine sphere of organizing, to have that be the only photo she possesses of her son is absolutely normal. The two neighbors, however, look scared and start talking about God. They say that the boy's death happened because he went against the divine order that establishes the Tsar as the holder of all power in Russia. Pelagea gets angry; she wonders aloud if the poorest will accept sleeping on the street because it is the will of God—or if the landlord would accept no longer being paid rent because it is easier for a camel to go through the eye of a needle than for a rich man to enter into the kingdom of God? The two neighbors end up squabbling amongst themselves, fighting over the holy book to find quotations in it that justify their points of view. In this fight, they end up tearing up the bible.

With this model, the scene to be constructed must make two people oppose the protagonist. This duo must be united by the same discourse, but with material contradictions that differentiate their circumstances. It will then be up to the spect-actor who enters the scene to find ways to push these contradictions more and more to the surface, so that the conflict is no longer between the protagonist and this duo but within the duo itself. We have to find ways to "split the one into two," as a famous politician once said.

In Rio de Janeiro, workshop participants made the following scene. The protagonist, a transgender woman, meets up with her sister and brother-in-law. The couple asks her to renounce a large part of her mother's inheritance; after all, she does not "live up to the family's values." It is notable that, in the scene, the husband/brother-in-law does most of the talking. When the sister speaks, she looks at her husband, and only at the end of the sentences does she look at the protagonist, as if apologizing. The husband becomes increasingly annoyed and says that, with that money, he will finally be able to open the business of his dreams and support his family. The interventions onstage began by questioning what the supposed "family values" were that the husband was referencing. Were they precisely what made the sister clam up?

146 *Are There No Alternatives?*

Did the sister agree with using the inheritance money to finance her husband's dream? Did she have no dreams of her own about what to do with that sum? The fight was no longer between the couple and the protagonist, but within the couple. The discussion evolved from one focused only on anti-trans prejudice to a discussion of the interrelationship between anti-trans prejudice and patriarchy—how the oppression of patriarchy "justified" both that prejudice and simultaneously subordinated the sister to her husband. This forum scene and its interventions highlighted how—if you drive that wedge between the sister and the husband—it opens up the possibility of an alliance between the sisters, an alliance founded on a clearer analysis of the ways that some systems of oppression act on both of them, if in different ways. The intention in this example was not to focus *less* on the anti-trans oppression than on the patriarchal oppression, but precisely to open up the possibility of an alliance between the sisters by splitting apart the alliance between the couple.

Chorus

One of the most significant clichés of left-wing art is arguably its representation of the masses. I say this because the masses are almost always represented as a homogeneous block, united by their beliefs and by a recognition that their strength will be able to change the world. In such representations, their internal unity with each other is unbreakable and driven by sheer revolutionary hope.

The model that I am about to describe opposes this cliché and shows how much, in fact, the masses are only brought together by a unity that is crossed by contradictions, which means that we should never take for granted their existence as a group fighting for the same objective. The model is inspired by a scene in *Saint Joan of the Stockyards*. A chorus representing the 70,000 workers of Lennox Meat Industries faces the factory's closed doors. With fervor, they shout in unison that they can no longer accept the miserable salary offered to them and that they will all quit. They stand still in front of the doors. Who do capitalists think the workers are? A herd of sheep who peacefully accept anything? We better leave! And, once again, there are those desperately closed doors. Why don't they open? They are entitled to, at least, the same pay rate as they earned last month and a ten-hour day! The doors remain closed. A man passes by, announcing that the factories have shut down. The formidable crowd disperses, each chasing a new job for themselves.

In the model or prompt partially inspired by that scene, participants have to construct their own non-realist scene in which a group appears to be extremely tight-knit. Gradually, however, the cracks and fissures within the group begin to appear. Though they have a will to fight, the need to survive also imposes itself. The group begins to dissolve; each new interruption or obstacle causes other characters to reveal the reasons why they can't keep fighting. At the end, the group completely breaks up. And for a scene built via this prompt to become a Forum Theatre play, you could have a character keep trying to make the fight continue, with the struggle to maintain the necessary group cohesion at the center of the scenario. In such a Forum Theatre scene, the union appears as it is: the result of political work, not a pre-existing fact.

In Portugal, a group decided to try this model with the theme of oppressions faced by LGBTQIA+ people. The scene began with the characters arranged in a triangle whose tip was closest to the audience. The character who stood at the tip launched the first word of a slogan of sorts: "homophobia?" to which everyone replied, "must not go unanswered." They began to march, always shouting with great vigor slogans and answers to the crimes: "Lesbophobia! Must not go unanswered! Transphobia! Must not go unanswered!" As the march went on, situations arose

Exercises Toward a More Dialectical Practice of Forum Theatre 147

that started breaking up the initial unity of the group. One of the most animated characters suddenly stopped, pale, gaze fixed on an implied figure in the distance: "It's my father! He doesn't know about me!" The character then left the demonstration. The march continued until a new actor interrupted: "But are we going to march this way? No, that would go past the school where I work!" This character also left. The political manifestation—weakened by then—continued its course. Two women, very happy, walking hand in hand throughout the whole demonstration up until that point, threw an object at a target "offstage." Another protester became scared: "What are you doing? I'm an immigrant! I can't get caught by the police." He looked around and disappeared through an imaginary alleyway. Then the two girlfriends looked at each other, not knowing what to do, until they let go of each other's hands and looked around, also scared themselves.

In the Forum Theatre session of the scene, the participants who intervened came to talk to each of the protesters who had left. One spect-actor essentially asked: wasn't it possible for the man who saw his father to stay in the demonstration, but hiding his face when walking past his dad? Another intervention suggested, on the contrary, that the father be confronted. To the person who did not want the march to pass by the school where they worked, another spect-actor asked: "Did you know that you can count on legal help if you experience discrimination at work? We could organize a new demonstration if the school is homophobic!" The interventions and the discussion revealed that it was important to talk before the demonstration about what kind of confrontation everyone was willing or able to face.

Muriel

This model is named after Muriel Naessens, a militant of historic proportions in the French feminist movement and a practitioner of TO who was part of A. Boal's team in Paris. When she made forums on gender-based violence, she always carried a banner with the telephone number of a shelter for women who were experiencing violence. She told me that she used to carry a pamphlet with the same number. After a while, she realized how difficult it was for spect-actors who needed help to have an opportunity to take the pamphlets themselves at those forum events. Standing up in front of the entire audience, picking up a piece of paper, having that paper in their bags: all of it was potentially dangerous. It was much safer and more discreet, Muriel ultimately learned, to type the number into their cell phone contacts and save it under a false name.

We often see Forum Theatre dramaturgies that bet everything on the protagonist's conscience. In such cases, it would be enough for the person to become aware of their problem for oppression to dissolve. I saw, for example, a forum on problematic drug use. The protagonist was alone in the scene, staring at his arm, with one hand holding a syringe, and he ended up injecting himself. The moment of the forum arrived. Interventions followed, one after another, in which spect-actors went into the scene to "decide" not to inject themselves. Consciousness, the ability to choose, was framed as the whole problem. Unfortunately, life isn't that simple!

Muriel's model proposes a different approach. In it, the following sort of scenario unfolds: the protagonist is in fact unconscious about a problem they face, but the scene has to be constructed in such a way that awareness does not (or would not) solve the problem by itself. There must be a concreteness that demands a resolution that goes beyond the sphere of intellectual understanding.

For example, in a workplace, a militant tries to pass out pamphlets about a strike. In the initial model, all the workers refuse to take the pamphlets. The militant does not notice that the security guard is on to him, which means that people taking a pamphlet would risk reprisals. As a result,

148   *Are There No Alternatives?*

in the forum, the task will not only be to raise the militant's awareness, but mainly to try to make sure that other workers can have access to the *information* contained in the pamphlet—and without exposing themselves to the security guards.

The model must neither deny the existence of "ideological" problems nor make them the only ones to be overcome in the fight against oppression.

Notes

1 Augusto Boal, *Jogos para atores e não atores* (São Paulo: Editora Cosac Naify, 2015).
2 Augusto Boal, *Hamlet and the Baker's Son: My Life in Theatre and Politics*, trans. Adrian Jackson and Candida Blaker (Abingdon and New York: Routledge, 2001), 147.
3 Heleny Guariba was an assistant to my father at the Arena Theatre. She was also a member of an organization that engaged in armed struggle and, as such, was imprisoned, tortured, and killed.
4 June of 2013 was the moment of the most important people's uprising of this century in Brazil. In that uprising, the use of people's violence in order to counter police violence was understood by the population as necessary. The Black Bloc, an affinity group of militants, decided to counter the police and was a great help at the beginning of those journeys.
5 Bertolt Brecht, *Saint Joan of the Stockyards*, trans. Ralph Mannheim (London: Methuen, 1991), 30.
6 Bertolt Brecht, *Life of Galileo*, trans. John Willett, in *Brecht–Collected Plays*: 5, eds. John Willett and Ralph Manheim (London: Bloomsbury Methuen, 2008), 161.

Conclusion

The landscape is distressing, but not desolate. There are struggles, joys, and life that exist in the world of Theatre of the Oppressed, potentialities that will probably only be extinguished when we are no longer haunted by the vampire who transforms everything into a commodity to suck its value dry. May this book be of some help to the vampire hunters yet to come! It is with those who make such invaluable, fragile, and intermittent experiences of TO that I feel solidarity. To speak of those groups, with whom each experience is always singular, in just a few mere lines here would be to generalize and turn them into abstractions when their strength lies precisely in being linked to their time like lips to teeth. It is for those groups that I write what I hope will be of some use. Our goals are cloudy, and the mist—who knows—may never completely disperse. The difficult task, however, is old and evident. End oppression. To do that, we will have to confront oppression as it is constituted today. With the ever-changing world, there is no guarantee that our theatrical arsenal will be up to the task, but there is also no need for the fatalistic assumption that it will not be! Our tools cannot simply be abandoned; nor can they be used without a critical perspective. No sign from the sky will validate our work. We remain with only the poor and irreplaceable proof of practice. May our practices grow each day more intertwined with people's organizations and more inventive to deal with the problems we face now. May those practices grow stronger and more powerful until the day they will no longer be useful in any other way than that which is required by the splendid realms of leisure and beauty.

Index

Note: *Italicized* page numbers refer to figures, and numbers with "n" refer to notes in the text.

abstract heroism 124; *see also* heroism
action and locale, contradiction between 144–145
Adivasis 97, 116n1
Adorno, T. W. 111
The Aesthetics of the Oppressed (Boal) 12
Albergaria, H. 130
Alemão 114
Alighieri, D.: *Divine Comedy* 89
Allende, S. 2
Alon, C. 64
Althusser, L. 19
anti-Aristotelian dramaturgy 48
Antigone 124–125
anti-Semitism 46
Aoun, I. 64
applause game 136–137
Arab Spring 24, 103
Arena Conta Tiradentes (Arena Tells the Story of Tiradentes) (Boal and Guarnieri) 31, 41, 63n25
Arena Conta Zumbi (Arena Tells the Story of Zumbi) 33
Aristotelian dramaturgy 119
Aristotelian theatre 36–37
Aristotelian unities 120
Aristotle 120
Arrentela, south of Lisbon 105–106, 117n10
Artaud, A. 52, 53; Theatre of Cruelty 40
artistic freedom 37
arts 75–93; capitalist state and its necessary overcoming 78–81; culture and 75, 87, 88, 89; defined 15; installations 15; institutions 90; policy for 77; politics and 39, 51, 53, 77; strategy 81–86
audience: of 1970s 40; alienation 36; Brazilian 30; campus 52; in Forum Theatre 12–13, 46; onstage 15; peasants 97, 142; Portuguese 108; protagonist 8n5; stage and 16, 29, 33; street 52; of undisturbed passivity 119; workshops 108

authoritarianism 28, 77, 81, 113
Autran, P.: *Theory and practice of the dramaturgy seminar at Teatro de Arena* 117n11
Avatar (Cameron) 53
The awkward militant 136

Badiou, A. 126
Bambirra, V. 56
Barbosa, I. 108–109
Basic Ecclesiastical Communities 115
Benjamin, W. 31, 81
Bensaïd, D. 18, 20, 23, 81, 86, 93, 128
Black Bloc 138–139, 148n4
Bloco de Esquerda (Left Bloc) party 104, 107, 108
Boal, A. 1–2, 8n4, 11, 24, 27, 36, 43, 44; *The Aesthetics of the Oppressed* 12; *Arena Conta Tiradentes (Arena Tells the Story of Tiradentes)* 31, 41, 63n25; critique of theatre 16, 18; death of 14; exile in various countries 12; *Legislative Theatre: Using Theatre to Make Politics* 48, 120, 128n8; *The Rainbow of Desire* 54; on rehearsal for revolution 13–14; *Revolução da América do Sul (Revolution in South America)* 29, 45, 112, 144; revolutionary objectives 53; *Stop, C'est Magique!* 54, 120; *Theatre of the Oppressed* 11, 20, 29, 31, 43–49, 53–55, 119; work and personal life 49
Boltanski, L. 15, 18
Bossa Nova 30
Bourdieu, P. 109
bourgeois drama 6–7, 39–40, 49, 60, 119–125
Bourgeois Revolutions 78
Brazilian Communist Party (Partido Comunista Brasileiro, PCB) 11, 27–34, 34n2, 39, 58; critique of hierarchy legitimized by knowledge 32–34; critique of historical determinism 29–31; critique of the historical subject 31–32
Breakfast at Tiffany's 137–138

Index 151

Brecht, B. 12, 13, 17, 29, 36, 38, 41, 60, 130; alienation techniques 14, 31; anti-schematism 39; bourgeois drama 48; contemporary spectator 38; criticism of theatre 12, 36, 40; *The Days of the Commune* 126; didactics of 137; dramatic theatre criticized by 122; dramaturgy 40; *The Horatians and the Curiatians* 40, 138; *The Jewish Wife* 46, 47; *Lehrstücke* 3; *The Mother* 13, 40, 113, 144, 145; narrative procedures 17; *Notes on Mahagonny* 37; no work on didactic plays after exile 40; plays judge or ridicule heroes 40; poetics 29; restlessness 39; *The Rise and Fall of the City of Mahagonny* 37; *Round Heads and Pointed Heads* 65; *Saint Joan of the Stockyards* 140–141, 146; theatre 40; *The Threepenny Opera* 37

Bringing the War Back Home 52

Buarque, C. 87

bureaucratization 19, 82

The burial 136

Butler, J. 43

Cameron, J.: *Avatar* 53; *Titanic* 53

Cândido, A. 28; *On Literature and Society* 27, 29

capitalism/capitalist state 78–81, 89; Bourgeois Revolutions 78; crisis of 24; dominant logic 80; Fordist 91; overcoming 23, 93; racism and 67; resistance to 83; valorization of value 94n13; wage relations and 81; women's oppression and 22

Capoeira-chi 131

Capovilla, M.: *The Given Word* 63n25

Capra, F. 89

Cardoso, U. 106

Cassavetes, J.: *Opening Night* 143

Castro, F. 56

The cell 136

Center for Theatre of the Oppressed—Rio de Janeiro (known as CTO-Rio) 120

Centers of Popular Culture (CPCs) 34, 39, 115

Chiapello, E. 15, 18

Chinyowa, K. C. 43, 44

chorus 146–147

Cinema Novo 30

Claire's Party 126

coercive power 119

Coletivo de Cultura da Zona Oeste (Cultural Collective of the West Zone) 114

communism 18, 84

Communist Party *see* Brazilian Communist Party (Partido Comunista Brasileiro, PCB)

Companhia do Latão 130

conflict 44, *121*; between capital and labor 22; critics 44; interest and 23; politics 87; protagonist 145; relationship and 45

contradiction between action and locale 144–145

Costa, I. C. 31, 60; *A hora do Teatro Épico no Brasil* 118n22; about *They Don't Wear Black Tie* 123

Creole 110

Critique of Hegel's Philosophy of Right (Marx) 79

Cuban Revolution 57

culture: art and 75, 77, 87, 88, 89; commodification 34; Communist 32; counterculture and 34; diverse 75; dominant 61; Leninist concept of 13; mass 61; popular 34, 88; reclassify 115

Dardot, P. 60

da Silva, J. 29

The Days of the Commune (Brecht) 126

de Andrade, Oswald 50n27

de Carvalho, S. 130, 141

The Decision 38, 41

de-individualization 98

Deleuze, G. 19

Delphy, C. 22

de Mello e Souza, G. 54–55

democracy: bourgeois 81; majoritarian 20; of the multitude 19; parliamentary 18; participatory 15; social 51, 76, 82, 93

Descartes, R. 44

dialectical practice of Forum Theatre 130–148; Chen's good morning 131–137; model exercises 137–139; models for Theatre of the Oppressed 137; models involving spect-actor intervention 145–148; models to enrich 139–145

dialectics 40, 41, 84, 113, 125–128

Diamond, D. 44

didactic plays 38–39, 40, 41, 138

diffusion of oppression 143–144; *see also* oppression

discourses 37–38

divide the unity 145–146

Divine Comedy (Alighieri) 89

domestic violence 1, 23, 64, 111, 113, 114, 124, 126, 135

Dort, B. 40, 45–47, 50n21, 61

Dosse, J.: *Jana Sanskriti: A Theater on the Field* 117n4

dowry 99, 100, 116–117n3

dramatic theatre 122

dramaturgy 77, 106, 125; anti-Aristotelian 48; Aristotelian 119; Brazilian political 112; Brechtian 40; critical forms of 77; Forum Theatre 48–49, 120, 123, 143; seminar 117n11

152 Index

The Eighteenth Brumaire of Louis Napoleon (Marx) 16
Eles não usam Black-tie (They Don't Wear Black Tie) 11, 112, 144
The Emancipated Spectator (Rancière) 15
The Enemy of the People (Ibsen) 58
Epic Theatre 3, 4, 6, 36, 40, 47, 112, 122, 126
"The evilness of the poor" 140–142

facilitation/mechanization 68–71
facilitator/joker 13, 46, 69, 70, 114, 130–133, 135–136
"Féminisme Enjeux" (Feminism Onstage) 106, 126–127
Filho, O. V. 28
Florestan Fernandes National School 111
Fordist capitalism 91; *see also* capitalism/capitalist state
Forum Theatre 8n5, 20, 30, 125–128; audience in 12–13, 46; dialectical practice of 130–148; didactic plays and 38–39; dramaturgy 48–49; as rehearsal for revolution 13–14
Forum Theatre Dramaturgy/"Chinese Crisis" *121*
Foucault, M. 19, 23; active intolerance 12
Franco, M. 113, 118n23
freedom of parties 79
Freire, P. 2, 12–13, 39; critique of education 12; *Pedagogy of the Oppressed* 22
French Communist Party 22
Furet, F. 24

Galileo 142
Games and exercises 131–137; applause game 136–137; Capoeira-chi 131; greetings 136; Helena's circle, or: "I must but I don't want to" 135; line of power 132–133; The neutral 135–136; Pascal's eyes 131–132; Samurai march 132; The two poles and the rubber band 134–135; Yes, But 133–134; Yes/no//no/yes 134; Zé's The Sun Shines 133
Games for Actors and Non-Actors 66, 120, 130
Gandhism 97, 102
Ganguly, Sanjoy 71n6, 98, 100
Ganguly, Sima 71n6, 100
Garo, I. 19
Gassner, J. 119
gender 43; -based violence 147; equality 14; identity 43; ideology 85; prejudice 45; transformation 43
Geração à Rasca (Generation in Peril) 103, 104
gestus 139–140
The Given Word (Capovilla) 63n25
Global Security Law 80
Gomes, A. 118n23
Gorender, J. 56
Grand Soir 129n21

Granma 56, 62n15
greetings 136
Grotowski, J. 53
Guariba, H. 148n3
Guarnieri, G. 28; *Arena Conta Tiradentes (Arena Tells the Story of Tiradentes)* 31, 41, 63n25
guerrillas, micro-entrepreneurs and 55–60
Guevara, C. 56, 57

Hallward, P. 15
Hegel, G.W.F 48
Hegelian dramaturgies 48
hegemony 17, 80, 84
Helena's circle, or: "I must but I don't want to" 135
heroism 40–41, 58; abstract 124
Holloway, J. 19
homophobia 18, 22, 67, 123, 146
A hora do Teatro Épico no Brasil (Costa) 118n22
The Horatians and the Curiatians (Brecht) 40, 138

Ibsen, H.: *The Enemy of the People* 58
impermanence of politics 51–53
Indian Federation of Theatre of the Oppressed 102
Indian Grassroots Movements 97
Indian Marxist Communist Party (PCIM) 97, 116n2
Institute of Agrarian Reform 33
The Institute of Philosophy and Social Sciences 114
Interactive Victim Training 2
In the same boat? 126
Invisible Theatre 25n15
Ivernel, P. 17

Jana Sanskriti, India 2, 14, 64; campaigns of 101; council of 100; history of 97; members of 98; political views 102; politics of 102; *Shonar Meye (Golden Girl)* 98, 99; spect-actors' committees 100; workshops 102
Jana Sanskriti: A Theater on the Field (Dosse) 117n4
The Jewish Wife (Brecht) 46, 47
June of 2013 148n4

Khapazes de Semear Konsciencia (KSK—Capable of Sowing Consciousness) 104, 106, 109, 117n16

labor laws 79
La Dignidad (Movimiento Popular La Dignidad—MPLD) 111, 112, 117n21
La Fura dels Baus 52
Landless Movement 111, 140; *see also* Movimiento Sem Terra (MST)
Latino/a/é 124
Laval, C. 60
Legislative Theatre: Using Theatre to Make Politics (Boal) 48, 120, 128n8

Lehrstücke *see* didactic plays
Lehrstücke (Brecht) 3
Lenin, V. 30, 58, 93; *The State and Revolution* 16
Levante Popular da Juventude (Popular Youth Rise) 112
LGBTQ 70
LGBTQIA+ 18, 24, 64, 90, 146
Life of Galileo 142
line of power 132–133
Living Theatre 40
Luxemburg, R. 38

Mais-valia Vai Acabar, Seu Edgar (Surplus Value Will End, Mr. Edgar) 112
Malcolm X 66
Manifesto of the Communist Party 22
Maoism 97, 124
Maoists 116n2
Mao Tse-Tung 84, 126
March 12 movement (M12M) 104
Marcuse, H. 40, 52
Marighella, C. 57
Marx, K. 18, 19, 55; *Critique of Hegel's Philosophy of Right* 79; *The Eighteenth Brumaire of Louis Napoleon* 16
Marxism 20
Marxist 24
materiality 85
Matrix effects 131
Mayakovsky, V. 17
mechanization 68–71
micro-entrepreneurs 55–60
micropolitics 23, 24
MNLM (Movimento Nacional de Luta pela Moradia, or National Housing Struggle Movement) 113–114
Modern Times 69
Moonlight 132
moralism in dramatic form 45–48
Moretti, F. 61
The Mother (Brecht) 13, 40, 144, 145
Movimento dos Trabalhadores Sem-Teto, or The Roofless Workers' Movement (MTST) 112
Movimento Sem Terra, or the Landless Movement (MST) 2, 112
Muallem, E. 64
Muktadhara 102
Muriel 147–148

Naessens, M. 70, 71n4, 147
Nandigram massacre 100
Narmada Bachao Andolan 97
narrative interruption 39–40
National Employment Agency (ANPE) 66
nationalism 30, 82
National Liberation Action (Ação Libertadora Nacional, ALN) 57

Naxalites 116n2
Nazism 46
Negri, T. 19
neoliberalism 2, 51–62; "bad uses" of Theatre of the Oppressed 53–55; guerrillas and micro-entrepreneurs 55–60; impermanence of politics 51–53
The neutral 135–136
non-governmental organizations (NGOs) 15
+Nós (+Us) 114, 118n25
Notes on Mahagonny (Brecht) 37

oblivion 62n7
Occupy Wall Street movement 20, 68
O Cortiço (The Slum) 27
On Literature and Society (Cândido) 27, 29
O Patrão Cordial (The Cordial Boss) 127
Opening Night (Cassavetes) 143
"O povo é quem mais ordena" ("The people are the ones who organize") 105
oppressed-oppressor 32
oppression 21–24, 64–67; in 1970s 66; critiques of 43–45; definition of 65; diffusion of 143–144; materiality 108; as means of theatrical production 12; protagonist 125; semi-autonomous 22; in society 32; struggle against 8n5; unambiguous 20
Óprima! An Encounter of Theatre of the Oppressed and Activism 103–111

Pal, S. R. 103
Parisot, L. 52
participation 14–17
Partidão (The Great Party) 28, 34n2
Partido Comunista Brasileiro (PCB) 11
Pascal's eyes 131–132
passivity 15, 33, 61, 119
Patkar, M. 97
patriarchy 22, 65, 99; homophobia and 67; racism and 84
peasants 5, 11, 14, 33, 56, 97–98, 100–102
Pécaut, D. 31
pedagogy 12, 39, 40, 69, 71n3, 115
Pedagogy of the Oppressed (Freire) 22
Peixoto, F. 54
Piscator, E. 125
Plato 16
politicization 11
politics 8n1, 11–24; audience in Forum Theatre 12–13; Forum Theatre as rehearsal for revolution 13–14; impermanence of 51–53; oppression 21–24; participation 14–17; representation 17–21; and sociology 83; theatrical production, oppressed as means of 12
Popular Culture Movement 115
Popular Party 19

154   *Index*

Popular Theatre School (La Escola de Teatro Popular—ETP) 111–116, 130, 136, 139
powerful people belong to power 142–143
Prestes, L. C. 27–28

"Questions of Occupation" 113
quilombo (a community of formerly enslaved persons) 140

Rachel (Shapiro) 24
racial discrimination 122
racism 67; overt 114; patriarchy and 84; police violence 104; in workplace 63n36
The Rainbow of Desire (Boal) 54
Rancière, J.: *The Emancipated Spectator* 15; philosophy of 16
Rashomon 132
reality of situation, model exercises for understanding 137–139; subaltern's point of view 137–138; success and failure of the same tactic 138–139
Renato, J. 11
representation 17–21
Revolução da América do Sul (Revolution in South America) (Boal) 29, 45, 112, 144
Ridenti, M. 57–58
The Rise and Fall of the City of Mahagonny (Brecht) 37
Roofless Movement of Bahia (Movimento Sem Teto da Bahia, or MSTB) 139, 141
Rosenfeld, A. 41
Round Heads and Pointed Heads (Brecht) 65
Roy, A. 97
Royal, S. 15
RUA (Rua—Juventude Anticapitalista, or Street—Anticapitalist Youth) 112

Saint Joan of the Stockyards (Brecht) 140–141, 146
Samurai march (exercise) 132
Santos, S. 87, 94n10
São Paulo Anthropophagic Fair of Opinion 49
São Paulo Fair of Opinion 112
Schechner, R. 41, 52
schematization 120
Schwarz, R. 14, 17, 28, 31, 32
Second World War 89
Senza Tregua 51
Shapiro, Y.: *Rachel* 24
Shonar Meye (Golden Girl) 98, 99
social division of labor 37
socialist realism 112
society as a totality 94n1
sociology and politics 83
Soeiro, J. 68, 71n2, 108
Soviet Union 28
Spanish Socialist Workers' Party 19

specialization 68–70
spect-actors 13, 40, 145–148; chorus 146–147; contradiction between action and locale 144–145; diffusion of oppression 143–144; divide the unity 145–146; "The evilness of the poor" 140–142; gestus 139–140; Muriel 147–148; powerful people belong to power 142–143
Stalinism 18, 23
The State and Revolution (Lenin) 16
Stop, C'est Magique! (Boal) 54, 120
strategy 81–86
"Students for Loan" 104–105
subaltern's point of view 137–138
Subjunctive Theatre 119–128; dialectics 125–128; Forum Theatre 125–128; limitations of the bourgeois dramatic form 119–125
success and failure of the same tactic 138–139
The Sun Shines 133
Szondi, P. 122

tactical autonomy 58
Tapioca, Z. 29
The Taste of Others 136
Teatro Brasileiro de Comédia (Brazilian Comedy Theatre) 11
Teatro de Arena (Arena Theatre) 11
teleology 1
Temer, M. 112
Thatcher, M. 123
"Theatre Against Fascism" 113, 114
Theatre of the Oppressed (Boal) 11, 20, 29, 31, 43–49, 54, 119; "bad uses" of 53–55; critiques of oppression 43–45; Forum Theatre dramaturgy 48–49; models for 137; moralism manifested in dramatic form, criticism of 45–48; *see also* Brazilian Communist Party (Partido Comunista Brasileiro, PCB)
Theatre of the Oppressed Group-Montevideo (GTO-Montevideo) 106
Théâtre Populaire 45
Theatrical Guerilla (Guerrilha Teatral) 112
theatrical guerrilla 57
Theory and practice of the dramaturgy seminar at Teatro de Arena (Autran) 117n11
They Don't Wear Black Tie 11, 123, 144
The Threepenny Opera (Brecht) 37
Tiradentes 31
Titanic (Cameron) 53
Travail Théâtral 45
Tretyakov, S. 17
Trotsky, L. 89, 90
The two poles and the rubber band 134–135

UMAR—Azores 104
UNESCO 23

União Nacional por Moradia Popular, or
    National Alliance for People's Housing
    (UNMP) 114

valorization of value 94n13
Vargas, G. 27
victims 23, 66, 114, 123–124
Vollaire, C. 23

Weinblatt, M. 44
Workers' Party (Partido dos Trabalhadores,
    or PT) 120

Working Class Party 84
World March of Women—Portugal
    (MMM) 104

Xavier, N. 28–29

Yes, But 133–134
Yes/no/no/yes 134

Zapatista revolt 1994 (France) 2
Zé's The Sun Shines 133
Žižek, S. 126

Printed in the USA
CPSIA information can be obtained
at www.ICGtesting.com
LVHW081746160924
791185LV00006B/115